Literature from the
"Axis of Evil"

Literature from the "Axis of Evil"

Writing from Iran, Iraq, North Korea, and Other Enemy Nations

A WORDS WITHOUT BORDERS ANTHOLOGY

THE NEW PRESS

NEW YORK
LONDON

Requests for permission to reproduce selections from this book should be mailed to:
Permissions Department, The New Press, 38 Greene Street, New York, NY 10013.

Published in the United States by The New Press, New York, 2006
Distributed by W. W. Norton & Company, Inc., New York

Grateful acknowledgment for assistance in funding for this book is made to Furthermore:
a program of the J. M. Kaplan Fund.

LIBRARY OF CONGRESS CATALOGING-IN-PUBLICATION DATA

Literature from the "axis of evil": writing from Iran, Iraq, North Korea, and other enemy
nations: a Words without borders anthology.
p. cm.
Includes bibliographical references.
ISBN-13: 978-1-59558-070-2 (hc.)
ISBN-10: 1-59558-070-0 (hc.)
1. Developing countries–Literatures–Translations into English.   I. Words without
borders.
PN6014.L5845 2006
808.8–dc22   2006043311

The New Press was established in 1990 as a not-for-profit alternative to the large,
commercial publishing houses currently dominating the book publishing industry. The
New Press operates in the public interest rather than for private gain, and is committed to
publishing, in innovative ways, works of educational, cultural, and community value that
are often deemed insufficiently profitable.

www.thenewpress.com

Composition by Westchester Book Composition
This book was set in Adobe Garamond

Printed in the United States of America

2 4 6 8 10 9 7 5 3

Contents

Contents

Acknowledgments

In compiling this anthology, we relied on the invaluable help of consulting editors and translators, some of whom have asked, for political reasons, not to be mentioned. The efforts of Ha-yun Jung, Zara Houshmand, Majid Roshangar, Tania Nasr, Khaled Mattawa, and Jacqueline Loss in finding these authors, selecting works, and arranging translations under tight deadlines were nothing less than a kind of literary heroism. Likewise, we are indebted to the exceptional generosity of agent Joy Harris in representing this project pro bono; the acuity and foresight of editor Diane Wachtell in envisioning an anthology framed by the concept of "literature from the 'axis of evil'" (and keeping it to a reasonable length); the enthusiasm and diligence of assistant editor Joel Ariaratnam; and the beyond-the-call-of-duty dedication of production editor Sarah Fan, who coped with last-minute changes with extraordinary selflessness and grace. We also wish to gratefully acknowledge Bard College, our host institution from inception, and our funders (too numerous to mention here but identified on our Web site), especially the critical funding support of the Furthermore Foundation for this volume. Finally, we take this opportunity to remember the initial inspiration for and

support of the founding of Words without Borders by the late Cliff
Becker, literature director of the National Endowment for the Arts.
Much loved and missed by the entire literary community, he was a
friend to writers everywhere.

Editors' Note

In economics, a trade deficit comes about when we import too many foreign goods. In culture and education (defying economics in so many ways!), we experience a deficit when we import too few. American culture has always been richer for its exposure to other cultures. Yet our trade deficit in literature has become extreme, and the last thing we should do in these dark times is shut ourselves off from seeking greater knowledge of foreign experience.

Since the 1970s, American access to world literature in translation has been steadily decreasing. A 2005 Bowker study calculated that only 3 percent of the books available for sale in the English-speaking world were works in translation. (A significant proportion of these, too, are new translations of known classics, rather than discoveries of unknown and contemporary writers in other languages.) By comparison, Western Europeans are accustomed to translated works making up about one-third of their smorgasbord of literary offerings. In 2003, then–PEN Translation Committee chair Esther Allen noted in a letter to the editor of *Harper's* that, according to a then-recent United Nations Development Program report, the Arab world, with a population of 280 million, translated only about 330 books per year—a figure directly comparable to that in the United States, where, with a population of 285 million and a vibrant publishing industry annually producing close to 200,000 books per year, we also published about 330 books in translation per year (excluding technical and scientific treatises). Official censorship and weak publishing infrastructure may be largely to blame in those notoriously "closed" societies in the Middle East, but what is our excuse in America? In summer 2003, the *New York Times* announced that "America Yawns at Foreign Fiction," while pointing out that the number of books in translation that year accounted for fewer than 0.5 percent of the books available to Americans. The article seemed to accept at face value publishers' contention that only "the market" is to blame, without acknowledging that successful "markets" are cultivated gardens, not wild states of nature.

To add insult to injury, in 2004, it came to the attention of the publishing community that the Treasury Department's Office of Foreign Assets Control (OFAC), which monitors transactions with nations under embargo, had for a number of years been requiring any publisher wishing to bring out a work by an author from a so-called "enemy nation" to apply for a license. In 2003, these nations included Iran, Iraq, North Korea (what George W. Bush memorably called the "Axis of Evil"), as well as Cuba and Syria. In recent history, Libya and Sudan have been on and off the OFAC list. Though the law was part of a larger set of economic sanctions against countries whose governments were in violation of international regimes, it seemed contradictory to say the least that a publisher in a country fiercely proud of its tradition of free speech should have to apply for a government license to translate, say, Iranian human rights activist and Nobel Peace Prize winner Shirin Ebadi. Ebadi clarified the absurdity of the problem when she wrote a *New York Times* op-ed piece in 2004 arguing for a lifting of the prohibition so that she would be able to publish her memoirs in the United States, asking,

If even people like me—those who advocate peace and dialogue—are denied the right to publish their books in the United States with the assistance of Americans, then people will seriously question the view of the United States as a country that advocates democracy and freedom everywhere. What is the difference between the censorship in Iran and this censorship in the United States? Is it not better to encourage a dialogue between Iranians and the American public?

Soon after, the OFAC issued a blanket license that permits all publishing activity involving writers living in embargoed countries. Thus the OFAC has managed to preserve intact its power to grant—or revoke—such a license. Writers who are government officials remain suspect, however, so if the Libyan writer Kamel al-Maghur included in this collection were still alive and active in the government, Words Without Borders could not have commissioned translation of his writing without the explicit permission of the U.S. Treasury Department.

This book was born in conscientious objection to the use of "axis of evil" rhetoric and to the OFAC's apparent fear of "free trade" in ideas and literature, a fear that seemed to mirror that of bureaucracies in those regimes that appear on the OFAC's list. Many of the writers in this volume were found living in exile from their homelands, but many others could not have been translated without the OFAC's explicit approval, prior to Ebadi's intervention into the affair. Words without Borders, which gratefully receives grant funding from the National Endowment for the Arts to support its translations of foreign literature, is required to affirm that none of this funding or the necessary matching funds goes to authors living in any of these countries.

The "Axis of Evil" is an abstraction that obliterates both the very great differences between the included countries, which are not even remotely in alliance with each other, and the distinctiveness of the individuals who live in them. The devastation wrought by the "axis of evil" rhetoric and thinking behind it, from Abu Ghraib to the deaths and maiming of so many thousands of people, military and civilian, and the deaths and maiming yet to come from cancer and other illnesses related to depleted uranium from American "smart" weaponry—this is now glaringly clear. But it is not the place of this book to provide foreign policy analysis or commentary. Our hope was that with this book we might simply celebrate diverse works of literature and through them, provide fresh perspectives on the notion of the "enemy nation." Is the "enemy" a particular leader, or a more pervasive ideology? A system of government, a people, a social group? Our intention has never been to present a naive apology for tyrannical regimes nor to recommend any particular political solution to the problems they present both internationally and for their own people, or to condone a commercial globalization dominated by the English language, or—least of all—military interventions by the United States.

Rather, we aim simply to stimulate international conversation through literature, with all its complexity and nuanced insights into the ideas, beliefs, daily lives, and articles of reference of people in other cultures, who are thinking and writing in languages other than English. In the immediate aftermath of 9/11, many of us hoped that if any good at all could come of such a tragedy, it might be a renewed awareness that we are part of the much larger tapestry of an interdependent world. It also seemed to some of us that embedded in the assault was a warning about the dangers of simplistic, abstract generalities about "the other," whoever those others might be. Clearly the attacks on the World Trade Center were an assault on a symbol, made in total ignorance of the reality of the particular human lives unfolding within the towers. To the extent that people within existed at all for the attackers, it was in abstract terms, as "infidels." And yet, the posters of the missing that wallpapered New York bulletin boards and phone booths and telephone poles for weeks were anything but abstract: they evoked the absolute individuality of singular lives, from one person's fondness for dancing to another's tattoo on a left shoulder blade. They were a painful poetry, asserting individual lives against amorphous mass death, intimate knowledge against ignorance. We hoped then that our president might declare a "war on ignorance"—because to cast the attackers as ignorants, as they were, despite their scientific degrees, would deprive them of the glamour the word "terrorist" might have for the young and furious. But a war on ignorance would also obligate us to address the ignorance in our own culture (ignorance of the rest of the world, ignorance of our own weaknesses) that makes us vulnerable.

Literature, at its best, should allow us to see the individual rather than the general; to participate in some intimate way in other lives rather than melding them into shapeless abstractions. How many Americans—even the most bookish—have ever read the work of a contemporary writer living in Iran, Iraq or North Korea? Newspapers give us accounts of tyrannical and corrupt leaders, and brave dissidents under trial—the heroes and villains of the story—yet rarely do we have any contact with the more subtle hopes and ambitions of unique individuals, the oddballs and misfits as well as the "ordinary citizens."

Certainly young people have understood viscerally the need to look outward and to know more about the rest of the world: applications to study abroad, especially in non-Western countries, are on the rise, and college classes on foreign subjects that were underenrolled a few years ago are now hugely popular. Multiculturalism—a novel term only twenty years ago—is already a fact not only of American life but of American literature and culture. The success of

so many books and movies about the American ethnic experience—
and of dozens of foreign writers living and writing in English, from
Azar Nafisi to Khaled Hosseini to Arundhati Roy—suggests that
Americans may not be as provincial in their tastes as is often assumed.
Perhaps we are on the way to a true multiculturalism, which will be
a global multiculturalism.

A great deal of humanities scholarship has been devoted to de-
bunking naive universalist claims for literature and to pointing out
the importance of preserving and respecting "difference," rather
than stirring up one bland soup and calling it "international." For
related reasons some academics contest the idea of reading literature
in translation at all, especially in translation into English, arguing
that this is a colonialist exercise that can only distort and tame foreign works—especially, now, those coming from Arabic writers. As
the brilliant radical critic Ammiel Alcalay has said, "once you sanc-
tion and legalize a certain kind of border crossing, it domesticates
the concept and precludes a truer border crossing that would really
disrupt ways of thinking and approach." Likewise, some argue, our
general ignorance of the contexts in which these works were written,
and the literary antecedents to which they refer, can only inhibit if
not actually deceive our understanding. Yet communication is essential (if always imperfect), especially the complex and profound communication to be found in literature, and we still believe that it is
better to get someone on the telephone—even if there's some static
on the line—than not to make the call.

Others have questioned whether our selection process inevitably
means that we will choose works more accessible to American readers, thereby—despite all of our good intentions—winnowing out
the truly "foreign." Certainly, as when we find foreign friends, common points of reference help to establish the relationship. One
hopes, however, that such relationships go beyond narcissism, and
that common ground simply provides a space to begin to explore

what is not necessarily shared. Out of step with less-enlightened elders, the clever student in Iranian writer Houshang Moradi-Kermani's "The Vice Principal" will seem a deeply familiar figure, as will the condemned soldier longing for the comforts of ordinary domestic life in Sudanese writer Tarek Eltayeb's "The Sweetest Tea with the Most Beautiful Woman in the World." Yet with works ranging from the magical realism of Kurdish-Syrian novelist Salim Barakat's *Jurists of Darkness* to the eerie and frightening expression of a rigid ideology in Kang Kwi-mi's "A Tale of Music" from North Korea, it seems unlikely that readers will complain that the works they find here are "not foreign enough."

We were dependent on a network of foreign editors, academics, and translators to provide access to works included here. No doubt there are great writers we have overlooked or could not contact. This is neither a definitive selection nor, obviously, a thorough and encyclopedic collection of work from these countries. In the case of North Korea, our initial expectation of finding "samizdat" literature turned out to be naive; all that we could find was in fact propaganda literature. In North Korea, it seems there are not only things that must not be said, but every work must in the end praise the Great Leader or it never sees the light of day. Nonetheless, there are moments of luminous poetry and humanity in these works that are all the more moving for the circumstances under which they must have been written.

In the case of Syria, we faced not only a concern that writers might suffer repercussions for appearing in an American publication (especially one with the title *Literature from the "Axis of Evil"*) but also an internalization of political tensions that meant that one writer might not want to appear alongside another associated with a different political point of view. In Iran and Saddam Hussein's Iraq (as, once upon a time, in the Eastern bloc) writers clearly had to work around political censorship and in many cases went into exile.

In Iraq, writers' lives have obviously been complicated (to put it mildly) by wartime, and it may be years before writings emerge that truly represent life under Saddam and afterward. Yet works both from Iran and Iraq published on Words Without Borders reflect the trauma for both societies of the Iran-Iraq war—the formative experience of a generation, as central to both literatures as World War I was to the literature of Europe and America.

We found it quite difficult to obtain work from Sudan, while wonderful work from our nearest enemy nation, Cuba, is so abundant (and, in relative terms, widely available in the United States) that with great regrets, we ultimately decided to present only a tiny sampling. Overall, our original draft of this book was far too long; the equivalent of a companion volume of works for which there was no room here may be found on www.wordswithout borders.org. There, too, one may find literary work from around the world and a vibrant community of people dedicated to international literature.

There is no doubt that this is an "American" project, taken up with the best of intentions, but nonetheless from an American point of view—there is no other logic for gathering work from these countries together than the fact that the American government has branded them as hostile nations. A number of writers and potential advisers refused to participate for that reason, greatly troubled by the current title and its implications or possible interpretations. Tarek Eltayeb from Sudan, in his section introduction, movingly expresses the unfairness of pigeonholing writers by country of origin, let alone "enemy" country of origin; and one of our favorite Libyan authors withdrew his selection at the last moment, presumably for this reason. In Libyan author Kamel al-Maghur's "The Soldiers' Plumes," characters are defined not by nationality nor even by city but by a neighborhood, coping with a long succession of outsiders. Yet we dearly hope that the benefits of the book, in allaying ignorance, stimulating curiosity, and opening the minds of readers, will outweigh its faults.

Once upon a time, knowledge of Greek and Roman literature (in the original languages!) was considered essential to the cultured person. In medieval Spain, Arabic was the treasure chest of the world's knowledge. More recently, familiarity with French, Russian, and German literature (in translation) were the hallmarks of the truly civilized Anglophone—even when English speakers were at war with speakers of those other languages. Now, once again, we must aim to widen, not diminish, our circles of reference, thus waging the eternal battle against ignorance and fear of the "enemy" with at least a few glimmers of the pleasure, courage, and largeness of spirit these writers may provide.

The Editors of Words Without Borders
www.wordswithoutborders.org
May 2006

Iran

Iran, formerly known to the West as Persia, is home to an ancient culture distinct from the rest of the Middle East. Two and a half millennia ago, it was the center of the largest empire the world has known, remembered for its enlightened tolerance of the religions of its subject peoples and the earliest known document to serve as a bill of rights. The Zoroastrian religion originated in Iran at this time, too, and, though eclipsed by the coming of Islam with the Arab conquest in the seventh century, its legacy remains alive in many traditions that set Iran apart from the Arab world.

Shiite Islam has been the dominant faith in Iran since the fifteenth century, and is closely aligned with the sense of national identity. Its origin story of tragic injustice and heroic suffering at the battle of Kerbala—and its extravagant emotional expression—is a template that has shaped popular culture and the interpretation of political events and social justice for many generations. Today, 90 percent of all Iranians identify as Shiite.

At the same time, there is substantial diversity in this country of seventy million people, including many different tribal groups (some still semi-nomadic), Kurds, Arabs on the gulf coast, Assyrian and Armenian Christians, a Jewish community that traces its origins to the time of Esther, and, recently, a large influx of refugees from Afghanistan and Iraq. Countering any centrifugal forces are a century of strong control from the central government, as well as the more subtle unifying influences of government-sponsored media, public schooling, and compulsory military service.

Iran's modern history began with the Constitutional Revolution of 1906, which first instilled democratic ideals and tried to curb the corrupt Qajar monarchy, followed by the rise to power of Reza Shah, who modeled his vision of a secular, modern nation on Kemal Atatürk's Turkey. Forced to abdicate by the Allies during World War II, he was replaced by his son, Mohammad Reza Shah. In the early 1950s, Prime Minister Mohammed Mossadeq galvanized a democracy movement with his attempt to nationalize the oil industry, until then controlled by the British. He was removed from power in a CIA-led coup, which left oil profits shared equally by Iran and a consortium of Western oil companies. The shah's cooperation with Western interests, along with his repressive rule and the cultural disruptions of rapid modernization, led to widespread popular unrest and eventually to the Islamic revolution of 1979. The power vacuum was quickly filled by Ayatollah Khomeini's radical theocracy. For Americans, the defining event of the Islamic revolution was the crisis when American embassy staff in Tehran were held hostage for 444 days, which ended all relations between the United States and Iran. For Iranians, this event is eclipsed in memory by eight years of war against Iraq, with a million dead and Saddam Hussein's aggression fueled by the United States.

Although the Islamic revolution is perceived in the United States as a conservative religious throwback to a premodern era, the reality on the ground has a different flavor, if only as a function of time passing. In the three decades since the fall of the shah, there have been huge strides in development, literacy and education, public health, and infrastructure. There are modern problems, too, many stemming from the pressures of a young population, half of which is under the age of twenty and facing soaring unemployment.

The literature of the Persian language is dominated by the giant figures of the classical poets such as Hafez (1320–90), Rumi (1207–73), Sa'adi (1220–90), Khayyam (1048–131), and many others barely known in the West. Their poetry is very much alive today, recited and loved by Iranians at all levels of society, and its influence extends far beyond Iran's modern boundaries to Afghanistan, Pakistan, and India. Many of the classical poets speak from the Sufi tradition of Islamic mysticism, and it is mainly through poetry that Sufi mysticism, distrusted by mainstream Islam, has become deeply embedded in Iranian aesthetics and moral values.

Another legacy of the classic poetry is that literature continues to hold pride of place among the arts in Iran even today. Contemporary poets and novelists enjoy a heroic status in Iranian popular culture that American writers might envy. Here we present a sampling of three very different voices. Poet Ahmad Shamlou, who died in 2000, has been a monumental and revered presence on the literary scene for most of the twentieth century. Houshang Moradi-Kermani, now in his seventies, has focused his energy on young readers, and his own memories of a more innocent era have helped to shape the imagination of several generations of Iranian youth. Finally, Tirdad Zolghadr offers a glimpse through the cosmopolitan kaleidoscope of contradictions that is Tehran today.

Zara Houshmand

THE VICE PRINCIPAL
Houshang Moradi-Kermani

TRANSLATED FROM THE PERSIAN
BY CONSTANCE BOBROFF AND
M. R. GHANOONPARVAR

If there's one author the mention of whose name is apt to cause an Iranian face to light up, it is Houshang Moradi-Kermani. He was born in Sirch Village near the city of Kerman in south central Iran in 1944. At the age of twelve, he left his village, first moving to Kerman and then to Tehran, where he attended university, graduating in English literature. His collection, The Stories of Majid *(from which "The Vice Principal" is taken) was first published in 1979, the year of the Iranian Revolution—a year that saw a publishing boom—and has been reprinted over two dozen times. It has also been made into a television series, making the boy-hero Majid a household name. Moradi-Kermani is also the most translated modern Iranian author, and he continues to garner award after award in European literary circles while remaining virtually unknown to Americans. Majid, like the heroes in all of Moradi-Kermani's books, pulls himself up by his own resourcefulness despite the hurdles imposed by the dominating authorities. "The Vice Principal" appears here in translation for the first time.*

———————

The kids had turned the classroom upside down when the vice principal, all charged up, stuck his head in the door:

"What's going on in here, you jackasses?"

The vice principal as usual was holding a switch in his hand and was the very picture of Jack the Ripper, all mean and stern. As his voice boomed in the classroom, the kids flew like frightened mice from the blackboard and the nooks and crannies of the classroom and stuffed themselves back in their seats. In an instant, the screaming and pell-mell subsided. The vice principal came into the classroom and stood just inside the doorway. He cast a harsh and bitter glance at the kids, who were doing their best imitations of innocent lambs, and said:

"What do you have this period?"

"Composition, sir."

"Who is your teacher?"

"Mr. Hosseini. They say he's been transferred and isn't coming anymore."

"All right, shut up then and do your work. If anyone makes a sound, I'll come and paddle him until he's black and blue."

"May we go outside, sir?"

"No. Get your asses back in your seats right now. I'll be back in a moment to take care of you."

He left to make the rounds of the courtyard, looking in on the classrooms and inspecting the premises before coming back. No sooner had he put a foot out the door than the classroom turned again into a flea market. The hollering and commotion of the kids rose to fill the air. They flew out from behind the desks and started climbing atop each other's heads and shoulders, onto the door, and up the walls. Bits of chalk, erasers, watermelon seeds, date pits, pens, and notebooks flew around the place, hitting the kids in the back of the neck and on the forehead, eyes, and ears. The foulest of swear words were launched from every direction. The sounds of the hooves of a herd of galloping mules and crash landings onto desks and benches resounded in the classroom as plumes of chalk dust filled the air.

A few of the children sounded a false alarm, "The vice principal is coming." But he didn't come and didn't come.

When he finally did come, the period was just ending. At the back of the classroom, two of the boys were wrapped up in a wrestling match.

"Again you're at it, you jackasses!"

The wrestlers had clamped onto each other's legs like lobsters. Their faces had turned the color of cooked beets from the strain. The vice principal's words did not make it to their ears. As the two friends were thus occupied, the vice principal came up behind them and his arm got down to work.

He delivered seven, eight, ten hearty counts of the switch to their arms and legs and just below their fannies until their limbs went completely limp and they let go of one another.

Tails between their legs, they hopped back in their seats.

The vice principal laid his switch on the teacher's desk. He flared his nostrils once and went up to the board.

He took a piece of chalk and on the board he wrote:

"Who Renders the Greatest Service to Mankind?"

"This is the subject of the composition for next time. Write it and bring it to class. Anyone who doesn't do the assignment, woe upon him!"

"Sir, you aren't going to tell us more about it?"

"It requires no further explanation. It's in fact very simple. You are free to write your own opinion. Who serves people the most? Teacher, doctor, soldier, businessman, worker, merchant . . . in short, whoever, it strikes you, does the greatest service for men and society. It's entirely up to you."

"Are you yourself going to take our class?"

"Yes, I myself am coming. Now, go quietly out in the yard."

It was as if the cage door had opened. The kids flew into the yard flapping their wings.

I was standing in front of the class reading my composition aloud from my notebook. The classroom was silent and no one dared breathe. Only from time to time the sound of a lone cough or psst-psst or hee-hee could be heard from the periphery. The vice principal was sitting in his chair. He had his switch on the table in front of him at the ready. He was sucking on hard candy and emitting slurping noises from under his thick mustache. He was a notorious smoker. He'd recently laid his cigarettes aside and had taken up eating hard candy in order to free himself from his smoking habit. Whenever he'd get the craving for a cigarette he would toss a few pieces of candy down the hatch instead.

I was reading my composition with gusto and dramatic flourish and my voice was echoing throughout the classroom:

Yes, in this great world of ours, all men toil and their work is a benefit to the welfare of society. Doctors treat the sick, engineers draw up building plans, and teachers make the children of men literate, that in the future they shall not grow up blind and ignorant. Soldiers fight in wars and do not allow cold-blooded, godless enemies to lay a hand on our wealth, honor, and dear country. Police go without sleep all night and catch thieves and lead them to jail. Likewise, the grocer, spicer, shoemaker, carpenter, and blacksmith each serve mankind in some way.

Most of our parents expect that we will become doctors and engineers and be respected members of society. And if it turns out that we can't get so far in our studies, we become teachers. And if we should give up learning halfway through, either because our parents can't afford to send us another year or because we acted lazy, then we go into business. Now business is a good thing. Society has a need for businessmen. Laborers too, for their part, work especially hard. Most of our fathers are businessmen or laborers and are proud of it. Thus, we cannot say who is the one who renders the greatest service to mankind.

However, if we think a little, we find there is someone in this society who serves men much. He puts in an abundance of effort and if one day he should turn his back or not be there, no one would be willing to perform his job and then we'd all become helpless. Yet despite all this, we don't like him at all and he takes no pride in his work. We all flee at the sight of him and if, God forbid, one fine morning our glance should fall on him in some back alley or on the avenue, we would block our eyes and immediately turn around and get off the streets and go home or back to our job. Yet, no one can be found who does not, sooner or later, have need of his services.

Yes, it is the town body-washer who, in my opinion, more than anyone, renders the greatest service to mankind.

When I got to this point, some of the kids couldn't contain themselves and started cracking up, and the classroom was overtaken by whispers. The vice principal struck the desk hard with his switch—whack!

"Silence!"

Then, turning to me:

"Read! May God silence your tongue, once and for all."

I read:

Yes, it is the town body-washer who in my opinion serves mankind most. Because no one praises him and however much he may be the biggest expert in his work and wash the dead body well and wrap a shroud around it, one does not give him a prize nor applaud him. At no time or place has anyone ever seen it written in the newspaper, "We are thankful to so-and-so, the body-washer who washed our father nicely." Or have you ever seen that when a certain body-washer has worked hard and gained some expertise in his work, they give him more pay and his business becomes brisk and his clientele increases?

All of us who have gathered together in this classroom and are in the pursuit of knowledge and learning, whatever else we may become, we don't want to become a body-washer. In fact, we are afraid of body-washers. Now, for us who are children, we will say nothing. But even my grandmother, whose age is advanced and who dreams of the dead every night and even has a shroud which was brought back for her from Karbala and which she's put in the bottom of her trunk and sometimes checks up on and even sleeps in, even she is afraid of the body-washer. A short while ago, she happened to catch sight of Leila, the body-washer in the market, and quickly averted her gaze and pulled my hand and said, "Let's go fast, Majid." But Leila ran up in front of her and said, "How are you, Bibi?" Granny responded to her greeting with a curt, "Not bad," and ran into a side street with me in tow. She could have warmed up to her a little and, during the conversation, casually dropped the request that when, if God wills it, after 120 years she's gone to the other world, would Leila please wash her well. However, Granny had imagined that when Leila had asked how she was doing, she'd been checking out business prospects and wanted to find a customer and see when the matter of washing Granny was going to yield cash so that she could start thinking how to spend it. Maybe she'd use it as a favorable promise of payment to the debt collectors. Granny was not at all thinking that everyone asks after each other's health and poor Leila too, like everyone, had simply wanted to say, "How are you doing, Granny?" Yes, until sunset that day, the color had clean gone out of Granny's face and she kept murmuring prayers under her breath and blowing the air around her to ward off evil.

But, this same Granny, whenever her eyes happen to fall on the doctor, do you think she so easily lets him go? She suddenly remembers all her pains and diseases and she goes on yapping so much about them the doctor can't flee from her fast enough. Thus we see that everyone fears the body-washer.

I looked out of the corner of my eye. I saw the vice principal was furiously having a go at one of the hairs of his mustache and was hellbent on pulling it out by the root, and instead of sucking the hard candy a little at a time, he was chewing it with vengeance. The twin sounds of the crunch-crunch of hard candy and the switch smacking against the desk were getting louder by the minute.

God knows how upset he'd become. The children were grinning from ear to ear and laughter was choked up in their throats. Whenever one of them couldn't contain it and exploded with laughter, the vice principal would respond with a hard whack on the desk with the switch.

"Shut up! Let me see what stinking load this jackass has dumped with this composition of his."

I got really frightened. I said:

"Sir, you want me to not read anymore?"

"No, go on, read that nonsense so everyone will see how much of a stupid idiot you are! Read!"

"Yes, sir."

So I read:

In order to write this composition, I went and made some inquiries here and there about the life of Kal Asghar, the body-washer, and his wife, Leila, the body-washer. I found out the storekeepers don't like to sell goods to them. When they see those hands, they are frightened since they know that one day those very hands will wash their own lifeless bodies and those of each of their family members. Every time Kal Asghar the body-washer gets on his bicycle and goes for a ride around town, policemen turn their heads away in order that they not see him. Even if he commits an offense, they don't fine him. He has two daughters who are—and if you will, I mention them here only as sisters—right at the marriageable age and who radiate beauty like the full moon. However, no one comes to take their hand. Up to now, no one has even seen anyone inviting them to a wedding. Just imagine what it would feel like to be at a wedding and the body-washer is right there next to you. Would you be able to feel comfortable eating the fruits and sweets and wedding dinner? Certainly, I wanted to go over to Kal Asghar the body-washer's and ask lots of questions and include them in my composition. However, I was afraid of him. Even though it's a small town and everyone knows his body-washer, still, few people have any real details about their lives. Everyone just avoids them. They themselves, of course, know all these things but are polite enough to pretend not to notice and just go on practicing their trade, expertly washing the dead. Thus, they render a greater service to man than anyone else. Nor do they expect much from anyone. While in retaliation for this unkindness, they could give a few good kicks to the ribs and abdomen of anyone in town who dies, or at least give him a pinch when the next of kin isn't looking and thereby unload some of their pent-up grief. The dead person also, what with his condition, can't exactly start screaming and shouting and swearing and saying, "Ouch."

Now please compare him with the bath attendant at the

public bathhouse. Since we are alive and talk with him and engage him with a warm, "How do you do?" in the byways and streets and as long as we can afford it, we show no restraint in giving him a tip; despite this, when he's giving us a rubdown, it seems he's making us pay our fathers' debts. The way he puts so much force into rubbing the scrubbing pad and scrapes so hard into the delicate skin of our bodies you'd think he wants to remove our hides completely. For a few days, the place where he has mauled us really burns. And when he massages, he yanks and twists our arms so much that one would think he was a butcher with a predilection for tearing apart the thigh bones of a cow. Then when he applies the soap to our heads for the shampoo and rubs it in, he tugs at our hair with such a vengeance that our "Ows!" echo throughout the bathhouse. And in the same way, we fear that due to the sheer, overpowering force of his strong paws which bend our necks to the left and right, little by little our necks will become loose and will come out suddenly from between our shoulders, and our heads will remain in his hands and our bodies will fall on the floor of the bathhouse.

As we know, the body-washer never does this to a corpse and this is where it becomes evident to us how forbearing and kind body-washers are. But never mind all that! Still, with the sting of our tongues we torment the body-washer and shower snide remarks on him. For example, any time we see someone who looks a little odd and his clothes are mismatched and his hair is disheveled and his complexion is pale and there is rather a lot of gunk around his eyelashes and drool is dripping out of the corners of his mouth and he's got a nasty disposition, we say, "He looks just like a body-washer," and this is totally unfair since our very own body-washer has a proper black hat and coat which appear to have once belonged to some affluent person. And as opposed to many of the people of this town, he isn't grouchy and there is always a sweet smile engraved on his lips.

In short, we don't pass up any opportunity to inflict evil on the body-washer. Yet he, with complete patience and forbearance and self-sacrifice and pleasant demeanor, nicely washes and shrouds all the people of the town, one by one from doctor to teacher, grocer, office worker, and policeman. He holds no grudge in his heart for anyone. He wouldn't hurt even an ant nor has he any expectation of respect and commendation from anyone. Therefore, we should conclude that . . .

Suddenly, the back of my neck was stinging, my tongue froze in my mouth, and my notebook fell out of my hand.

I looked up and saw that while I was deeply engrossed in reading my composition, the vice principal had come up on tip-toe upon me and was now swatting me with the switch. The kids had put their fear aside and unleashed their laughter into the classroom. The vice principal laid another one on the back of my neck with his switch. His face had turned black as coal. I stood staring at him at a complete loss. He was about to explode with anger. The two ends of his mustache and the flaps of his nostrils were shaking. He had a fat and fleshy face with hanging skin. Whenever he'd get very upset, the skin of his face would form rolls and the rolls of flesh would take on a life of their own. His eyes had become the size of two bowls, huge and bloody. He turned to the kids:

"Shut up, shut up, jackasses!"

The kids swallowed their laughter. The class quieted down. I bent over and picked up my notebook. I said:

"May I sit down?"

"No, stay right there, I have business with you."

I ran my hand over the back of my neck, which was burning something terrible, and said:

"I think it would be much better if I sat down, sir. Seeing as how my composition is over. And then since you have already given me my beating, there's nothing much left to do. Why not let someone else come and read his composition?"

The vice principal stared unblinkingly at me and chewed on the tip of his mustache.

"You're trying to turn the class into a circus, aren't you?"

"Me? Me, dare do such a thing . . . ?"

"Yes, you. In my classroom, clowning around. I'll teach you a lesson on clowning around that you'll remember as long as you live."

"What clowning around, sir?"

I was shaking like a leaf. It dawned on me and there could be no denying it: I was done for. He said:

"What was that garbage that you read?"

"My composition. I wrote it and read it."

He raised the switch up and then lowered it very hard. This time, instead of the back of my neck, the switch struck me in the face. It didn't hit me in the eye, thanks to some miracle; it hit me on the lip. The switch was slender and flexible. It wrapped around my head and went all the way around and hit me in the earlobe, setting it on fire.

"What . . . that the body-washer does the greatest service to mankind? Is this how to write a composition? May the body-washer come and cart your ugly face out of my sight. Who wrote all this nonsense for you?"

"I wrote it myself. I'm good at literature."

"To hell with your literature."

My hands were shaking. My lips had gone dry. My ear was burning. I said:

"You said we were free to write whatever we wanted. You said, 'It's entirely up to you.'"

"So that means in your opinion, jackass, no one does more for people than the body-washer? You mean, doctors and teachers and shoemakers and bricklayers are useless?"

"I didn't say they're useless. I said all of them are good, all of them perform a service."

"But you wrote, 'The body-washer does the greatest service.'"

"Yes, I agree I did write that. But since people don't like him, they even tease and bother him. But he doesn't hold it against them and still goes on serving people."

The vice principal sat down on his chair. If there was any time he deserved a smoke, this was it. However, instead of a cigarette, he took some hard candy out of his pocket and tossed it into his mouth.

He chewed it in a mad frenzy, crunch, crunch, crunch. His mouth might have sweetened up a bit, however, his mood remained as bitter as before. He said:

"Was your father a body-washer?"

"No, sir."

"What about your grandfather?"

"Not him either; nobody in our family was ever a body-washer."

"Do you yourself, when you grow up, want to become a body-washer?"

"No sir, I myself am afraid of the body-washer."

"What do you want to become with this defective brain of yours?"

"Whatever God has planned. However, mostly I wish I could become a writer."

Notwithstanding the foul mood and the all-consuming anger, all of a sudden he gave a laugh. His dirty, yellow teeth which had so long ago become completely ruined from all the cigarette smoke emerged from under his mustache.

His laughter was bitter and soundless. He stuck his hand in his pocket and took out two big pieces of candy which were stuck together and stuffed them in his mouth and chewed, crunch, crunch, CRUNCH. I said:

"Shall I sit down, sir?"

"No, I'm going to make a human being out of you today. So, you say you want to become a writer, eh?"

"Yes, sir. God willing."

"Pity your poor readers! A writer should have a gentle soul and talk about roses and plants and moths and love and kindness and forgiveness and self-sacrifice, not about body-washers and grave-diggers and such things."

"I also talk about kindness . . . forgiveness . . ."

"Kindness? Of the body-washer, I'll bet! And I suppose you read books, too?"

"When I can manage to get ahold of them, yes."

"Have you read the books of Sadeq Hedayat?"

"I read one half-way but I didn't understand anything. I gave up."

"He always writes about body-washers, hearse drivers, the dead and these sorts of things. Have you read these things?"

One of the kids in the back, seeing an opportunity for himself, stoked the fire a bit:

"He reads all kinds of books, sir."

The vice principal shot back at him:

"Shut up, no one asked you anything."

My earlobe was burning. I rubbed it. The tip of my finger became bloody. I wiped off the blood with my thumb.

"Sir, shall I sit down?"

"No. You haven't said what your purpose was in writing this trash."

"Actually, to tell you the truth, I wanted to write something that would be new. Something no one had ever thought of. I knew everyone else would write about teachers and doctors and soldiers and these kinds of people; I didn't want my composition to be like theirs."

"So why didn't you go after, for example, the gardener, the farmer? Do they not work hard? In cold and in heat, they plant the wheat. The wheat becomes bread and you, jackass, stuff that bread into your damned stomach."

"What you say is completely true. However, no one dislikes the farmer. They say, 'Don't work too hard! Keep up the good work. God willing, your crops will be plentiful.' But no one tells the body-washer, 'God willing, your business will become brisk and you'll get a lot of customers,' even though this same farmer in the end will have to do business with the body-washer."

The kids unbottled their laughter. The vice principal turned red. He stuck his hand in his pocket and took out some candy and threw it in his mouth and chewed it:

"So you always have a ready answer?"

"Please let me sit down."

"No, wait. You wrote that nonsense on purpose so that the kids would laugh and you'd disrupt the class. Or else you wanted to make a fool of me. This was precisely your intention wasn't it? I myself have studied and grown up in schools and classrooms just like this. You can't pull the wool over my eyes. Your intention was to make a fool of me, wasn't it?"

"No, I swear to God I had no such intention. Okay, yes, I did wrong. May I sit down now?"

"Is this the kind of nonsense you always write instead of compositions?"

"It depends on the composition . . . on the teacher."

"If the teacher is a simpleton and can't defend himself, do you, jackass, then make a fool out of him?"

"No, sir."

"Then what, then?"

"If a teacher should say to the class, 'It's entirely up to you,' I go around looking for something fresh and write that. I don't copy from books like the others."

"I suppose if you were to write juicy swear words and insulting language, that would be fresh?"

A drop of warm blood dripped from my earlobe onto my neck and found its way down my collar. With the palm of my hand, I wiped it and said:

"Swear words are not to be written, I guess."

"Why not?"

I started to falter.

"Sir . . . may . . . I . . . ple-plea-se . . . sit down?"

"No, stay right there. I'm not done with you."

"Since you gave me what was coming to me, what is the need to keep standing here?"

"Since you want to become a writer, let's see when it's possible to write swear words and dish them out to people."

"As far as I know, it's possible to write swear words in stories. Although not just any swear word."

"For example?"

"For example, some swear words which aren't dirty, you can have them coming from the mouth of a character in the story in order to show that that character hasn't had a good family upbringing and can't control his tongue."

"Can you give an example? Give us a swear word that can be written."

My tail had been caught in the trap in a bad way. I couldn't think of any example that could be said, and that too, in the class-room. Every swear word that came to mind was dirty. All the bad swear words of the world had come into my head. However, show me the guy who would dare open his mouth in front of the vice principal and let out one of those!

The vice principal was staring me right in the eye. He was chew-ing the end of his mustache. I avoided his eye and looked at the ground. He'd gotten up. The switch in his hand was dangling like a baby snake. The vice principal was hoping to God that I would let out a swear word and then he would rearrange my head and shoul-ders. I said:

"Sir, may I sit down?"

"Give a swear word, then you can sit down."

"I don't know any."

"You say that and expect me to believe it? You have to give a swear word. Even if the bell rings, I'll keep you standing here. Did you think there was no one who could straighten you out?"

The class was so quiet that if an ant had crawled up the wall, the sound of its feet would have been audible. The kids just sat there watching the whole time. Forty or fifty pairs of eyes. I guess they were waiting for me to say a swear word and watch how the vice principal would beat the living daylights out of me. Perhaps they were even wishing to pipe up with a few suggestions themselves. However they didn't dare and were waiting for me to be the one to do their dirty business. They'd sit back and, from the comfort of their own seats, safe and sound, have the satisfaction of watching my downfall without any risk to themselves.

The vice principal became extremely impatient at my having gone mute. He raised the switch and said:

"Give us a swear word, jackass!"

Suddenly, something sparked in my mind. I was so pleased with myself, I didn't stop to think. I blurted out:

"Jackass."

The vice principal cried out:

"What?!"

"Yes, sir. 'Jackass' is a good, respectable swear word. Not too dirty and conveys the personality of the character as well. It can be used in a story."

He took it personally. He got offended. I hadn't bargained on this. Things had gone very wrong. If only I'd given an indecent swear word and not said "jackass!"

Nor did the vice principal fail to rise to the occasion. Instead of the switch, he raised his foot and gave me a hard kick in the bladder. I almost fell to the ground but I caught myself. Pain seared through my side. He wanted to rip off my head. He forced his voice into a low growl.

"So you mean I'm uncivilized then, ja . . . ja . . . jacka-a-a . . . ?"

He gagged on the rest of his words. I held onto my side.

"Sir . . . sir, I swear by the life of my Granny, I didn't mean anything. I couldn't think of any other swear word which I could say in front of you."

I didn't think things could get any worse when I heard someone open the door. Mash Reza, the custodian of our school, stuck his head in:

"Sir, shall I ring the bell?"

The vice principal, grating his teeth, bellowed:

"Ring it!"

Mash Reza left. The vice principal took my composition notebook from me.

"You need not come to school tomorrow. Tell your parents to come and pick up your school file. They can send you to whatever the hell place they want."

"Ding-aling-aling!" The bell went off. The kids broke up the class. The vice principal went outside. My composition notebook was in his hand. I ran after him.

"Sir . . . sir . . . please forgive me, I won't write these sorts of things again. Please just tell me what I should do now, sir!"

"I told you to tell your parents to come to school."

"I don't have any parents, sir. I have a grandmother who, may such a thing not happen to you, suffers from pain in the legs. She can't come."

"If no one can come, you yourself take your file and get lost."

The kids had gathered around us. The vice principal cleared a path for himself through the kids and went into the office. However much I ran after him and begged and pleaded, it was no use. I stopped just outside the office door. I craned my neck and glanced into the office through the window. I saw the vice principal putting my notebook on the principal's desk and showing him my composition. The principal read a bit and smiled.

The kids had crowded around me and were showering taunts on me. Some of them did, however, feel sorry for me. As I was looking through the window into the office, I saw my composition was being passed hand-to-hand among the teachers. The teachers were all grinning from ear to ear. One of them began to read it out loud and the others laughed. Mash Reza was serving them tea. They drank tea and laughed.

During the last period and that afternoon and evening I was pretty well spent with grief. I was completely down and out. I huddled up dejected in the corner with my chin on my knees and arms wrapped around my legs. I was talking to myself: "I don't dare tell Granny they've kicked me out of school. How could I tell her? The poor thing would die of grief. Whenever she worries, it only makes her legs hurt all the more. Next thing you know, she'll have gone and fainted. What would I say is the reason they threw me out? By writing a composition, I sure have created a mess for myself. I'll lose all respect in Granny's eyes. The poor thing was happy that at least I could write nice compositions. How will she brag about me to everyone now? If it were just a matter of math and algebra and geometry, that would be one thing. If they said, 'He hasn't studied his lesson, he hasn't done his problems, we kicked his bottom. We threw him out,' fine, that is one thing. But how can this be happening to me who was always tops in composition? How Mr. Hosseini used to praise me! How the kids used to clap for me! I used to hope and pray Monday would come to read my composition in class. Now they are saying you've written nonsense, take your file and get lost. And I didn't even write anything bad. Fine, I won't write anymore. I won't write a thing. Actually, I don't even want to become a writer. It only leads to headaches. I'm not going to read books either. But is that possible? Can I really not write anything? Not read anything? If I don't write anything, what would I do? I'll flunk out of Composition. I'll have to repeat the class. I'll copy out of books like the others. No, I'll write, I'll write myself. Fine, they'll kick me out. They'll beat me until I die. Did you think they'd forever go on picking you up and patting little Sweetie on the back? If only I was good at math. I wish I could play soccer . . ."

The samovar in front of Granny was boiling. Granny poured a glass of tea and placed it in front of me. She was probing me carefully. She figured out things weren't all right with me. She knew something was up, that I'd withdrawn into myself.

"What's wrong with you, Majid?"

"Nothing, Granny."

"Don't hide it from me."

"It's nothing, Granny."

"Did your exam thing go badly?"

"No."

"Don't you give me none of that 'No.' Then what the hell happened that has made you so gloomy?"

"A person doesn't have to be in a good mood all the time, you know. Even you yourself sometimes get gloomy."

"I'm not going to let you off the hook until you tell me what happened."

"Nothing happened."

"Did they say something to you in school?"

I got up and left the room. I went out into the courtyard. I sat down by the courtyard pool. Granny got up and came and stood behind me.

"Okay, fine. Get up and come inside. If you don't want to tell me what happened, then don't. I'll get to the bottom of it eventually."

I went inside and spread out my bedding and got in under the covers. I pulled up the quilt over my head so that my eyes wouldn't meet Granny's. I held my ears so that I wouldn't hear her voice. It became as clear as day to me that if she established eye contact or said anything to me, she'd get the whole story out of me and then all hell would break loose and we'd never hear the end of it.

However much Granny said, "Come, eat dinner, have some tea," I didn't respond. Nothing would go down my throat anyhow.

"Then get up and come and sit over here. Do your homework. Do some studying."

I wasn't capable of sitting up. My sides were aching. It was throbbing right in the spot where the vice principal had kicked me. I was having visions of my file under Granny's arm as she was leaving the school and I running after her. Granny's back was bent under the burden of shame and grief. From under the covers I heard the sound of Granny crying. She was sobbing. I stuck my head out from under the covers:

"What is it, Granny. Why are you crying?"

"What do you care?"

"Granny, nothing's happened. I've just caught a little cold, plus my head hurts."

Granny didn't say anything. She kept on sobbing and sniffling. I again stuck my head under the quilt. Granny got up. She went and fixed herself a water pipe and came back. She sat at my head and smoked the water pipe with great intensity, keeping it gurgling away nonstop. I was fighting the urge to cry. Tears welled up in my eyes. On both sides of my eyes they were spilling out and cascading down my ears. I said:

"Granny, believe me, nothing happened."

Granny took her lips from the mouthpiece of the water pipe. The gurgling sound of the water pipe stopped. Calmly and in a pleading tone, she said:

"I hope something bad hasn't happened to your uncle? Have you heard something and aren't telling me? Why don't you tell me and set me at ease."

I raised myself up in bed to a sitting position.

"Granny, I swear, nothing has happened to Uncle."

She said:

"All these things you do, you have no idea what you're putting me through. I've been imagining all sorts of things. I can't stop worrying."

I saw that if I didn't open up and tell her everything right out, the poor creature would stay awake until morning and plain die of grief. My heart melted for her. I was in a terrible bind. If I should lay everything on the table, that they'd kicked me out of school, woe upon us all. I'd never hear the end of it. Granny, at that time of night, would raise a racket such that everyone in the entire neighborhood would come to know, and yet if I held my ground and didn't say anything, she'd let her imagination get the better of her. Granny was puffing on her water pipe. She was sobbing away and rocking her head back and forth. God only knows what all she must have been imagining. I put my head under the covers. I waited until the bubbling sound of her water pipe stopped. I said softly and all choked up:

"Granny, you have to buy me soccer shoes."

It was as if my voice came from the bottom of a well. I wasn't sure whether or not Granny had heard my words. I said:

"I want to play soccer. You have to buy me a sports jersey and shorts. Will you?"

She didn't answer. She kept on puffing faster and faster on her water pipe. I said in a loud voice:

"I don't want to be a girly wimp. I'm not going to read books anymore. Books make a person get crazy ideas . . . turn you into a nerd."

I pushed back the corner of the quilt and looked at Granny's face. Still smoking the water pipe, she said:

"Did they say in school you were a nerd?"

I didn't answer. It was clear she'd stopped imagining the worst. She continued on the same track:

"Did you yourself get the idea you'd like to have soccer shoes or did they say to at school?"

I said:

"You have to come to school."

I didn't say anything more. She started talking about everything under the sun and then started listing her grievances and lecturing.

"A person need not make such a big deal over these things. I was thinking something had happened."

I slid under the covers. My throat was about to explode from wanting to cry. I was afraid I'd start crying out loud. I was afraid Granny would figure out the whole matter and I'd spill my guts out and then heaven have mercy on Granny.

That night, I didn't blink until morning. My eyes just remained wide open. Like someone who has gone to the grave with a guilty conscience, I kept turning from side to side. I racked my brains. I was about to go crazy. Suddenly, in the middle of the night, I sat up and exclaimed:

"Granny, Granny I don't want to become a writer and write books. They won't let me write what I want to write!"

But Granny was asleep and didn't hear my voice. The room was dark. I could hear the sound of Granny's slow breathing.

In the morning half-light, Granny was performing her ablutions when I startled awake and got out of bed. I got ready. Granny was still at her prayers. I took my bicycle and got out of the house without breakfast. Before Granny could come and shout, "Where are you off to?" I was already past the street corner.

I went straight to Mr. Hosseini's, our old composition teacher. I peeked in through the crack of the door and saw that not a creature was stirring in the house. I stayed and waited.

The sun was well up by the time I caught a glimmer of Mr. Hosseini coming up from the other end of the street. He had an overcoat on and had gone to buy bread and was just returning. Cheered, I went up to him:

"Hi, Mr. Hosseini, good morning!"

"Hello, how are you, Majid? What brings you over this way?"

"Nothing, I just came to say hi to you."

"So early in the morning!"

"I'd been missing you now that you don't come to our school anymore."

"That's nice of you to think of me."

I wanted to find a way to broach the topic but I didn't know how. I followed him up to his house. He said:

"Come in, have you had breakfast?"

"No, I'm not hungry . . ."

"You seem a little upset to me. Are you in some kind of trouble?"

I involuntarily grabbed his sleeve:

"Sir, I beg you, I'm desperate. I've been kicked out of school."

"What? What did you do to make them kick you out?"

"I wrote a composition. The vice principal didn't like it. He beat me and then said, 'Don't come to school tomorrow.' Granny is supposed to go and pick up my file."

"Strange! What exactly was it that you wrote?"

I recounted the story of the body-washer and jackass to him. He laughed and said, "You did wrong, you know."

I said: "If it had been you, even if you didn't like it, you'd have let it pass. You'd have explained to me what I did wrong."

He said softly and kindly:

"Now don't worry. What's done is done. These sorts of things happen often enough in life. You who want to become a writer must know and endure a lot of things. Don't worry, they just wanted to shake you up a little. Come in, let's have breakfast together. I'm getting late."

"Sir, I don't want breakfast. Please, can't you do something? Please do something to prevent Granny from having to go to school. My self-respect is at stake here."

"I'll phone your principal. Don't fret. Everything will work out, God willing."

"Sir, how can we bring the vice principal around? Sir, I'm worried to death."

"It's not the end of the world, you know. The principal is familiar

with your family background. The vice principal is new. He'll speak
to the vice principal."

"When should I go to school, sir?"

"In about two hours. I have to talk to your principal. Then you
go see him yourself. He's a good and forgiving man."

"May God grant you a long life, sir. If I ever become a writer, I'll
write a story in which I'll say that you were a great man."

He laughed and said:

"Your vice principal is also a good man. If he weren't strict, he
wouldn't be able to run the school."

"Sir! He's not into literature at all."

"Fine! So he's not. After all, not everyone should have to be
imaginative like you and be interested in writing and stories."

He patted me on the shoulder and offered me some bread. I
broke off a piece of his fresh bread and put it in my mouth. Mr.
Hosseini went inside. My spirits rose. I ate the bread and pedaled
my bicycle into the street, and off I went.

In two hours. I was riding around the streets on my bicycle asking
people "What time is it?" I would have to kill the two hours until it
was time to go see the principal. I knew Mr Hosseini to be a man of
his word and that he would definitely phone the principal. However,
I was so filled with dread, I feared he would forget.

The schoolkids were walking to school with books and schoolbags
in hand and I was wandering around in the streets, lost and bewil-
dered. I wanted to go to school and stand there and wait. However, I
was afraid the other kids would see me and there would go all my self-
respect. I was yearning to be in school and in class. My books and
notebooks were fastened to the front of the bicycle. Rubber bands
were holding the books and notebooks in place on the handlebar.

I passed by a few schools. The kids, alone or in groups, were going in. Aimlessly I cruised around, pedaling my bicycle. The shopkeepers were opening their shops. They were shaking the dust off their goods and hanging them up for display on the doors and walls. An old man wearing a black suit was walking briskly down the sidewalk. He looked like a teacher.

"Sir, what time is it?"

The old man was in a big hurry. He didn't answer. I asked again: "Sir, what time is it?"

He turned around. He saw my books and notebooks on the front of the bicycle. He said:

"The bell is about to ring, hurry up!"

He didn't say what time it was. He said, "Hurry up." Time was passing slowly. I wished to tell the old man, "They've kicked me out of school," but he'd gone and turned into a side street. The bazaar was good, the perfect place to kill time. I looked at a few shops and their miscellaneous trinkets. Time was going by swift as an arrow now. Accordingly, I turned into the coppersmith's bazaar.

A boy of my size with a ragged appearance, dirty hands and face, and rubber sandals on his feet was struggling to carry a big, heavy pot out of the shop and was putting it next to the door. I stopped to watch him. Suddenly my stomach fell. I said to myself, "Majid, once they've kicked you out of school, you'll be just like him. Starting tomorrow or the day after, Granny will grab you by the hand and bring you to one of these very shops."

Then I was disgusted with myself and thought, "Majid, you stinking idiot, what the hell is to be done with you? What gives you the right to think there is something wrong with this boy that you've got to look at him this way? If only they'd let him study, he'd run circles around you."

I got off my bicycle and leaned it against the wall. I said to myself, "Might as well get started practicing." I went up to the boy:

"Hi, want some help?"

I took hold of the other end of the pot. He looked at me as if he'd just seen the boogey monster. He said:

"Who are you?"

"A person, same as you."

I brought out a big copper tray and said:

"You folks don't need an apprentice, do you?"

He snickered and didn't answer. I looked at his feet, which were red from cold. The straps of his sandals left a mark on his thin and dirty little feet. His boss came, looking mean. He stormed at the boy, saying:

"Who is this?"

He gestured at me. The apprentice said:

"I don't know, I've never seen him before."

The master laid a slap across the face of the apprentice.

"How many times do I have to tell you, when I'm not around, don't let every Tom, Dick, and Harry enter the store!"

I saw the situation was dire. I jumped onto my bicycle and got myself out of there in a hurry. I could hear the voice of the boy behind me crying and sending all sorts of obscenities after me. I turned at the intersection and entered the main bazaar. The sun had risen higher, and from the holes in the roof of the bazaar, funnels of light were creeping down and hitting the walls. The bazaar smelled of dampness. The walkway in front of the shops had been freshly sprinkled with water. The bazaar was still quiet. I asked of a shopkeeper who was putting out a shirt to hang, "Sir, what time is it?"

"Twenty minutes to nine."

By the time I reached the end of the bazaar, those twenty minutes would be up. However, I would have to walk very slowly. I was not on my bike anymore. I thought, "Right now the kids are sitting in class and here I am wandering around with nothing to do." Then I remembered the coppersmith apprentice. I said to myself, "What a fine mess you got him into first thing in the morning. Gosh, I hope his boss didn't beat him too much."

I got closer to the bookshop, which was about midway down the bazaar and from which I was in the habit of buying books or taking them out on loan. I saw that in front of the store there was some commotion, and shopkeepers and passersby were crowded together back to back. I went forward and craned my neck. A woman's voice could be heard shouting up a storm. Her back was toward me. The voice was familiar. It was Granny! Suddenly I froze like a statue. What in the world was Granny doing here?

Granny was scolding and cursing and saying all kinds of nasty things to the old bookseller:

"May God bring you misery, man. You have caused my child to go astray with your infernal books."

She was throwing the books on display in front of the old man's shop and screaming like there was no tomorrow. She didn't give anyone a chance to speak.

"Why do you give these books to my boy to read and ruin his head? Did you think this child just came in off the streets or something?"

She picked up a hefty book and was about to hit the old man on the head. They stopped her. She said:

"You are the one who caused my child to be thrown out of school. God won't forgive what you've done."

The old man was at a complete loss:

"Me? I am the one responsible? Do you even know who you're supposed to be having it out with? Why are you making all this fuss?"

"The person I'm supposed to be dealing with is you. Don't try to pretend you don't know what I'm talking about, your name is Sadeq . . . Sadeq whatever, I don't know . . ."

"Who is Sadeq, Mother?"

"I've seen with my own eyes twenty times how my child saved up penny by penny and brought it and gave it all to you. Bought books from you. You've ruined him. You've caused him to go crazy. You've turned him out into the streets and I hope God tears you into tiny pieces. You should be ashamed of yourself, a man of your age. You gave those books to my child to read for what?"

I wanted to go up front but I didn't have the gumption. I was afraid of Granny. Not to mention I was curious to see how it would turn out.

The old man was standing there dumbfounded. Granny had let go of the books and burst out crying. A cloth seller who'd been watching the spectacle came forward to Granny:

"Mother, you know this poor guy's name is not Sadeq."

Granny kept on crying and spoke through her tears:

"It's Sadeq Hedayat. Now I remember, that's it. It's his books that he's read and been ruined. It's affected his head. Their teacher said he writes things that the devil himself wouldn't be able to come up with. He went and wrote a story about the life of Leila the body-washer and brought it in and read it in front of the class. They say it's all his fault. He took my child and completely perverted him."

The cloth seller spoke up:

"There's one bookseller on the other end of the bazaar. He spreads out his wares next to the wall, right there along the wall. He's your man. Go pick a fight with him. Maybe he is Sadeq Hedayat."

The old bookseller had just figured out what was going on. His temper softened. He smiled and rubbed his eye with the palm of his hand and said:

"Mother, the one you're after was a writer who died a few years back. I have never even stocked or sold his books. Go and ask, let's see who gave your child his books to read. Go and catch hold of that one."

Granny was sitting there crying. She was repenting what she had done.

"Now I don't know where my child has gone . . . what he's doing. He's completely vanished."

Finally, I worked up the resolve and, through the crowd, I went forward and took Granny's arm:

"Get up, Granny. I haven't gone anywhere. You are also wasting your time running around the bazaar looking for Sadeq Hedayat. Don't make a laughingstock out of us."

As soon as Granny's eyes fell on me, she blasted me, "Where the hell have you been? Why didn't you go to school?" Then she took my arm and dragged me: "Let's go to school."

We set out. The crowd was watching us. With a gesture of my head, I begged forgiveness from the old bookseller.

That morning, after I'd rushed out of the house in that state, Granny had figured out that something definitely must have happened at school. She'd marched straight to school to see the vice principal. The vice principal, in turn, agitatedly narrated for her the story of the "body-washer" right there in the school yard. He'd told her, "He read the books of Sadeq Hedayat and got all perverted." Granny for her part had imagined that Sadeq Hedayat was that same bookseller of whom I was the trusted and loyal customer and she lost no time in going to the bazaar and staging the Apocalypse.

In any case, we reached the school. I was afraid to go in. However, Granny tugged my sleeve and we went straight into the office to the principal. The vice principal was in the school yard and was wandering around among the kids with his infamous switch. In the office, we sat down. The principal was talking on the phone. I was hoping and praying that Mr. Hosseini was on the other end. In the end I never did figure out who he was talking to. The composition notebook was on the principal's desk. We waited until the principal's conversation came to an end and he put down the receiver. Granny hadn't even had a chance to wet her tongue when I got up from my chair. I said:

"Sir, I swear, I would rather the world come to an end than read inappropriate boo . . ."

The principal interrupted me mid-sentence:

"Don't speak until you are given permission. Behave!"

"Yes, sir."

I lowered my head and sat down. Granny spoke up:

"You please assign him some examples of nice handwriting, he has to copy it exactly as it is; he wouldn't dare write anything else."

The principal lit a cigarette and said:

"He has to compose it himself, Mother. Do you think this is first grade that we should give him words to copy out?"

"The minute he writes himself, you see how it turns out. Teach him however he should write that will please you. He's just a child. He's not yet been bumped around by life. He doesn't know anything about the bad and good out there. He thinks whatever he writes is okay . . . May God reward you, please help him. He doesn't have anyone. Treat him as your own child."

"It's not up to us. You yourself should sit down with him and give him guidance. Don't let him read just any trashy book and write any nonsense and bring it to class."

"Damn these books, sir, devil take them! To tell you the truth— you aren't a stranger from whom I'd hide it—he gets a penny and a dime from me, or sometimes his uncle, just to be nice, puts a coin in his hand. Instead of buying things or clothes or something to eat, he takes it and goes straight to the booksellers. They too, when they see he's alone, they just give him anything that comes to hand to read and totally spoils his mind. Of course, unlike you, I'm ignorant, I don't have any learning; what do I know what he reads and writes?"

I got up and, without permission, I said:

"Sir, we hear that every book is worth reading once."

The principal knocked his cigarette ashes in the ashtray and said:

"There you've gone and spoken again! What kind of idiot has said such a thing? There are many trashy books out there which one should not so much as look at, let alone read, especially someone of your age who doesn't know the difference between good and bad."

Granny drew her chador around herself and produced a few tears for the occasion:

"All that I suffer is just my hard luck. Sir, begging your pardon, he wants to become a poet . . . what do you call it, a . . . writer. I guess in our family, we've had all sorts . . . except poets and writers . . . why should I hide it from you, I've had a hard life. I've suffered bad luck and going without just to get him this far. My prayer to God has been that he'll be able to earn himself a bit of bread and keep his head high before friend and enemy alike. But no, now I see all I've worked for has come to naught. Some folks are lucky, sir. He has a cousin just a few years older who went and got a regular job in an office. Now he collects wages from month to month. They give him two sets of clothes and two pairs of shoes a year. His life, thanks be to God, is getting in order. Now you please tell this one here, if he becomes a poet or writer, what will that get him? Will they pay him for that? Will they give him shoes and clothes? When he gets bigger, will they give him a wife? To tell you the truth I don't know what he's setting his heart on."

Quietly I said to Granny:

"Granny, you've always liked the stuff I've written, now what happened all of a sudden that . . ."

God rest her departed soul, she stuck her elbow out of her chador and gave me such a jab in the ribs it took my breath away. The principal, who saw that Granny had started up with her whole life story and was wasting his time going on and on, got up and went to the door. He called the vice principal in.

The vice principal came in all charged up, letting the switch swing up and down. He sat on the chair across from Granny and me. Granny made me understand with her gestures that I was supposed to go and kiss the vice principal's hand and ask for forgiveness. Both repulsion and shyness held me back. I played dumb and stared at the corner of the ceiling where the plaster had peeled and there was a spider's web.

The principal turned to the vice principal:

"Forgive him this time; let him go back to class."

"He has to put it in writing that he won't read any nonsense in class and that he'll maintain order in the classroom and school."

Granny said:

"He'll write whatever you want—actually, go ahead and punish him, beat him as much as he can take. Just don't kick him out of school and ruin his life. May God grant you a long life."

The vice principal got up and took a blank piece of paper from the desk and gestured in my direction: "Come and write!" I took a pen out of my pocket and the vice principal dictated while I wrote:

> *I, the undersigned, in the presence of my grandmother, promise that from now on, I will restrain myself from writing anything that violates the order and discipline of the classroom and I will avoid disrupting class and I will not be disrespectful to the teachers. If I don't comply with these things, they have the right to expel me from school.*

The vice principal said:

"Now sign underneath."

I didn't know how to make a proper signature, so I just wrote my name and drew a circle around it. Then the vice principal motioned to Granny:

"Mother, you also put your thumbprint underneath."

He put ink on the tip of Granny's finger with the nib of his fountain pen, and Granny pressed her finger under the "Letter of Promise." The vice principal picked up the "Letter of Promise" and said:

"We'll put this in your file. So help me, if you violate it . . ."

Granny said, "He wouldn't dare violate it. You should grind him up and turn him into mincemeat."

Granny was making her way through the children in the school yard, her chador wrapped around her head, tightly covering her face. She left the school and I, composition book in hand, ran to class.

FROM *A LITTLE LESS*

CONVERSATION

Tirdad Zolghadr

*The writer and curator Tirdad Zolghadr was born in Califor-
nia in 1973 and raised in Iran, England, and Switzerland,
and now lives in Zurich. Since 2002, he has collaborated on
various publishing and exhibition projects under the title
Shahrzad. He served as co-curator for the seventh Sharjah Bi-
ennial in 2005. His work explores the transfer of knowledge
and theory between Europe and Tehran, and, more particularly, the mise-en-scène of internationalism in the arts. In this
selection from his "travel novella" A Little Less Conversation,
Zolghadr returns to Tehran in a brilliant blend of fiction and
autobiography, which later evolved into a novel,* Softcore
(Saqi, 2006).

Golmohamad turns and makes for the cab. The driver nods and
mumbles politely as he turns the key in the ignition. He's
wearing a light gray suit and looks like a young Leonid Brezhnew. As
they drive down Hafez Avenue, Golmohamad is struck by the fact

that in Tehran, you're rarely more than twenty feet away from a pizzeria serving cheeseburgers in a setting of purple bathroom tiles, fake black marble, and pink neon, with syrupy Iranian soft rock in the background.

The driver switches on the tape recorder, and Golmohamad recognizes Neil Diamond's song "Two-bit Manchild." "Hep-hep," says Neil Diamond. "Hep-hep—you want me—and I can't deny I'm a man."

Owing to his father's corporate career in multinational pharmaceuticals, Golmohamad grew up attending polyglot schools in six different cities in five West African republics, and moved back to his birthplace just over a year ago. When asked about motives for returning to Tehran, he refers to childhood memories, to family, to his mother tongue. "Something about the light, the landscape. Roots." The more he makes himself sound like a palm tree, the more people are touched.

The city's appeal, he decides, as they head for the highway leading toward the Karaj suburbs, must be the mere fact that it doesn't try to please, consisting largely, as it does, of sand, dust, glass, neon, and eight-lane motorways running straight through concrete housing projects. Surrounding the official center are scores of satellite towns and villages that are very similar.

Over the past twenty years, eight million locals joined the preceding four, most of whom were newcomers themselves. Swifter than speech, Golmohamad decides, somewhat theatrically. Lighter than language. To describe Tehran would be like spelling out a frenzied, hour-long dinner table discussion to a complete newcomer. Personally, he'd take Tehran over Isfahan flower gardens and donkey bridges any day, and finds a smug sense of satisfaction in the fact that there are many who would beg to differ.

Very recently, European architects in Prada dinner jackets and Le Coq Sportif have been here, reciting statistics from Dutch coffee-table exhibition catalogs, of the new avant-garde status of Third World metropolises carelessly breaking all urban records, proportions, and aesthetic standards. Western concepts and terminologies, they say, trying to sound apocalyptic, ominous, touched, enthusiastic, and nonchalant at the same time, can no longer do justice to the many Tehrans of this shifting world.

Golmohamad is well-groomed and tall, and, though visibly very sure of himself, he seems oddly self-conscious. This makes him what the French would call *sympathique*. Whether, on the other hand, the Germans, who like a certain touch of noncommittal humility in a young man, would grant him a *sympathisch* is an open question. For he is indeed the type of person who makes you wonder whether the difference between charm and egotism, or between concern and condescension, was as obvious as you had assumed.

Yashar, an elder relative and close friend of his father's, lives in one of the many satellite villages near the suburb of Karaj. With his two-meter height, his corduroys, denim shirts, and handsome, arrogant features, you might see a gentleman farmer in him, if it weren't for his high-pitched giggle and his pubescent sense of humor. He likes to surprise you by sticking his little finger in your ear and making obtrusive grunting sounds. Or by suggesting he had recently had sex with your mother, out in his apple orchard somewhere.

Some time ago, Yashar inherited a sizeable amount of land from his father, and, over the last thirty years or so, has earned the reputation of a skilled and distinguished host, conversational gambits notwithstanding. He speaks very little and is considered an outstanding listener. During the many afternoons Golmohamad has spent at the farm, he has witnessed army officers, political dissidents, a dervish, a folk musician, housewives, farmers, Swiss journalists, Arab tourists, and a TV newscaster sitting on the veranda, mumbling at Yashar as he sat with his hands folded in his lap and his head cocked to one side, doing a fantastic job of appearing to be sympathetic.

During the Iran-Iraq war, when both Baghdad and Tehran were pelted with Euroamerican missiles, dozens of families moved out of the city center to stay at Yashar's, where they went for long walks in the orchards, played volleyball, or sat around sipping date liquor and reciting eleventh-century poetry. *The dust on your doorstep / a paradise to me / a fervent pheasant / I fling myself / on searing arrows of your glance.* Or suchlike. In the evening, there was cheap dance music from L.A. and Istanbul blasting from a tiny tape recorder, and opium with sweet tea and honey pastries.

Yashar speaks fluent British English, with the high-pitched, whiny singsong of the Persian accent. He learned it as a student at the Imperial College in Kensington. He soon discovered how to withdraw considerable amounts of money from London banks by using alternating surnames and account numbers. This was how he paid for university tuition, a reasonable nightlife, and a Mini Rover, although he didn't own a driver's license, neither Iranian nor British. When a bobby politely demanded his license, Yashar showed his Iranian birth certificate, apologizing for everything being written in Farsi. In the symmetric center of the document, there is now a stamp saying, "This driver's license is hereby endorsed for six months."

In the 1930s, Yashar's father, as well as both his grandfathers, were officers under Reza Shah. Reza was the Iranian Atatürk, very keen on modernizing the country, by any means necessary. Iran, he insisted, was to be taken seriously. Reza found the term "Persia" embarrassing, seeing as it smacked of water pipes and flying carpets, and had it replaced by "Iran," which refers to the country's Aryan heritage. The Aryans were little more than a despairing mob of hungry Siberians who settled in what is now Iran a very long time ago. Most had long forgotten they had ever existed, when a small flock of German Romantics in wigs, white stockings, and fluffy shirtsleeves suddenly decided the Aryans had successfully colonized vast parts of

Asia and Greece, and declared them the "Cradle of Civilization." Reza Shah very much approved of the idea, as do many Iranians nowadays.

Be that as it may, Reza found the nomadic Iranian tribes of the early twentieth century at least as embarrassing as water pipes, if not more so, and took to luring the tribal leaders to peace talks or religious ceremonies, where he had them imprisoned or shot. This was the line of work Golmohamad's ancestors were in before settling down in a village which was, at the time, a good stretch away from the outer limits of Tehran.

On the way to Yashar's village, the taxi driver makes a detour through the Ekbatan housing project, an enormous assemblage of right angles, functional voids, and horizontal strips of glass and concrete, the stuff people refer to as "Stalinist," although Stalin actually preferred gigantic wedding-cake architecture, playful squiggles, and pointed turrets. Designed in the mid-seventies, at the peak of the hysterical optimism of the Shah era, Ekbatan is the largest housing estate in the Middle East. At an art opening in north Tehran last week, someone claimed Ekbatan had as many inhabitants as Sweden.

The car stops by the outer courtyard of block 44 D, where Afsaneh has been waiting for them, reading a paperback romance by Nicolas Bouvier. Afsaneh is a young up-and-coming video artist with a perfect gap between her front teeth. Watching her approach the cab, crossing the smooth concrete courtyard in the glaring afternoon sun, Golmohamad tries to relax the muscles in his gut by taking several deep breaths, as if to pull the air all the way down into his stomach. This is a technique he learned in acting classes as a teenager, a method against stage fright.

As Afsaneh climbs into the cab, the driver mumbles another standard greeting before resuming the journey towards Karaj. Golmohamad is still nursing a hangover from a housewarming party in his apartment the night before. The air flowing in through the open windows is hot and unpleasant.

At Yashar's, they find a small group of visitors having a late lunch on the veranda. They all interrupt their meal to awkwardly stand up and shake hands, and in a confused fit of coquetry, Golmohamad declines to join them for lunch, watching as Afsaneh is offered cucumbers in raisins, yogurt, and fresh mint, along with lamb and eggplant sauce on saffron rice with sour berries and a baked crust.

Afsaneh is wearing olive-green army pants, Charles Jourdan shoes, and a light blue T-shirt that says "Death to America" in pink. She praises Golmohamad for the things he has been pursuing since his arrival—his showroom in the making, his many ingenious plans and ideas regarding the gallery Web site, the merchandise, and the making-of documentary.

"In Iran, such things are totally, completely new to everyone," Afsaneh is saying. "They're far more appreciated than anywhere else."

He nervously assumes Afsaneh is coming on to him, but then realizes with disappointment that she isn't, so he snidely tells her that to impress the locals with flashy gadgets and cosmopolitan prattle, he could just as well move to Wimbledon, but then stops, seeing as she's not really listening. Surely enough, she smiles, rubs his elbow absentmindedly, and goes and sits down next to Yashar.

The swimming pool lies in the shade of an enormous oak tree, from which an occasional leaf or twig plummets down into the cool, dark water. Two men with shaved chests, gold chains, and perfect tans are floating around on inflatable mattresses shaped like bright red cell phones. Visibly bored, they collect the twigs and stick them between their toes. A pop diva from Uzbekistan makes pleasant cooing noises from the tape deck.

Yashar is now standing by the gate, talking to five young men surrounding a small, bearded figure in a traditional white frock.

Yashar introduces him to Golmohamad, saying this is his new neighbor, the famous Mr. Tarofi himself. In the years following the revolution, Tarofi was a notorious political figure, a traveling judge and henchman in one. One summer afternoon, Tarofi paid a visit to a drinking buddy of Yashar's, a Maoist poet, and dealt him a shot to the head in his own backyard.

Tarofi always wears Kojak sunglasses. His beard is remarkably thick, woolly, and amorphous. For security reasons, he is always accompanied by his many sons. Tarofi insists on speaking English. He sounds like Joe Cocker.

"Europe very good nice. Very nice, very good," he croaks. "Learn English Birmingham."

"Birmingham. So you've been to England."

"Yes. I go Switzerland for gon."

"Gun?"

"Yes. Go for buy gon. Engineers ABB. Brown Bovering."

"Guns for whom?"

"Gons for Iran. Very good nice."

"Yes. So you've been to Switzerland. Zurich or Geneva?"

"Go Bern."

So they chat, in Farsi now, and Golmohamad eventually ventures something like, "Mr. Tarofi must have many wonderful anecdotes to tell, about his exploits in the name of the revolution, he put in such great effort, let me go and sacrifice myself for him, may his breath be warm, may God give him life," and other standard Farsi formulae, but Tarofi refuses to go there.

"We made mistakes. But things have changed. And so have we." After the historic Iran-USA soccer game some years ago, Tarofi saw dancing couples and unveiled women on the street. He desperately wished to express his approval. "I share your happiness," he grunted at them. But once people recognized Tarofi, they formed a circle around him, clapping their hands and jeering, "Dance, Hâjji, dance."

Feeling confused and disappointed, Mr. Tarofi returned home. Suddenly, he turns back to Yashar, asks him a long list of questions on irrigation techniques, then waddles quickly off into the twilight, his sons running after him like groupies.

During the course of the evening, as a drunken discussion on international politics unfolds, Golmohamad can hear Afsaneh categorically stand up for the Iranian cause, the exemplary character of the Iranian model, the dignity of the Iranian revolution, and the political maturity of the Iranian masses, getting caught up in contradicting moral platitudes, until she finally falls quiet, staring furiously at her Charles Jourdans.

Sitting next to her on the settee is Pantea Paknazar, the youngest of the six Paknazar sisters, a portly, loud, acrimonious intellectual. As the discussion grows louder, Pantea is sporting a familiar complexion on her peachy face.

Recently, in an uptown Hare Krishna restaurant called Rama, Golmohamad watched her scream at a helpless waiter for a period of four minutes. "A reservation?" Pantea yelled at the slender young man in Dolce & Gabbana spectacles and a dark orange T-shirt. "A RESERVATION? Listen. Listen to me, darling. I'm NOT HAVING ANY of your FASCIST propaganda." The restaurant fell silent, except for the waiter's faltering apologies, and a George Harrison CD on the hi-fi.

"Goooh—vinn—daaa," said Harrison.

As she recently confided in Golmohamad, Pantea is currently writing the screenplay for a two-hour motion picture called *Twenty*, set in multi-story apartments in postmodern skyscrapers in north Tehran. The story, if Golmohamad understood correctly, was that of a love triangle between two affluent single mothers and an Afghani kitchen help. The kitchen help lived in the hollow steel pedestal of an enormous advertising billboard for Nokia cell phones. Golmohamad knew for a fact that hundreds of Afghanis did indeed live in billboard contraptions of this kind, but considers the story a scam, a ploy to earn a pat on the back as the daring dissident film-maker, and hold moving talks for understanding audiences in progressive European venues with Sergei Eisenstein retrospectives and glossy catalogs. In the final scene of the movie, the Afghani blows up the Revolutionary Courthouse with a makeshift time bomb just as the single mothers are sentenced to death by stoning for adultery, by a judge played by Kevin Costner in a rare cameo appearance.

With Tehran being one of the flattest metropolises worldwide, filming ostentatious high-rises would amount to little more than a cheap rip-off. So these days, Golmohamad likes to smile patronizingly at Pantea, and make sarcastic remarks on bourgeois radicalism, despite the fact that, when she suggested he himself play the Afghani houseboy, he was, in truth, very tempted.

On the way home from Karaj, the taxi follows the Alborz mountains until it reaches the long Hausmannian boulevards of West Tehran. It's three in the morning, and the radio is playing "El Bodeguero." The desert landscape is punctuated by small concrete sheds and brightly colored neon in pink and green.

A week goes by. Golmohamad's bathroom plumbing makes odd chirping sounds. No matter how long he lives in this downtown apartment, every morning, he will always stop what he's doing and assume, ever so briefly, that he heard the sound of birds nearby.

His phone line makes clicking and humming noises, as it usually does when it's tapped. Under the Shah, the SAVAK's reputation was such that mere rumors sufficed to turn every disco into a potential antechamber to secret torture chambers with concealed doors, and every neighbor and relative into a potential spy. Subversive literature was read only in the small hours of the night, under thick blankets draped over reader and reading lamp. Now, by contrast, Farsi translations of

Marx, Nietzsche, Foucault, and Rushdie are available in every academic bookstore. And you can't sit down in a taxi without someone comparing the classe politique to all sorts of zoological species and organic materials.

Golmohamad can't help thinking of one of the interrogations upon being arrested last month—he was recently arrested and detained for filming the wrong government building at the wrong time—when zip disks, VHS, mini DV tapes, minidiscs, audiotapes, CDs, handwritten notes, newspaper articles, and photographs from his apartment were piled in a single heap in the middle of the room. A middle-aged man in a tea-stained shirt and plastic flip-flops reading "Xanadu" in orange and green walked up to the pile, picked up an article from the *Süddeutsche Zeitung*, loudly and annoyedly assumed it was Swedish, then grabbed a zip disk and held it up to the light. Unsatisfied, he pondered a minidisc for a little while, placing it thoughtfully against a standard CD, to confirm the wondrous difference in size.

Prerevolutionary Tehran, the place Golmohamad has come to know from 1970s magazines and slushy family anecdotes, has its own type of zest. Cocktail bars, Shirley Bassey concerts, Buicks, Chevrolets, Oldsmobile station wagons, ballroom dancing, eurohippies, sidewalk cafes, fake eyelashes, fantastic political pageantry watched on small black-and-white TVs. These days, you do find, say, food courts, West Coast hip hop, international film festivals, Nike and Puma and Swatch and Longines, along with a heavy metal scene, pizza burgers, Jim Jarmusch retrospectives, Dutch and Korean package tours of Isfahan and Shiraz, and flamboyant teenagers in daddy's BMW convertible. But you won't find a Hard Rock Café, nor $50 cocktails, nor pubescent Kuwaiti tourists in Motörhead T-shirts, nor voodoo theme parties, nor sanctimonious Greenpeace demonstrations. A marvelous stroke of luck. If little else, the 1979 revolution still is, and hopefully always will be, a matter of dignity.

EXISTENCE

Ahmad Shamlou

TRANSLATED FROM THE PERSIAN
BY ZARA HOUSHMAND

Ahmad Shamlou was born in 1925 and died in 2000. In addition to twelve collections of his own poetry published between 1948 and 1978, he wrote several plays and a major analytical survey of Iranian folklore, Ketab-i Kucheh *(Book of the Street). He was the editor of an important edition of Hafez as well as other volumes of classical Iranian poetry, and translated many French authors into Persian. "Existence" was first published in the collection* Hava-yeh Tazeh *(Fresh Air) in 1957, when the author was already well established but with a long career ahead of him.*

If this is life—how low!
and I, how shamed, if I don't hang my lifetime's lamp
high on the dusty pine of this dead-end lane.

If this is life—how pure!
and I, how stained, if I don't plant my faith like a mountain,
eternal memorial, to grace this ephemeral earth.

Iraq

Iraqi literature has always grappled with political realities. The biographies of the authors included in this anthology present a portrait of the literary scene throughout Mesopotamia. The seventy-two-year-old poet Saadi Youssef, for example, has been an active voice in the Communist Party in Iraq for over fifty years, even during the more than seven years that the party was affiliated with Saddam Hussein. Youssef did not retract his support until the Party endorsed the American occupation (the minister of culture under Paul Bremer's civil administration was a Communist). His contemporary Fadhil Al-Azzawi, whose international experience first began with an official grant for study abroad in the Communist GDR from early 1977 until 1983, decided not to return to a country dominated by war and destruction after completing his education and settled with his family in East Berlin. When Muhsin Al-Ramli's brother was killed in 1990 by Saddam Hussein's Ba'ath Party regime, the author left for Jordan to write for newspapers and literary magazines, and then moved on to Spain to found an Arabic literary journal.

By contrast, those authors officially celebrated at home in Iraq enjoyed spectacular careers. Even today, three years after the start of the American occupation and the demise of one of the bloodiest dictatorships in the Middle East, the literary scene is still dominated by the same people who supported and upheld that regime for years. When Iraq declared war on Iran, the country was in the throes of an economic upswing. The resulting improvement in the standard of living brought with it an increase in consumption that also benefited writers and artists who were guaranteed an apartment, a car, and one publication annually by the Ministry of Information. But the end of the 1970s was also a period of doubt and divisiveness, of flagrant oppression. Iraqi writers were confronted with an ineluctable choice: either succumb to the seductive wiles of the Ba'ath Party and join the chorus of its praises, or continue to write in a solitary act of humanistic altruism. Then the "Battle of Qadisiya"* jolted the "brave warriors of the nation" like a quake; it plunged an entire generation of theoreticians and poets into an abyss, as Iraq was transformed into a massive graveyard.

What can literature possibly accomplish in such a country? What can literature possibly accomplish in a country whose cities are barricaded behind sandbags? A country where, between the politics and the pollution, most people can barely breathe, living in the squalor of overcrowded quarters where the mortality rates climb to staggering heights? Anyone seeking an answer to this question was faced with two alternatives: either he went into exile or he quit writing. Even those who chose to quit writing saw themselves forced to write something that did not rile the dictator, because even silence was considered a crime. Thus appeared a series of countless trifling texts—the "literature of puritanical purification"—designed solely

---

* Translator's note: 636 A.D., when the Arabian army conquered the Persians. Used by Saddam Hussein as a metaphor for the Iran-Iraq war.

to purify the soul and cleanse the consciousness of the people, as if nothing had happened, as if all this devastation and destruction had been wrought somewhere else altogether.

Iraqi literature had to pass through two phases before it could produce a modernist tradition of its own. At home in Iraq, "Operation Desert Storm" wiped out all the fantastical illusions generated by the "literature of puritanical purification." Abroad, Iraqi exile literature had to witness the collapse of the communist system before it could free itself from the dominance of communist writers in the literary exile scene. It has only been since the late 1980s that Iraqi exile literature has undergone substantial qualitative developments. This literature has been produced by those writers who are not bound by ideologies or partisan politics. Their rejection of dominant ideology and their resistance to the wars in Iraq compelled them to formulate a "brutally raw realism" characterized by a shocking sense of modernity. With the distribution of xeroxed copies of forbidden works smuggled into the country, this realism, with its depictions of "filthy" reality, has been able to take hold in Iraq in recent years, and a young literary movement has emerged on the periphery of this movement.

Today Iraqi literature may be characterized as follows: old guard writers in Iraq are bowled over by the sight of American tanks in the streets of Baghdad. These writers find ample opportunity for self-aggrandizement and for hauling in the spoils of their newfound freedom—whether by singing the praises of the occupation forces and the new power-holders, or by making their debut on the scene of the burgeoning media landscape. On the other hand, there is a whole series of young writers who are seizing their own moment of opportunity. For them, this implies first and foremost quickly acquainting themselves with the lessons of contemporary international literary works, with discovering new worlds—in stark contrast to the older generation that lived encapsulated in its own half-blind world. And it is these young authors who will produce a new Iraqi literature.

Najem Wali
Translated from the German by Lilian M. Friedberg

BAGHDAD MY BELOVED

Salah Al-Hamdani

TRANSLATED FROM THE FRENCH

BY C. DICKSON

An Iraqi poet, actor, and playwright, Salah Al-Hamdani was born in Baghdad in 1951. He has been living in exile in France for thirty years, voicing both his opposition to the dictatorship of Saddam Hussein, his wars, and to the Anglo-American occupation. He began writing as a political prisoner in his early twenties. He is the author of numerous literary works, including tales, short stories, and poems in Arabic and in French. Some of his texts were published in Arabic in clandestine journals in Iraq during the dictatorship. Al-Hamdani assisted Saad Salman in writing the dialogues for his film Baghdad On/Off.

Al-Hamdani's poetry takes us to the banks of the Euphrates, upon which his native Baghdad stands. The author once confided in his "The Beginning of Words":

> *I once found it difficult to accept exile far from Iraq. Now, [by my wife's side], I appreciate the waiting and the separation. I have tried to surmount each step of the loneliness. Still be alive here, with nothing from back there. Live here in a foreign land, awkwardly perhaps,*

but live. Suddenly, over by the door standing ajar on the narrative, on the screams of men, on the smells of childhood, a whip lashes across my throat. How might I emerge on the other side of the book? I don't want to flee. Simply retrace the days and remember with the soul of a child . . .

In my homeland people used to go to the mosque regularly, they lined up before Allah and said hello to the mother of the man they'd executed the day before with their bare hands. They fed on lies, they practiced Ramadan during the day and got drunk at night. Everything said regarding the sacred book was very refined. So was the food. The dead and the victims were the color of the Eastern sands.

"Baghdad My Beloved" was written in 2003. It echoes the author's familiar themes of exile and opposition to the American occupation of Iraq.

You needn't crucify yourself
either on the edge of a page
of history that is not your own,
or to atone for the dead born of your suffering
for nowhere is there a cry to soothe your pain.

You needn't crucify yourself on the banks of the bloody
    torrents
that gush from your body,
as the Euphrates bares the secrets of its soul
at the dawn of a new defeat.

I know,
no wound can justify war.

You needn't crucify yourself at the end of day,
when you have not concluded your prayers
over the fallen palms
for there can be no honorable killer.

You needn't crucify yourself for the ashes of disaster
for the tombs of your Gods,
or for the beliefs of a dying humanity.

Baghdad, my beloved,
neither father, nor son, nor God,
no prophet crowned by the church will save your soul,
neither the one from Mecca,
nor the prophet of those who refuse
to share olive branches in Palestine.

Here is my war notebook
years of exile
folded into a suitcase;
abandoned far too long to the dreams of the condemned.

Here is my share of victims
my share of moon
my harvest of emptiness
my share of dust, of words, and of cries.

Here is my sorrow
like a comma barring off an ink mark.

Baghdad, my beloved,
I was squatting in a corner of the page
Sheltered from barren days
far from bloody rivers
that swept away the names of the dead
and people's silence.

Baghdad, my beloved
sitting like a Bedouin in a mirage
stretched along my shores, I cherished my own death shroud
far from the cross, from the hand of Fatma
and the star of David
far from their books, from their wars
wandering through the sandy dunes
from the wasteland to the town
I drag my body from season to season
and you from the couch to the mirror,
from my bedroom to the street
between my writing and my loneliness
far from their cemeteries,
from their martyrs, from their morgues.

Baghdad, my beloved,
you did not stand shivering in the doorway of the ruined days,
a whole civilization geared to killing
has robbed you of your innocence.
Baghdad, you who never submitted to Saddam, the brute
you have no reason to groan
at the simple revelation of that iron fist
those who busy themselves about your agonizing body,
those "liberators," become his henchmen.

Baghdad, my aching heart,
my father, a laborer, never knew joy
my mother lost her youth in the mirror
and the sole witness to my
first heartbroken sobs upon your breast
is the blowing sand,
the starry sky and God's gaze as prayer is being called.

Madinat al-Salam
city of peace
love in the essence of the written word.

How I wish today
that man had never discovered fire
and I curse him for tramping on through his own deafening din.

The earth that gave me life is being put to death today
oh! mother! Let me return to your flesh
So I might listen to the beating of your soul
and drink in the murmur of your breath.

March 25, 2003

FROM *AT THE BORDERLINE*

Sherko Fatah

TRANSLATED FROM THE GERMAN
BY ANDREA HEYDE

Sherko Fatah was born in East Berlin in 1964 to an Iraqi Kurdish father and a German mother. Fatah spent part of his childhood in Iraq, where his extended family still lives today. In 1975, he and his parents settled in West Germany. Sherko Fatah is at home in both cultures; he writes in German and has close ties to his father's native country, in which he has traveled extensively. Fatah studied philosophy and art history in West Berlin and wrote a master's thesis on philosophical hermeneutics. In 1999 he attended a writers' workshop at Literarisches Colloquium Berlin, one of Germany's most prestigious literary venues. During this time he worked on his first novel, Im Grenzland *(At the Borderline), for which he received the Aspecte Prize in 2001. It is neither a coming-of-age novel nor a character study but rather the depiction of life in an area torn by war. His second book,* Donnie, *the story of a foreign legionnaire haunted by memories, has just been published. Sherko Fatah writes in German.*

The smuggler passed the slope and walked on toward the mine-field, measuring each of his steps with increasing care. Blue-bells bloomed and blades of grass, flattened by the wind, spread across the ground, trying to hide themselves in the stone-filled meadow that ran up to the hilltop in a gentle slant, beyond which lay the cliffs and the pass. No minesweeper had come to this place; there were no barriers, no warning signs.

The smuggler stopped at the meadow's edge and walked a few steps to the side and back to determine his exact point of entry. The location and positioning of stones served as his clues. He quickly found the spot he was looking for—the meadow had remained the same. He took out a metal rod and glanced around one more time.

Above the slope the first cliff emerged from the yellowish gray soil. The plateau hung above it like a pulpit. Two wretched, almost bare trees with dangling branches bowed over the abyss. He thought of the nocturnal voices and felt as if he had departed a house having left something behind.

He adjusted his backpack and crawled into the meadow. It seemed lush only from afar. Blades of grass covered the dry, loose ground in random patches. This was what made the terrain so treacherous. Contrary to appearance, it provided an ideal ground for those flat mines that looked like three disks stacked one upon the other, with the smallest disk on top, burrs running vertically around the edge of the disks, most likely to give the mine a better foothold in loose soil. This made these contraptions—they were hardly bigger than one's palm—look like toys.

After excavating a mine, the smuggler would always become aware of the gravity of his situation when he recognized the letter-ing on it, which was located exactly where a foot would press down on its topmost disk. These characters, whatever they indicated, were not decorative. They were inscribed on a small greenish-brown area, covered with soil, not meant to be read, intended to disappear in the explosion, into a wound and pain, thereby delivering their message. An inscribed countdown before detonation.

The smuggler kept his head close to the ground and slid forward on his knees.

Shielded by his straw hat's brim, he saw directly in front of him a clearly marked path that had narrowed further. Pebbles that he himself had positioned as markers guided him, but only centimeter by centimeter, as he had to recall their positions by his memory. Once he hit upon one, he immediately paused to take a slip of paper from his coat pocket and compare the sketch with the ground in front of him. The pebbles' positions, the ones on the drawing and the real ones, matched. He folded the piece of paper and put it away. Then he removed his hat and, with the back of his hand, wiped his forehead. It was tremendously important to prevent sweat from running into his eyes. Therefore he rummaged through his coat pocket to find his handkerchief and dried his face with it. Then he draped it on his head so that it covered his forehead, securing it with the help of his hat.

He carefully leaned forward and rested his elbows on the ground, reexamining every square centimeter around him. After he thought he had found the first position, he briefly closed his eyes one more time. Then he began to drive the metal rod into the ground, at a slant angle, very slowly, millimeter by millimeter. He had to be ready—and that was what now caused the sweat to run down his temples—to stop at the slightest resistance that wasn't caused by the soil. He stared at his fingers to feel this resistance, as if, by doing so, he could heighten their sensitivity. The metal rod bore its way further into the ground. It lay there at an angle and, therefore, remained close to the surface. Should the rod come upon it, it would hit the mine sideways, where the burrs were located. Sure enough, the rod's tip touched something. Pausing again, the smuggler removed his tool cautiously from the ground a moment later. He put it next to him and started digging up the drill hole and pushing clumps of soil to the side with his fingers. The drilled channel turned into a funnel with a widening mouth. The mine's lower edge, weathered like the wall of a miniature ruin, appeared. The slow wiping brought the mine's gradation into view. The smuggler inched ahead and removed sand from the second disk. He now wished that he could blow away the remaining dust, but he couldn't. Pressure from above must not be imposed under any circumstances. After uncovering the entire lower disk, he raised his upper body and straightened his shoulders. He looked down on this object—exposed as it was now, it seemed almost pathetic—and felt a certain pride because of his victory. The triumph of escaping or circumventing a trap was his most dependable feeling. He breathed deeply, then held his breath. This time he didn't rest his elbows on the ground but leaned forward. Spreading the fingers of both hands, he reached under the edge of the disk so that he could lift the mine from all sides. After he had raised it from the ground in very slow motion, he tilted it slightly: the remaining soil fell off the top disk. He put the mine down at the invisible edge of his trail, some thirty centimeters away from his lower leg, ensuring that it didn't touch any grass. He took out a small paper bag filled with salt and poured some of it into the funnel. This would allow him to spot the holes easily in case he returned soon enough. Even if the wind spread the salt around, it would still be better than if somebody recognized it as a marker. It was visible only to somebody who held his head close to the ground.

Before he crawled farther, he threw another glance at his slip of paper, where, in addition to the exact positions, he had noted the types of antipersonnel mines he would encounter. Most of them were the regular flat ones, but in three spots along the way there were some that resembled a damaged oil can: cylinders that stood upright in the soil. On the top was mounted an antenna that triggered an explosion when touched. This type was called "Bouncing Betty" be-cause it sprang almost one meter into the air when activated, ensur-ing that its metal splinters would rupture a person's abdomen. These mines offered one small advantage and two huge disadvantages to the smuggler. He could locate them according to his site plan when he was in close proximity, without first digging them up. However, they were heavier than the other antipersonnel mines and, because of the antenna, the utmost care was required to remove them and place them on the ground.

He dug up two more discoid mines before he reached the first Bouncing Betty. Now he slowed down his movements so rigorously that the blink of an eye was enough to startle him. He squinted at the sky to regain focus. The afternoon had come, and a slight breeze swept over the meadow. For a moment, the smuggler saw himself kneeling in this wasteland as if he were someone else. Although he was able to observe the countryside in every direction, including the jagged rock faces and even the faint peaks of the highlands in the distance, he had no feel for the landscape's vastness. He felt the waft of a breeze. The few noises he noticed sounded muffled, as if they were coming from inside a room.

Once more he lowered his head to the ground. The movement of the blades of grass confused him. He noticed a few ants, a white pebble, and then, momentarily glistening like a spider's thread, the antenna ready to receive its command. The smuggler drew nearer and pushed the grass aside. He took a shovel and began to grub around the hidden cylinder. He didn't need to be too careful, so long as he kept an eye on the antenna.

After he was done, he straightened himself for a moment and breathed deeply. He traced the path he would take with the mine in his hands and pinpointed the spot where he would put it down. This place had to be somewhat sheltered, within a furrow yet easy for him to relocate on his way back. He lowered his fingers into the hole around the uncovered object, wrapped his fingers around it, and picked it up. The antenna must not touch anything on its way up. The smuggler moved his hands exactly the way he had planned to. He put the cylinder down in its designated place and slightly pressed it into the soil until it had been stabilized. He exhaled and quickly removed both of his hands from the object.

Since the mine was quite big, three quarters of it had to be buried in the ground, lest a competent observer of the area spot it, with the help of binoculars, for instance. Therefore he dug a hole, positioned himself crosswise on the trail, and lowered the mine into it. Much of the cylinder disappeared into the ground and would only be identifiable at a short distance. Again, he marked the other hole and crawled farther.

It took him till evening to cross the minefield. He had noticed every stage of the course of the sun as he had looked up at it before and after digging up each mine. The last one, located thirty centimeters off the rocky soil where the grass abruptly ended, gave him the satisfaction of having done his job. He crawled toward firm ground, which provided him with an immediate sense of security, and looked searchingly back at his trail. The dug-up and relocated mines were invisible, including the last one, which he had lowered into the ground.

The smuggler got up and cleaned off his coat and pants. He always performed this part of the procedure with particular care. Negotiating the border protection system was the last portion of his route.

Now he had to face the border guards. They expected him, although they never knew exactly when he would come. Whoever was on duty demanded he pay an "entrance fee." The small town he wanted to visit was at a mountain pass three kilometers away. From the border station, the area gave the impression of being completely abandoned with a road meandering through the valley. But in reality, the region was quite densely populated on the other side of the border. Near the place where he always went first were some tiny villages in close proximity to each other. Whenever he had enough time, he visited at least one of these villages, where the liquor was cheaper than anywhere else. This time, however, he only wanted to go to the small town.

He intended to return as soon as possible. Normally he would stay through the night after next to spend another morning and afternoon in the foreign country. It didn't bother him to cross the minefield in late afternoon, since burying the mines took a lot less time than digging them up and he didn't like to spend the night outdoors before returning to his city. This time something pulled him back to his town.

On his way to the pass he worried about the patrols, but they would have to pay very close attention to notice a path through the minefield. Whatever else was unsettling him—he didn't want to think of it.

He walked toward the border and tried to concentrate on what would happen next. He went over his orders once more and anticipated the weight of his backpack.

In the early evening he reached the border station, a container-turned-barracks amid gray scree. The road stood out like a bright channel through the grayish brown of the stony wasteland. The barrack was located at a right angle to his path. The smuggler saw no one as he drew closer. There were no barriers and, aside from the barracks, nothing that marked the border. The door on the narrow side of the container opened, but no one stepped out onto the short staircase in front of it. Someone waited for him inside.

The smuggler approached deliberately and shouted a greeting before reaching the steps. He had got into the habit of appearing to be easygoing, even cheerful, in front of the border guards, giving their informal arrangement a playful touch. After all, it was possible, although not likely, that someone new and uninitiated, perhaps even a superior, would be there.

He stepped into the barracks and caught the glances of four border guards. They sat around a shabby wooden table, eating. Guns leaned against the wall. The smuggler immediately remembered his painful visits to the Red House. In the next moment, however, he approached them nonchalantly. One offered him a chair. The smuggler joined them and passed around cigarettes, which he carried with him for occasions such as this. All four interrupted their meal and smoked pleasurably, as if they themselves did not have cigarettes in their pockets.

The smuggler now was obliged to chat with them. His role was that of an unexpected guest who eased their tedium. Language was a problem. Thus far, with all the border guards the situation had developed in the same way: they uttered a few intelligible sentences, while he gathered all the snatches he knew of their language and supplemented them with gestures. The border guards often came from remote regions of the country and had always been more difficult to communicate with than the locals, who, because they had been here since before the war, spoke both languages. Because of these circumstances, they appeared as if they were members of the occupying forces in their own country. Over time, the smuggler had memorized enough words to keep a simple conversation going. Because, from the very beginning, he had noticed that his ability to talk to these men had a direct influence on the amount of money he had to pay. With strangers, the border guards attended to their duties rigidly and, most likely, without consciously escalating the price. It was simply based on instinct.

One of them, as always, did most of the talking, and he was the most important of the group. He sat opposite the smuggler, smoked with his upper body reclined, and groomed his mustache with the tip of his thumb after each puff. He asked about news from the other side.

The smuggler thought briefly and then landed a hit with his

story of the government declaring that the temperature was now to be 40 degrees Celsius. The men were amused, though it was less a joke than a familiar story. They nodded and commented more than they laughed about it.

The ice had been broken, the barracks had become a place where the usual rules did not apply. One of the men got up, adjusted his suspenders, and brought a tin plate for the smuggler. The conversation was no longer overly important; he was now considered a guest, and would remain so until they had finished their tea.

FROM *SCATTERED CRUMBS*

Muhsin Al-Ramli

TRANSLATED FROM THE ARABIC
BY YASMEEN S. HANOOSH

*Born in a small village in the northern part of Iraq in 1967,
Muhsin Al-Ramli earned a degree in Spanish literature from
Baghdad University and a PhD in Spanish literature from the
University of Madrid. Inspired by his brother, Hassan, a novelist and short-story writer, Al-Ramli began writing short stories at the age of fifteen. He worked for the local journals in
Baghdad in the late 1980s. After Saddam Hussein's regime
murdered his brother in 1990, Al-Ramli moved to Jordan to
write for newspapers and literary journals. In 1995, he moved
to Spain, where he co-founded* Alwah, *an Arabic literary journal. He has published two collections of short stories, three
plays, and one novella,* Al-Fatit al-Muba'thar, *and has translated several books from Spanish into Arabic. "Boredom," one
of his short stories, was published in London in the biannual
literary magazine* Banipal. *The author now lives in Madrid,
Spain, where he runs his own publishing house and co-edits the
literary journal* Alwah *with Abdel Hadi Sa'doun. His novel*
al-Fatst al-Muba'thar *(translated here as* Scattered Crumbs)
is a semi-autobiographical story taking place in an unnamed

Iraqi village during the eight-year conflict between Iraq and Iran in the 1980s.

The summer grew hotter and the war more voracious. It brought convoys of flags, medals of honor, and village youths in coffins back to us. To make good on these losses, the police launched a big campaign to arrest all deserters, so they took Qasim, Saadi, Ismael, Kamil, Nuri, and Seth and threw them behind the military prison's bars, in long halls of cells that used to be stables for the English horses before independence. Until public attention induced the authorities to put them in solitary confinement, each hall featured one of Hajji Ijayel's sons as its main attraction.

While Qasim gathered around him the prisoners of his hall to draw them in varied poses and to tattoo their arms, shoulders, and chests with phrases of love, freedom, and torment, Saadi's fellow prisoners selected their finest sheets to put under him in an attempt to regain some of the warmth of their wives' beds at night. The guards were the first to get drawn or tattooed by Qasim and the first to lay Saadi on their sheets.

When news reached the warden, he ordered Qasim to paint a picture of the Leader, and when he could not, he was placed in solitary. The warden ordered Saadi to stop entertaining the prisoners at night, and when he failed to comply, he was isolated as well. But Saadi took off his underwear and climbed up on the shit canister in his cell, placing his behind in the little window that separated him from the rest of the prisoners in his hall so that they in their turn could climb up and get him from there. When the warden learned of this, he became infuriated and transferred Saadi to a private chamber next to his office, where he was provided with all the amenities reserved for prominent prisoners.

Later on it was said that there had been a narrow secret passage connecting the office with Saadi's chamber, covered on the office side with a file cabinet and on Saadi's with a closet for undergarments, including brassieres, and red nightgowns. Saadi never denied these rumors, nor did he bother to respond to them with more than a robotic, oafish smile, and the sentence, "Yeah, those were nice days with Mr. Warden!" Qasim likewise did not bother to add that without Saadi it would not have satisfied Mr. Warden merely to isolate him. He would have tortured Qasim to death.

The war intensified, so the Leader pardoned all military prisoners and returned them to their units. He also released all political prisoners from life and returned them to the belly of their mother earth after they had lain around in the refrigerators for a period long enough for their parents to pay the cost of nooses, the importation of which would have cost the government hard cash.

On leave after the pardon, Saadi asked his mother to weave him a shoulder braid to put around his shoulder like a corporal. She did so with joy, thinking that he had been promoted and was going to continue his military service. However, that did not happen. After more than one successful attempt to fake a higher rank, even that of an officer, Saadi got bored with the military life because "It's not so nice." He fled to the cornfields where boys, donkeys, and pleasure lay. Qasim escaped also after he saw ravaged cities and villages and entered houses whose owners had fled, leaving tea glasses half full, portraits staring in bitterness, and wedding clothes in the closet. He was able to make it to the wedding of his daughter Shaima, that delicate, thin girl, submissive unlike her mother. His joy at her wedding was a genuine joy such as he had not felt since his own wedding with Hasiba, who feared that illness might assail her daughter before the wedding, and so she could not keep from dancing as she beheld her daughter in the white wedding dress. The girl looked small, beautiful, like a child's doll, her fingers clinging to the elbow of her fat groom, whose blubber almost rent the sleeves of his suit and burst its buttons as he wiped off the sweat oozing from his flushed temples and thick neck.

The heat was intense and so was the war, so the government formed a committee of thick-necked and choleric experts to reassess the physical, psychological, and mental criteria by which a citizen was judged to be exempt from military service or flung into it. The committee was also to reexamine all the homeland's precious lunatics, including Abood al-Ramli, whom the police put into their car after they wrestled him out of my weeping aunt's lap as she begged them, "I swear by Allah, the boy is crazed, the poor thing." Hajji Ijayel tried to calm her down by saying, "They're only doing a simple test, and then they'll return him," although deep inside he wished they would take him into the army because the army was the maker of men. He hoped that it might remedy his son's condition so he could fill the gap left by Saadi and Qasim. On the way he told the police the story of Abood's life from the time that he was born a beautiful, laughing boy. He also told them, proudly, the story of his grandfather who stabbed the English officer sonofabitch, and he told them that he had another son called Ahmed who was first in his university in studying law and so the government was going to appoint him as a judge, and that he had another son called Abdul-Wahid at the front line. But he did not say a word about Saadi, Qasim, or Mahmoud.

As he stood before the committee after waiting in line with thousands of misfits, holding the sun-stroked Abood up by his collar, Ijayel repeated what he had told the police. One expert with a big bald head barked at Abood, "What's your name?" This startled Abood and made him tongue-tied. His father repeated the request to him, reminding him of the names he had learned under the date palm, so Abood recited the names up to the tenth grandfather until the bald man said to him, "Count for us from one to ten." Relishing the memory of the rhyming game that Saadi and the village boys had taught him, Abood began counting to the bald man, smiling and humming the forced end rhymes. "One, you'll mount someone. Two, I'll ram it in you. Three, you're screwed by Uncle Ali. Four, your ass is sore. Five, your father will drive. Six, we have longer dicks . . ." He ignored the shouts of his father, who set about trying to stop him. "That's shameful, boy! Boy, shut up!" Hajji Ijayel tried to remind his son of the verses he had taught him from the national anthem, but he could not stop him. "Seven, I'll ride you to heaven. Eight, your cock's a dry date. Nine, your balls are smaller than mine. Ten, I'll mount sissy men." Then he jumped up and down, clapping elatedly as he used to do when playing that game with Saadi and his friends.

The committee did not buy this show of idiocy, or that of thousands who performed better scenes of hysteria and lunacy in the hope of saving their skin. Although the officials duly noted the strange thickness of Abood's eyebrows, the protrusion of his forehead, his beaky chin, and dingy color, they nevertheless transferred him, like the rest, to the torture room—"the Sieve"—in which the strongest of charlatans weakened under the sting of the thick electrical cord.

Abood giggled at the fall of the first few lashes upon his skin while his father averted his eyes in pain. After a few minutes the screams rose until they shook everyone. Abood let out a wild, wolfish howl, so perfectly wolfish that it frightened the flogger himself. The committee was thus assured of his insanity and dumped him with his father on the sidewalk, where Ijayel sought help from some good Samaritans to lift Abood onto a sack in the trunk of a taxi that took them back to my aunt, who was sitting in front of the oak-wood gate waiting for them under the sun.

But to her surprise, when she stood up and stepped forward, opening her arms to receive Abood, whom the driver and Ijayel had dragged from the trunk by his armpits, she instead received Warda, who ran into her mother's arms silent, listless, haggard, parched-mouthed, and with disheveled hair. Ijayel left his son in the hands of the driver and rushed to Warda, questioning her. She gasped, then burst out crying on my aunt's chest, "Fauzi died, Mama." My aunt screamed, "Yibooooooooo! Miserable Um Qasim!" For a moment Hajji stood as if pinned to the ground, then turned to the driver and said, "My son-in-law was martyred in the war fighting for the homeland."

Although Warda gave Fauzi a daughter as beautiful as herself and insisted on naming her Warda before leaving the baby with Fauzi's parents, she had not been able to decide during the entire period of her marriage whether or not Fauzi was a man worthy of respect. She strove to find the answer in light of what Qasim had said about the man who deserves respect. This uncertainty is what hurt her the most in her husband's death. Perhaps he was a man worthy of respect, but his monthly seven-day leave was not enough time for her to find out. The war had more of him than she, until it took him forever.

FIVE CROSSES

Saadi Youssef

TRANSLATED FROM THE ARABIC
BY KHALED MATTAWA

Saadi Youssef was born in 1934 in Basra, Iraq. He has published thirty volumes of poetry, seven books of prose, and has rendered into Arabic major works by such writers as Walt Whitman, Federico García Lorca, George Orwell, Nuruddin Farah, and Wole Soyinka. He left Iraq in 1979, and after many detours working as a journalist, publisher, and political activist, he recently settled in London.

We stopped in five stations and did not leave a souvenir.
We did not shiver there, or get drunk, or strum a guitar.
Five rivers of sand on the guitar.
Five crosses made of silence:

You are sad;
I wipe the dust of the broken world off your eyelashes.
You are naive;
in our desert you are hoping to set sail.

You are tired;
your hair spreads shade between wakefulness and rain.
You are alone
as if we never shivered, or got drunk,
or strummed a guitar.
Bitter thirst on your lips, journeys in your eyes,
you are a dark sapling
flowering in the dark.
I touch my voice when I touch your leaves.

O five stations without a souvenir . . .
O five rivers in a guitar . . .
O five crosses made of silence . . .

Do not leave me tonight crucified on the walls.

Basra, November 11, 1961

HAMEED NYLON

Fadhil Al-Azzawi

TRANSLATED FROM THE ARABIC
BY WILLIAM MAYNARD HUTCHINS

Fadhil Al-Azzawi was born in 1940 in Kirkuk, in northern Iraq. He studied English literature at Baghdad University, earning a BA degree. He earned a PhD in cultural journalism at Leipzig University in Germany. He edited a number of magazines in Iraq and abroad and founded Shi'r 69 *(Poetry 69), which was banned after the fourth issue. He spent three years in jail under the dictatorship of the Ba'ath regime. His poetry and criticism have been published in the leading Arab literary magazines since the early sixties and his books published in many Arab countries. He has published eight volumes of poetry in Arabic and one in German, two open texts, five novels, one volume of short stories, two volumes of criticism and theoretical writings, and many literary works of translation from English and German. He left Iraq in 1977 and has lived since 1983 as a freelance writer in Berlin.*

"Hameed Nylon" is the first chapter of the novel The Last of the Angels *(Riad El-Rayyes Books, 1992), which is set in Kirkuk, Iraq, some fifty years ago, during a period of British "influence." In the novel, Hameed Nylon progresses from being*

the terminated employee of a British oil company to a labor organizer to an insurgent. This novel is now forthcoming in William Hutchins's translation from the American University in Cairo Press (2006).

Hameed, who had yet to learn the nickname by which he would be known for the rest of his life, entered the house, which emitted a fresh country scent. With his foot, as usual, he shoved open the heavy door, which was fashioned of walnut and decorated with large, broad-headed nails. Only at night was it closed by a bolt with protruding teeth. Verdigris had spread across this until its edges looked bright green. He climbed a few steps, making his way to the two small rooms over the entryway that led to the courtyard.

It was the first time Hameed had returned from his job at the oil company so early. It was barely eleven, and this fact surprised his wife, Fatima, who was not expecting him until afternoon. He interrupted her innocent laughter as she stood on the steps discussing her nightly pleasures over a low masonry wall with a neighbor in the adjacent house. Her happiness actually was tinged with bitter anxiety, since she had been married for more than a year without conceiving. She had sought out most of the better-known and even less well-known imams in the city for charms against barrenness to cancel out the magic that the many women envying her had clearly concocted to her detriment. Although she had never said so openly, her suspicions, from the beginning, had focused on Nazeera—her husband's sister—and on Nazeera's mother, Hidaya, a plump old woman who made no secret of her collaboration with the devil, for her house was always cluttered with herbs and dried flowers, ground bones, and assorted chemical substances purchased from Jewish druggists in al-Qaysariya, at the entrance to the old souk.

Among the imams whom Fatima consulted was a blind man who charged her a dirham to write a charm. He told her, "This amulet will set on fire any devil that dares approach you." As an additional precaution, however, she consulted another Turkmen imam, who lived in a nameless alley branching off from the Chay neighborhood. A month or two later, since her belly had not swollen up yet, her neighbor advised her to tour the tombs of the dead imams, since the living ones were not useful anymore and only wrote charms for money. Thus Fatima, enveloped in her black wrap, headed to Imam Ahmad, whose tomb lay in the center of the main thoroughfare linking the al-Musalla district with the old souk. She wept and pleaded, deliberately prolonging the time she spent there so the imam would not ignore her request. A passing car almost ran into her, since in her spiritual rapture—tears streaming from her eyes— she had forgotten she was sitting in the middle of the street. After that she visited the tomb in al-Musalla cemetery of a Kurdish imam said to have been able to converse with birds, which understood and obeyed him. A month later, when no change had occurred in her, even though she made her husband sleep with her* more than once a night, her visiting mother said, "This time you're going to head for the tomb of a Jewish saint, for no one is on better terms with the devil than Jews; evil is only negated by evil." Next morning when she related that to her neighbor, however, the woman advised her to go to the citadel and ask a Christian household there for a hog's tooth. She said they put those, normally, in water jugs. She should slip it under her husband's pillow, since Satan fears nothing more than hogs' teeth. Perhaps because of all of this advice she was receiving from here and there, and also, possibly, because she was disillusioned with saints whose blessed powers had failed, she decided to

* The use of this phrase for "copulation" reflects the biblical tone of the original Arabic.

call off, at least temporarily, these unsuccessful attempts while increasing the number of times she slept with her husband, since she knew, perhaps with good reason, that—more than any other location—bed was where the issue would be decided, if only because this was the resting place for the saints closest to God.

Even so, Fatima would not have paid much attention to this matter had it not been for her mother's persistent entreaties as well as the insinuating comments of the old woman Hidaya and her daughter Nazeera, who deliberately spoke in riddles, saying, for example: "The cow that doesn't give birth is slaughtered." On the whole she was content with her nightly trysts with her husband, who had never given a thought, not even once, to having children, since love for women eclipsed all other loves in his life. He especially wished to preserve for the longest time possible his sense of being a young man little burdened with responsibilities, so that he could leave in the morning for his job at the oil company and not return home until he felt like it. He occasionally returned in the afternoon but frequently stayed out until ten or eleven P.M. without upsetting Fatima, who had no way of discovering anything about his work except from the stories he told her. She knew he drove the private car belonging to an English engineer and his wife, conveying them from one place to another and waiting for them. She grasped that this type of work might force him to work late more often than not. He was occasionally obliged to travel to other cities and areas, accompanying his boss. Then he would return home bringing—especially during Christian holidays—chocolates from London or locally produced pieces of sugared coconut, which she had not tasted before. Thus the moment she saw her husband enter, she raced to him, since this was the first time he had returned so early, a fact that made her feel uncomfortable and anxious. She fought to control her emotions and to keep herself from asking why he was early. He, however, spoke first, saying with a smile, "I want to lie down a little." Only then did she find the courage to ask anxiously, "I hope you don't feel ill?" As he climbed toward their two rooms over the house's entry-way, he replied, "No, not at all. I'm just tired." This answer satisfied her enough that she said, "Fine; I'll start cooking right away so we can have lunch together." She went off to prepare the food, feeling on the whole contented and delighted that her husband was home with her. Even if something were the matter, he would certainly tell her, she was sure of that.

Her husband kept uncharacteristically silent this time, however. In fact, he did not leave his bed to go to the coffee shop or to visit with his friends, not even that afternoon. Neither did he go out to chat with the neighborhood youth, who met each evening in front of a shop located near the community's mosque. Even worse than that, he did not leave home for work the next day. Only then did Fatima realize that there was something wrong, something he was hiding from her and did not care to divulge. It had to be something serious. Her fears led her to beg him to tell her the truth, but he merely told her he had taken a few days' holiday. She felt somewhat relieved but not entirely reassured, for he might be trying to deceive her, thinking that he should not alarm or upset her. She knew that when he was in a good humor he would tell her one story after an-other about Mr. McNeely, his flirtatious wife, Helen, and the other Englishmen who worked in the Baba Gurgur region for the Iraq Pe-troleum Company in Kirkuk. She knew that every Englishman was called "Boss" and that the company belonged to them. Fatima and Hameed would laugh a lot when he told her how Englishwomen were not at all embarrassed about showing their nude bodies to em-ployees and how they wore undershirts and shorts in the presence of their cuckolded husbands, who bragged about their wives to one an-other. In fact, he had discovered that his boss's wife had more than one English lover. He was equally well versed in his boss's affair with the daughter of Khamu—an Assyrian Christian—who enjoyed the rank of a "first-class" employee with the firm. That was not all; her father encouraged the girl to persevere in this relationship with the man. As for the boss and his wife, they did not attempt to conceal their affairs from him, giving the impression that these were extremely natural. In fact, his boss's beautiful, bronzed wife would leave the home of one of her lovers and climb into the waiting automobile as if returning from prayers. Once when they were on the lakeshore in al-Habaniya, Helen removed every stitch of clothing. When she noticed that Hameed was staring wildly and lustfully at her, she was surprised and winked at him, smiling as she sank into the water. Fatima had frequently teased him, laughing: "What more do you want? Many men would pay good money to have such enjoyable work." Hameed, however, did not actually find in his work the kind of satisfaction his wife imagined, for he felt humiliated most of the time as he sat behind the steering wheel, waiting for Helen to leave an assignation. They occasionally invited him inside and served him lemonade in the servants' quarters while he listened to his mistress's moans from a bed in another room where she lay with the lover she was visiting. That would drive him crazy, agitating him, although he did not dare protest or refuse the invitation. He assumed it not unlikely that she would fancy him someday and invite him to sleep with her, but that day never came. After the incident in which Mrs. Helen McNeely appeared naked at al-Habaniya and after her conspiratorial wink, he spent more than a month feeling uncertain of his standing with her, wanting her but lacking the audacity to cross the line separating them. The image of her standing naked before him never left his head, since he often thought of her while he slept with his wife. That did not, in his opinion, constitute any diminution of his love for his wife, everything considered, for Mrs. Helen McNeely was no better than a whore. He, as a man, had a right to seize this opportunity. He was sure he would show her in bed that he was superior to all her other lovers. He would thus avenge himself and erase the humiliation he felt whenever she climbed into the car to head for one of them.

Hameed never returned to work and there must have been some secret reason, which would eventually surface, even though he attempted to postpone this moment, day by day. People in the Chuqor neighborhood learned from other men who worked for the company that Hameed had been fired. Instead of trying to console him, however, they burst into laughter, and his story traveled by word of mouth until the whole city knew it. Thus he acquired a nickname that remained linked to his given name forever, as if it actually were a real part of his name. Even innocent children always called him by this name, which he himself finally accepted, adding it to his given name: Hameed Nylon.

The story these workers told, based on reports from the oil company, was that Hameed, who was the personal driver for Mr. McNeely and his wife, wishing to try his luck with the wife and to win her affection, had returned one day from a trip to H3* and Rutba, carrying a simple present for her—a pair of nylon stockings—but that Mrs. McNeely, who considered him a servant, had tossed the stockings back at him and thrown him out. Some said that she initially accepted his present but asked him the reason for it. Then, taking his cues from films he had seen, he leaned over her and tried to kiss her. At that point she slapped his face, screamed, and accused him of trying to rape her. Others asserted that she had slept with him but had grown bored with him and had then used the nylon stockings as a pretext to sack him. Neighborhood women asserted that he had befriended the Englishwoman and actually had given her nylon stockings but that her husband, who was suspicious about this affair, had used the stockings as an excuse to separate him from his wife and thus had fired him. Hameed Nylon remained silent for

* British oil company jargon for a location.

many days, refusing to say anything about the incident. Once he regained his peace of mind, he made only one comment: "The only
true thing in any of these stories is the nylon stockings."

Although the people of the Chuqor neighborhood considered
his termination by the firm a natural event that no one could influence, some men who worked there, and most of the neighborhood
youth who trained each day in the gym they had created in an
abandoned structure adjacent to the house where Hameed Nylon
lived, tried to incite the people of the neighborhood against the oil
company. The imam of the Chuqor community even mentioned in
his study sessions, which began spontaneously every day after evening prayer at the mosque: "The English have deprived one of our
community's young men of his livelihood because of a pair of
stockings. This matter cannot be acceptable to God or His
Prophet." Some women's zeal was so aroused that they swore at the
poor kerosene vendors and snubbed them. They would open the
taps of the drums that were pulled by donkeys, letting the kerosene
spill onto the street. They told the sellers, who had absolutely no
knowledge of the affair: "You should pour kerosene down that Englishwoman's ass." Once again the community's sages intruded:
"How are these poor fellows to blame?" Oil workers' families certainly did not want to lose the privilege of buying gas at reduced
rates through coupons sold to workers. Moreover, the secret labor
union that was organizing oil workers distributed a handbill that
attacked the firing of Hameed Nylon and called for his reinstatement, although no one in the Chuqor neighborhood knew about
the pamphlet, and that was just as well, for if the people had felt
the case was political, they definitely would have been afraid. Although the Chuqor neighborhood had never at any time in its history, which stretched back at least a hundred years, participated in
a protest demonstration, many residents had heard of them. Indeed, some had seen the demonstration in the great souk a few

months before. There were also some butchers who had assisted the
police by attacking the demonstrators and clubbing them, after
they were told that these demonstrators advocated female licen-
tiousness, once a week, every Friday.

Thus a month after Hameed Nylon lost his job, it was decided
that one Friday the neighborhood would put on a demonstration to
seek the reinstatement of their son who had been fired from his position with the firm. Everyone became excited by the idea after it
was lengthily discussed in the coffee shops, which turned into free-
for-all houses of debate every afternoon. The matter evolved into a
quasi-religious duty once the Mullah Zayn al-Abideen al-Qadiri declared that since all Muslims constitute a single body, when one
member suffers, the rest of the body rallies on its behalf with a vig-
ilant defense. Consequently, an aged artist, known for carving words
on marble tombstones, undertook the creation of protest signs, de-
vising the texts himself.

One day, after the Friday prayer, a procession that included
women and children set forth. Athletes from the Chuqor neighborhood, along with those from other communities, carried signs written in a variety of scripts—Ruq'a, Farsi, and Kufic—"There is no
god but God; Muhammad is the Messenger of God," "In the name
of God the Merciful, the Compassionate," "Traitor, Your Time's
Up," "Hameed Nylon's Innocent," "Hameed Nylon Has a Family
to Support," and "Long Live Hameed Nylon!" Raised alongside
these were green flags brought from the mosques. Thus the tops of
their standards read, "God," "Muhammad," and "Ali." When the
children saw these, they rushed home and returned with any scraps
of cloth they could find. They tied these to sticks, which they began
to wave as they hopped about inside the crush of people or at the
front. The neighborhood's dervishes brought their swords and
lances, which they brandished, striking in time to the ululations of
the women or whenever anyone cried, "God is Most Great!" There

were also three or four—among them the thief Mahmud al-Arabi, who broke into houses by night (naturally outside of the Chuqor neighborhood)—who brought their revolvers, since they felt responsible for their community's inhabitants. They fired into the air until the mosque's imam forbade them to do that. They stopped firing but kept their revolvers in their hands. Many children had stained their faces black with soot so that they resembled Africans or jinns. Others wore goat heads attached to skins that reached down to their feet. They were butting the air with their horns. At the same time some sheikhs sprinkled rose water from small bronze vessels with long necks over the assembled people. Others carried pictures of al-Hasan and al-Husayn, the dragon-slaying saint, the child king Faisal II, King Ghazi, and Kemal Atatürk. Indeed, there was even a framed portrait of the renowned artist Samanchi Qizzi—taken from the coffee shop in the great souk.

Finally the demonstration set off, but where was it heading? No one knew. It traversed the Chuqor neighborhood, back and forth, entering alleyways and bursting out of them. Women watching from rooftops thought the procession was a prayer for rain when they saw the soot-stained faces and the goat heads. So they started to pour water over the heads of the demonstrators for good luck. After they had crisscrossed the neighborhood, someone shouted, "Let's go to the company and present our complaints." Another person cried, "No, let's go to the barracks and present the matter to the government." Mullah Zayn al-Abideen al-Qadiri, the mosque's imam, who was marching in the lead with the neighborhood's sheikhs beside him, stopped to deliver a speech that everyone remembered for a long time. He said, "It is unreasonable to think we can proceed from here to the company in Baba Gurgur to present our petition to the Englishman and his wanton wife, who is a Christian. We would die of fatigue before we reached there. Moreover, God and His Messenger have forbidden Muslims from bowing their heads before infidels. If we go there, we will be forced to act in a submissive and subservient way when we appeal for merciful treatment from a harlot and her procurer husband. This approach would ill befit the honor of the Chuqor neighborhood. I have heard others demand that we head for the barracks or the palace, but how is the government involved in Hameed Nylon's firing? It's the English who fired him, and they're not our fellow countrymen. Only red communists pick fights with the police and the government, and praise God we're not communists or Muscovites." When the Imam Zayn al-Abideen al-Qadiri reached this point in his speech, voices from enthusiastic members of the crowd asked, "What should we do then?" A profound silence reigned while the imam quickly responded. His answer was decisive and dumbfounding this time: "We will turn toward God." The multitude did not quite comprehend the meaning of this lofty phrase. Therefore, he added, "It's true that Hameed Nylon was sacked, but the affliction is even greater than that, for we are all threatened by the drought, since not a single drop of rain has fallen. If God does not show compassion by sending His clouds over the city of Kirkuk, we shall starve to death. So let's all go to the open area in al-Musalla to pray to God and His Messenger for the advent of rain and the dispersal of goodness and blessings to everyone."

Thus, to the beating of drums and the rattle of tambourines, people carrying their green flags and their placards demanding justice for Hameed Nylon headed to al-Musalla Square, which they crossed to the open cemetery, which concealed among its gravestones hoopoes and larks that took flight and soared into the air, until the human throng reached the open space Turkmen called Yeddi Qizlar, where remains of abandoned stone grist mills could be found. There everyone stood, facing God with dignified submission, raising their hands to the sky in common prayer and tearful, heartfelt entreaty for rain to fall and for Hameed Nylon to be reinstated to his job. They remained there more than an hour, asking

God to cleanse their soot-stained faces with copious amounts of rain. Suddenly the sky darkened as black clouds approached from the east. Then affirmative cries glorifying God's compassion and might resounded in thanks to Him for hearing the appeal of the inhabitants of the Chuqor neighborhood. In fact, there was thunder and lightning; the prayerful demonstrators were caught in the rain and only reached home by the skin of their teeth, soaked and nearly drowned in the torrents that swept through all the neighborhoods. The miracle that had occurred made them forget the story of Hameed Nylon, who could now joke with the others about his escapades with Mrs. Helen McNeely.

This miracle left an indelible impression on people's memories. They debated and quarreled for a long time about who deserved credit for it. Had God answered the plea of anyone in particular, or simply their joint appeal? They reached a degree of consensus on the notion that God would not have answered the prayer of one of the few Arabs participating in the procession, for they never washed off their butts and would be regarded as traitors forever and a day, because they had assisted the infidel English in the war against the Muslim Ottomans, fighting against their Turkish brethren without any consideration whatsoever for the religion uniting them. Since the Turkmen disparaged the Arabs in any quarrel that erupted between them with references to "traitorous Arabs" or "those shit-assed Arabs," many Arab children began to wish that God had created them Turkmen. Some Arab children even joined with Turkmen children in their enthusiasm and support for Turkish political parties, of which many Turkmen youth considered themselves members. The portrait of Kemal Atatürk, recognizable by his lengthy face, military uniform, and medals, was displayed on the walls of most homes, whereas only Arabs dared hang a picture of the king, the prince regent, or even of Queen Aliya, who was loved by many, especially women, perhaps because she was a widow or possibly because it was the English who had killed her husband—King Ghazi—according to widespread rumors, in revenge for his campaign to slay the Assyrians who had wanted to establish an independent state for themselves in Iraq under the leadership of Mar Sham'un, who escaped with his life, fleeing to America. Women told their children with pride how the people of Kirkuk had once gone out to welcome the return of the victorious soldiers and armed men of some northern tribes, each of whom carried the head of an infidel Assyrian in his hands. The women said that the eyes in these heads were impudent and kept staring at them, casting impertinent glances their way, so that many women had been forced to pull their headscarves back around their faces as they cursed Satan and the Assyrians.

Similarly, if the Arabs were ruled out as deserving any credit for this miracle, there was naturally no cause for the Kurds to claim a favor like this. The truth was that the Kurds themselves, the two or three families that had settled in the Chuqor neighborhood, denied playing any role in this case, which was God's doing alone.

It would not have been possible, in any case, for them to claim the opposite, since they were not very bright and could not even distinguish black raisins from dung beetles. (Everyone in the Chuqor neighborhood knew that a group of Kurds who were served a platter of raisins mixed with dung beetles had begun capturing fugitive beetles to devour, telling each other: "Eat the runaway raisins first; the others will stay where they are.") Would it have been conceivable for God to answer the prayer of such ignoramuses? The matter deserved no debate or reflection.

It was clear that God had answered the Turkmens' prayer and not anyone else's, but had He answered their communal prayer, or that of one or two of them only? It was admittedly difficult to be sure about a complicated matter like this, for opinions were totally irreconcilable. Some claimed that this miracle should be credited to the madman Dalli Ihsan, who had raised his head to the sky, as he always did, and ordered the clouds to give rain, so that it rained. These people had an irrefutable argument, namely that Dalli Ihsan was not a human being but a jinni, one of the Muslim factions of the jinn. This was no secret, since everyone said so every day. He would walk through the Chuqor neighborhood, stroll through the great souk, and stop repeatedly to scream in the faces of jinn who apparently were trying to pick a fight with him or to upset him. Then he would continue on his way only to turn around once more and curse the void. He was allowed to stop at any stall and take whatever he wanted without anyone asking him to pay, although to tell the truth he never took more than he needed for himself: an orange from here and an apple from there. At times he would sit in a deserted corner of a coffee shop and drink a tumbler of tea, without paying for it, naturally, and listen attentively to the coffee shop's rhapsodist recite the story of Antara ibn Shaddad or Sayf ibn Dhi Yazzan or the choice exploits of Mullah Nasr al-Din. He would smile and shake his head and then leave. Then some patrons of the coffee shop would mutter, "What a lucky fellow! The jinn's queen has summoned him."

The story of his relationship with the jinn had come to light many years previously, and even the children of the Chuqor neighborhood knew it. What actually happened was that al-Hajj Ahmad al-Sabunji, a wholesale cereals merchant and the community's richest man, was awakened one night by a voice, which did not sound human, outside his bedroom. He pretended to be asleep while sharpening all of his senses. Someone whispered in the dark, "Harun, Harun, are you ready?" The query came from a cat he had never seen before. Then he saw Harun—the household cat—join the other cat, which he greeted. He said, "I've borrowed some of my master's clothes for us." The second cat replied, "I was afraid you'd forgotten or succumbed to fatigue and fallen asleep." Harun replied,

"No other night's like this one. How could I forget our annual party?" Finally they leapt quietly onto the wall and from there descended to the street. Curiosity got the better of al-Hajj Ahmad al-Sabunji, who also went out to the street and followed the pair from a distance. The two cats, each carrying a bag by the neck, set off in the direction of the souk. Then they slunk off to the right, down a side alley, and ended up on the public street parallel to the citadel. Slowly and calmly they continued on their way to the women's baths. He saw his cat Harun and the other one change into men in front of the side door to the baths. They opened their sacks and then put on the jilbabs they had brought. Next they shoved open the door and disappeared inside. For a time, al-Hajj Ahmad heard heady, inebriating music coming from inside, from the courtyard of the baths. His heart pounded fiercely, for he had recognized one of the two men as none other than Dalli Ihsan. Al-Hajj Ahmad hesitated for a few moments, not knowing what to do. Should he enter also or not? He was terrified but recited, "In the name of God the Compassionate, the Merciful," and then the Throne Verse from the Qur'an (2:255). After that, he thrust open the door and entered, surrendering his fate to destiny. There he beheld a sight no human eye had ever seen before; nor would al-Hajj Ahmad al-Sabunji ever see anything like it again. The courtyard of the baths, which his wife visited once a week with the children, taking along her bundle of clothes, had been transformed into an astonishing chamber of colored glass. Hanging from the ceiling were huge chandeliers of pearls. Around the sides were pure gold benches on which were engraved magical inscriptions he could not decipher, not a word. Green, blue, red, yellow, and white birds soared through the higher reaches of the chamber, making music like jinn singing. Al-Hajj Ahmad inhaled the fragrance of intoxicating incense that made him forget he was in the Kirkuk baths. In fact, he forgot he was in this world at all. He was especially incredulous when he discovered something he could in no way explain: the chamber opened onto the shore of a vast ocean traversed by ships arriving from afar in the command of cats of every variety. These leaped to shore the moment the ships and vessels reached it and then changed into young men and women of ravishing appearance. He knew, since he had spent his entire life in the city, that there is no ocean in Kirkuk and that the Khasa Su, which runs through town, is an unusual type of river, since it dries up completely in the summer but turns into a torrential, raging river in the winter, flooding its banks at times and threatening to drown the neighborhood of al-Chay. The many people present wore the most splendid clothes. At the center of the hall sat the king and queen on a throne studded with pearls and rubies. They were surrounded by their ministers and courtiers and served by comely youths and maidens who were clad in silk and who carried around platters of pure gold containing finger foods and fruit. Al-Hajj Ahmad realized that these were Muslim jinn and that the names of their king and queen, respectively, were Hardhob and Murjana.

Dazzled by the lights and the elegance of the place, al-Hajj Ahmad al-Sabunji mingled with the guests without anyone noticing him. When he saw people singing and doing line dances, he joined them so that no one would notice a human being had crashed their party. They were all singing in unison to a beat like a magical incantation:

I saw my Love with my heart's eye.
Then he asked: Who are you? I said: You,
You who surpass every limit
To erase "where"; so where are You,
Now that there is no "where" where You are
And there is no "where" wherever You are
And there is no image for imagination to use to imagine You
So that imagination can know where You are?

Al-Hajj Ahmad al-Sabunji personally memorized these verses, passed down from al-Husayn ibn Mansur al-Hallaj, and started repeating them along with the others. He learned from the partygoers that this poet, who was crucified on a palm trunk in Baghdad, was actually not a human being. Instead, he was one of the God-fearing jinn. They cherish him very highly, and his standing with them is just below that of King Solomon the Wise, who possesses limitless sovereignty over all factions of the jinn.

During the exuberant pleasure that encompassed everyone, al-Hajj Ahmad al-Sabunji decided to make a mark that would provide irrefutable proof later on. Thus he approached Harun, who was wearing his navy-blue jilbab, and burned the sleeve of the garment from the rear with a cigarette butt that left a small hole, without Harun feeling it. Finally he found an opportunity to slip back to the street again, more than a little concerned for his safety. On the way home through a darkness attenuated at intervals by feeble street lamps, he met thieves carrying their bags on their backs, sentries who blew their whistles from time to time, solitary drunks singing Turkmen folk songs as loudly as possible while drunks in other streets responded with their songs in response to the songs they had just heard when awaiting an answering song, but al-Hajj Ahmad al-Sabunji, plunged into another world, was oblivious to everything—the stealthy thieves, the night watchmen, and even the Turkmen folk songs, which he normally enjoyed. Shaking from stress and fright, he might almost have been a prophet upon whom divine inspiration had been bestowed. Thus as soon as he reached home, he slipped into bed to ponder the events of his amazing night. He tried to sleep but could not and stayed awake until dawn, when he heard Harun jump onto the wall once more, slink into the house, and then—through the keyhole in the door—tell Dalli Ihsan, who had apparently stayed outside, "It was a great night, wasn't it?" He heard Dalli Ihsan whisper, "Naturally, of course." Then he added, "Good-bye."

Harun replied affectionately, "May the Prophet Solomon be with you." Al-Hajj Ahmad did not close an eyelid all night long and did not leave bed save to perform the dawn prayer, when he saw Harun stretching by the threshold, as if nothing had happened. Al-Hajj Ahmad deliberately donned his navy blue jilbab, in which he found the hole he had created with his cigarette butt. Then he turned to Harun and—to his wife's astonishment—asked the cat, "Do you see, Harun? You've burned my jilbab. You ought to have asked my permission before you wore it." Harun understood that al-Hajj Ahmad had found him out. Lowering his head, he left the house, never to be seen there again.

From that day forward, ever since al-Hajj Ahmad al-Sabunji told his story in the coffeehouse, Dalli Ihsan acquired a halo of sanctity. It is true that most people, especially the unsophisticated and the children, feared him, but the neighborhood's sages considered him a gift from God and a blessing for them from Him. As a Muslim jinni in human form, he could only bring them good. This madman, unlike all the other ones in the city, was quite fastidious, always wore clean clothes, and acted with admirable composure, except for his public conversations with the jinn. He naturally did not have a staff he used as a hobbyhorse the way other madmen did. Moreover, not a single child dared follow him or chase after him, even though the neighborhood was crawling with children. Not one man could think, merely think, of saying something mocking or sarcastic to him, since a matter like that could have cost him his life.

There was thus no doubt in anyone's mind concerning Dalli Ihsan's true nature. Indeed, they were even able to trace his jinni heritage. There was first of all the account of al-Hajj Ahmad al-Sabunji, whose piety, righteousness, and honorable actions no one could question, but this was merely one of the proofs, since Dalli Ihsan's mother had been forced, when an elderly woman of more than a hundred years, to admit under pressure from her neighbors that a king of the jinn named Qamar al-Zaman had been her lover, visiting her secretly at night. She had married him according to the precedent established by God and his prophet Muhammad. Ihsan was his son, although she had attempted to conceal his identity from everyone. Her spouse had later been taken prisoner in one of the wars he waged against Jewish jinn and had died of grief and sorrow at being separated from his wife and son.

Clearly the madman, who would not have spoken to anyone, was responsible for the miraculous rain that suddenly inundated Kirkuk, for who else would be able to order the sky to fill with clouds and have it obey or to order the clouds to rain and have them do so? As always, however, there were people who like to wrangle and to express extreme opinions recklessly. They claimed that the rains had fallen in torrents for Hameed Nylon's sake, since had he not been sacked by the company and had there not been a demonstration on his behalf in which the Chuqor neighborhood had fully participated, the miracle would never have occurred. This theory seemed rather logical but did not clarify the miracle. Others responded to this theory, saying: "If we were to adopt this logic, then it would be necessary for us to proceed even a step beyond Hameed Nylon." By this they referred to the flirtatious Englishwoman, since without her affairs with men and her fickleness, Hameed Nylon would not have been terminated. They concluded, "Such an opinion would inevitably lead us to a denial of the faith."

Mullah Zayn al-Abideen al-Qadiri was disturbed by all these views, which he considered heretical and noxious. He announced that neither the jinn nor Hameed Nylon was responsible for the miracle. God had quite simply accepted the plea of the Muslims and had caused the rain to fall abundantly on them. Truth to tell, this view appeared totally logical and was welcomed by the hearts of the inhabitants of the Chuqor neighborhood, especially since Hameed Nylon himself had joked about the idea that he had caused the miracle, saying, "If I were able to cause miracles, I would have made the English whore sleep with me." And he meant what he said.

The rain fell for three consecutive days without cease until low-lying houses were filled with water, the roofs of many homes collapsed, and the Khasa Su River flooded its banks, submerging the neighborhoods closest to it. People reached the point of praying again, but this time for the rain to stop. On the third day of what he termed Noah's flood, Hameed Nylon lifted his head to inspect the sky and told his wife, who had seized the opportunity to spend most of the time in bed with him, "It seems the sky is peeing a lot, after having to hold it in for months." His wife Fatima replied, nervously, "Don't blaspheme, Hameed; it's a miracle." Then Hameed, laughing, answered, "True, it's a miracle, but the sky should not get carried away." During this nonstop torrential rain, Hameed Nylon remained trapped in the two upper rooms they rented in the home of his sister Nazeera and her husband—the itinerant butcher Khidir Musa—who lived in a large room downstairs at the end of the courtyard with their three daughters, the eldest of whom was five and the youngest less than a year old.

During these rainy days, Hameed Nylon only descended to the large room once. Then he sat on the carpet near a charcoal brazier with ash covering its embers, a plate of Ashrasi dates and walnuts before him. He affectionately told his sister to pour him a tumbler of tea, and then his niece Layla came to sit on his knee. Khidir Musa expressed his concern: "How will I be able to sell my lambs if this rain lasts much longer?" Hameed Nylon teased him, "Think of the rain as a holiday, man. Your money will last a thousand years." Khidir Musa laughed, "That's the rumor my sister Qadariya spreads about me, God curse her; she says I place dinar bills under my mattress and sleep on them, ironing them that way." Hameed Nylon answered, "What's wrong with that? They're your dinars. Do whatever you want with them." Then he fell silent, gazing by the lamp's faint light at the cabinets. Their gold and silver doors were painted with red and blue peacocks, which had symmetrical tail feathers, and with boughs on which sat larks. There were flowers around the edges. Khidir Musa said, "There's not much work left in Kirkuk. There are as many butchers here as grains of sand. I'm going to move to al-Huwayja where there's not even one butcher."

Hameed Nylon knew that Khidir Musa craved money and that his avarice was so extreme he only rarely patronized the coffeehouse. Indeed, Hameed Nylon thought Qadariya's assertion justified. He did not realize that the person who really ironed dinar bills was his own sister Nazeera, who earned at times more than Khidir Musa—trading in fabrics and women's wear. She would travel and buy her goods from other cities that no one else visited. It was even reported that she had been to Aleppo, a city that women said was in Syria or Lebanon. She would bring back colored fabrics, beautiful blouses, and the famous Raggi Abul-Heel brand soap, which she sold to the women in the neighborhood and in nearby ones on credit, but for high prices. Moreover, her mother, Hidaya, a crone who lived in the adjacent Jewish quarter, ran a depilatory service for women's faces (using ceruse), practiced magic, and read fortunes. In fact, it was said that she could turn stones to gold by reciting arcane incantations she had learned from her Jewish neighbors. The two women—she and her daughter—took care to adorn their sturdy ankles with anklets, their wrists with bracelets, and each woman's neck with coins fashioned into a gold chain.

Hameed Nylon had barely finished drinking his first tumbler of tea when his wife Fatima came for him, pretending to be annoyed at being left alone in her house. As a matter of fact, she was concerned instead that Nazeera might be plotting to turn her husband Hameed against her. She knew also that Khidir Musa, who was incapable of opposing his wife, would join the plot against his sister-in-law. Hameed Nylon, who was tired of sitting in a darkness dissipated only by the flame of an oil lamp with a dirty globe, rose, saying, "The best thing a man can do during rain and gloom like this is to sleep." His wife followed him. On the stairs to their pair of rooms he heard one of Khidir Musa's lambs bleat. He answered sarcastically, "And upon you peace." His wife, climbing behind him, cautioned him about the crumbling steps. He responded in the dark, "I know each of them by heart." Fatima was happy they were returning once more to their suite, where he was removed from his sister's snares. Perhaps he would also feel like sleeping with her.

Hameed Nylon stretched out on his back on the bed, but did not hear her until she asked if he wanted some tea, since he had been dreaming, and his dream had traveled far past the Chuqor neighborhood and the city of Kirkuk, to reach a vast open space, a strange, limitless area he had never seen before in his whole life.

North Korea

It was in 1948, after three years of rule under the U.S.–Soviet Joint Commission that followed Korea's liberation from Japan, that the Democratic People's Republic of Korea was formally established in the Northern half of the Korean peninsula and the Republic of Korea in the Southern half. This national division resulted in a chaotic wave of two-way emigration that continued throughout the Korean War, during which hundreds of thousands of Northerners crossed the 38th parallel to the South and the Southerners to the North in pursuit of shelter, economic gain, family ties, and ideological and artistic ideals.

Writers were no exception, and this cross-exodus completely reshaped the face of Korean literature in the second half of the twentieth century. It remains disputable whether those who went North did so voluntarily or were coerced by the Communists, but it is true that a majority of prominent writers from the Japanese colonial era ended up in the North. They included both early modernist pioneers and nationalists like Hong Myeong-hui, the grandfather of Hong Seok-jung, whose historical novel *Hwang jini* is excerpted here.

Fifty years later, the literary tradition that the North Korean regime has built upon the legacy of such great writers appears to be little more than state-controlled propaganda to the outside world. According to "Guidelines for *Juche* (Self-reliance) Literature" as they appear in boxed paragraphs in a recent issue of *Choson Munhak*, the monthly literary journal from the Choson Writers Alliance, North Korea's official literati organization, writing is all about the Great Leader Kim Il Sung and all other elements are subordinate to this cause. "In works that feature the Great Leader, one need not fabricate anything outside the historical truth, for the history of the Great Leader's revolution itself is great enough to forever move the hearts of people," reads the last line on the page.

What is evident is that writing in North Korea is not simply censored but required to fit a specific design. Membership in the Writer's Alliance and strict adherence to its guidelines is the only way for a writer to publish his writing. The works included in this anthology were all written by such writers—whose individual biographies are rarely acknowledged in publications, which itself is quite telling—and published either in *Choson Munhak* or by a state-run publisher, the only literary works from North Korea that are remotely accessible in the South and the rest of the world. If there is an underground network of dissident writers secretly circulating their writings under the watchful eyes of the Workers' Party, the world has not heard from them yet.

Nevertheless, what we witness on these pages is the persistent power of the written word, of the willingness to deliver, despite all obstacles, the stories of lives in North Korea as they relate to events we know only from the news, from the capturing of the spy vessel USS *Pueblo* on North Korean shores to the mass repatriation of

Japanese Koreans to the North and the fall of the Soviet Union. And that power enjoys far greater freedom against the sixteenth-century backdrop of *Hwangjini*. The legacy of the late literary greats has perhaps not been lost after all.

Ha-yun Jung

A TALE OF MUSIC

Kang Kwi-mi

TRANSLATED FROM THE KOREAN
BY YU YOUNG-NAN

During the Japanese colonial rule over Korea (1910–45), many Koreans were conscripted into the Japanese army and munitions factories in Japan, and a considerable number of them remained there after liberation. After the Korean War (1950–53), North Korea suffered from a lack of manpower and looked for ways to speed up the country's reconstruction. In 1958, some young Koreans in Japan sent a petition to the North Korean leader Kim Il Sung, asking him to give them an opportunity to "return" home to escape severe social discrimination and economic hardship. At the time, 24.4 percent of Korean residents in Japan lived under the poverty line, while only 2 percent of Japanese fell in the same category. The first two ships carrying the returnees left Niigata in 1959, and until 1967, 88,000 people boarded ships for North Korea, including 6,000 Japanese.

"A Tale of Music" draws on this history to tell a disturbing parable about an artist's willing self-abnegation in the service of the Great Leader. It was published in Choson Munhak *in February 2003. Kang Kwi-mi is a woman's name, but no further information is available about the author.*

I don't know much about music, but today I'd like to write about it. My thoughts on music have to do with my two brothers. One of them plays the trumpet at a top-tier art troupe in the capital, and the other works at a granite quarry. My readers may think that I'm going to write about my brother who is a well-known trumpeter. But I'm going to write about my brother who digs rocks at a granite quarry, not my first brother who lives in the world of music.

What? About her brother who works in a quarry? What does she mean by recounting the story of a brother excavating rocks when she says she'll write about music? What do stones have anything to do with music? People will certainly say these things. It's not surprising, given that I had entertained the same thought myself.

I will have to go back far to a time when my family lived in abject poverty in Japan.

1

My childhood was spent in a small house next to the Katsuragawa railway bridge in Kyoto, Japan. Even now, when I close my eyes, I can picture my old house, which seemed to shrink each day under the weight of poverty. I hear the sounds of the flowing river, the trains' turning wheels, and the whistles that used to fill my heart with sorrow for no apparent reason.

My father pulled a scavenger's wagon and my mother worked at a sardine factory where she sprinkled sugar, vinegar, and sesame seeds on the fish to be dried. She was fired even from that job because she was Korean, so afterward she worked at an Arashiyama textile shop, where she spread out dyed cloth along the riverbank to dry.

Our life was arduous beyond description. My parents wanted to send us to a Korean school but couldn't afford our train fares; they had no choice but to send us to nearby Japanese schools.

I still remember an incident that occurred when my younger

brother was in the third grade of primary school. While playing with my rag of a doll, I overheard a conversation in the other room:

"Mother, you still don't have enough money for my lunch?" It was my second brother. (Japanese schools required the students to pay lunch money in addition to monthly tuition. Only then could they get bread, milk, and soup.)

"Wait a few more days. I packed you a lunch every day instead, didn't I?"

"You mean unpack cooked barley and radish pickles in front of the Japanese kids?"

"Then you haven't eaten lunch this whole time?"

(Silence.)

"Answer me," my mother said anxiously.

"At lunchtime, I went out to a corner in the school yard, and when lunchtime was over . . ."

"Then?"

Only after a long time did my brother croak in the tiniest voice:

"I'd go to the row of faucets, drink some water, and return to my classroom. When other kids asked me, I said I didn't feel like eating bread, so I went to the cafeteria . . ." He couldn't finish because his voice cracked.

Normally, he was a boy of few words. What misery drove him to confess this to his mother?

"My child . . ." Mother seemed to be crying.

Oh, my poor brother! Tears rolled down my face. Pressing the old rag of a doll to my face, I wept silently. I was seven years old at the time.

Other things probably happened when I was that age, but this memory alone remains vivid to this day. That's how poor our family was.

It was truly surprising that musical talent sprouted from my poor household. People often say that musical talent is inherited. The parents of Beethoven and Mozart were musicians, while Chopin, Schubert, and Tchaikovsky had music-lovers, though not musicians, as their parents. My family didn't have the slightest tie to music. More precisely, we couldn't have.

We didn't even have an old-fashioned beginner's recorder to play at home. My eldest brother, for some reason, became the first trumpeter in the wind band of Rakunan Junior High School, and became known as a musical genius. This school's band was known far and wide, not only in Kyoto, but all over Japan. My eldest brother was unquestionably the best trumpet player in this band.

My second brother, who was in the sixth grade in Kishoin Primary School, began to develop an interest in the trumpet. My eldest brother would practice the trumpet on a rock near the waterfall not far from our house, and my second brother would hold his music sheets, acting as a music stand.

The curvy trumpet was shiny gold. The movement of my brother's lips and the pressure with his fingers produced the musical scale—do, re, mi, fa, so, la, ti, do—and created the harmony of fluid melody. At such moments, my second brother would tremble with excitement. His eyes followed every move his brother made, observing how to play the instrument. He wasn't able to hold the trumpet in his hand, though, because my eldest brother wouldn't let him touch it.

One day, while my eldest brother was at work at an iron works, my second brother couldn't stand it any longer, so he searched everywhere for the trumpet his brother had hidden and took it out. He played as he had learned with his eyes. Unexpectedly, he could make pleasant sounds. From then on, he would play for an hour or so and put the instrument back before his brother came home.

I went up to the top of the bank and stood as lookout, being a sentry for him. My brother could play pretty well thanks to these stolen practices. They didn't last long, though. One day, about a month into his practice, he was caught by his brother. While I was looking the other way on my watch duty, my eldest brother suddenly materialized before me. The loud trumpet sound was still coming out of our house. My brother scowled fiercely as he raced toward home.

My heart sank, and I ran after him. As soon as he entered the house, he snatched the trumpet away from his brother and shouted, "What are you doing?"

My second brother was at a loss for words at such an unexpected turn of events.

My first brother's voice rose higher and higher. "Do you know what this trumpet means? You must know we haven't fully paid for it yet. Because of our debt, Father, Mother, and I are hammering away to make tools at the factory. Do you think this is a toy?"

An unexpectedly clear voice came out of my other brother's mouth, though I thought he'd be breaking down in tears. "I was not playing with it! Brother, I would like to learn how to play the trumpet, too!"

"What?"

There was silence for some time.

Finally, my eldest brother spoke in a low voice. "What's the use of learning how to play the trumpet? Look at me. People talked about what a great trumpeter I was, but no company wanted to hire me because I'm a Korean and the iron works was the only place I could find work. My fingers are ruined there. I even tried to jump from the railway bridge. I hope you won't . . ."

All this was true. My eldest brother hurt his hand at the iron works, so he couldn't freely move his fingers. He couldn't play the trumpet with that hand of his. Despondent, he attempted to jump from the bridge and was deterred by a Korean compatriot who happened to pass by.

What could my other brother say, knowing full well what had happened?

Afterward, my eldest brother banned his brother from playing the trumpet and hid it where no one else could find it. My second brother's trumpet fever didn't abate, however. If anything, it burned more passionately.

The incident I'm going to describe happened after music class. All the students left the music room, but my brother stood there all by himself. A trumpet was shining in the cabinet. Without realizing it, his hand stretched out toward the instrument. His heart pounded. The music teacher's ferocious face hovered before his eyes. The hand extended to the trumpet shrank back. But the temptation was too strong. His hand darted to the instrument, and then dropped several times.

Finally, he took out the trumpet. As soon as he held it in his hand, he put the instrument's mouth to his lips, like a thirsty person grabbing at a bottle of water and pressing it to his mouth. Boom . . . As the sound rose, his heart no longer pounded, engrossed in the sound the instrument was making. He had no idea how much time passed.

"What are you doing?" Someone tapped him on the shoulder, and my brother turned around. He stood frozen. He saw the headmaster and his homeroom teacher standing there.

"You dirty Korean! Who gave you permission to pick up this instrument any way you pleased?" The headmaster snatched the trumpet away from my brother's hand.

During the next class, the homeroom teacher called the Korean student who had touched the trumpet without permission to come to the blackboard and meted out the punishment of holding two water-filled buckets with outstretched arms. As time passed, my brother's arms seemed to break with the sense of humiliation, not just the weight of the water.

This incident, however, did not dampen my brother's obsession. Rather, his desire to learn how to play the instrument burned more vigorously, fueled by his resentment for mistreatment of Koreans.

Soon after, my brother graduated from primary school and entered Rakunan Junior High School.

As I have mentioned earlier, this junior high prided itself on having a famous concert band. When the students in the band donned white Navy-like band uniforms and marched out, the envious eyes of the student body followed every move they made. So much so that it was no easy matter to join the band.

On the first day of school, the school authorities allowed musically talented students to try out to find new talent among the incoming students. The parents made such a fuss around their children that it was hard to tell which one was going through the tryouts. Anyway, it was a great honor to make the band.

"Sir, my child has received private lessons since he was eight years old."

"I'm the Chief of so-and-so Police, sir. And this is my son."

"Sir, this is my business card. If there's anything my architecture firm can do for you, please feel free to come and see me."

One boy, standing alone in the corner, was silently watching the parents' power play. This boy was my second brother.

When the atmosphere of flattery and fuss calmed down a bit, he approached the teacher. "Please let me play in the band, sir."

The teacher, who was worn out by the parents' clamor, simply stared at the brazen boy, who had come to him without a sponsor.

He finally asked, "You don't have parents?"

"I do, but they couldn't come because they are at work."

"Hmmm."

The student did not grow diffident at all. "Teacher, what's the place of parents in a tryout? I would like to make it on my own account."

The teacher studied him before he asked, "What instrument can you play?"

"The trumpet . . . Let me play it, please."

Even a cursory look told the teacher that the boy was poverty-stricken. Thinking, "Well, what can you do, anyway?" he offered the trumpet.

When the teacher heard my brother's music, his eyes grew as wide as saucers. He asked him to play one more time and granted him admission to the band. My brother was the only student who made it without his parents' business cards, with no one's sponsorship, and with no one's introduction.

I'm sure that my brother didn't play the trumpet all that well. The music teacher, known as a music enthusiast, probably recognized the potential in my brother.

The next day, when my brother rushed to the band office as soon as his classes were over, he received a cornet, not a trumpet. The cornet is shorter than the trumpet. Since it was hard to play and wasn't a lead instrument, no one was eager to take it on.

Holding the cornet, my brother pleaded with the teacher. "Sir, I would like to play the trumpet."

The teacher lost his temper. "How dare you question me? All trumpet positions are filled already."

The trumpet is the backbone in a concert band. A powerless student couldn't dream of playing it. After that, the sound of the cornet rang out from the rooftop of the school building every day after school. It was like my brother's cry, "I will show you all how good I am, even though I'm just playing the cornet."

Some ten days later, when my brother, all by himself, was practicing a minute-long continuous sound, the music teacher made an unexpected appearance. He had come up, attracted by my brother's playing.

"Were you the one who was just playing the cornet?"

"Is there anyone else in the band who plays the cornet?"

"That's amazing. Your technique is strikingly similar to Bok (Pak), a graduate who played the first trumpet . . . He was a musical genius. None like him has appeared since." The teacher muttered in a lamenting tone without realizing it.

"My brother was that first trumpeter."

"Is that so? I can't believe it!"

The teacher went down to the musical storage behind the stage and brought out a glittering trumpet. He placed it in my brother's hand. "Play for me." After he listened to the music, he said, "Now I finally have a true number-one trumpeter."

My brother's joy about playing the trumpet was beyond words. Suddenly, he remembered how he had to hold two water buckets up in the air in primary school, along with the faces of the headmaster and his homeroom teacher. He felt as if he had gotten his revenge.

From that time on, the trumpet was always with my brother except when he ate and when he was in class. When we went to bed, I held my doll in my arms and my brother the trumpet in his.

Every day, the night air of the quiet Katsuragawa riverside was broken with the trumpet sound until Orion's Belt made its way lower in the sky. The passengers of the Kodama, a bullet train that passed there every night, could have heard my brother's trumpet mixed with the whistle from the train.

My parents, who were struggling just to make ends meet, didn't pay much attention to my second brother. And my first brother looked at his younger brother, who was following in his footsteps, with eyes of pity. I was the only one who hoped for my brother's success.

I was a primary school student then. Lying on the dirt floor of my room looking up at the night sky, I would pray, "Please let me have a pretty doll," whenever I spotted a shooting star. After my brother started playing the trumpet, however, I would pray, "Please make my brother a big success!"

On Sundays, I volunteered to act as my brother's music stand while he practiced in front of the waterfall. Two months later, he secured the first trumpeter's position in the band. Of course, he did justice to his role. The jealous Japanese students, notably a boy named Shinda, secretly took away a piston or springs from my brother's instrument, drilled a hole in the connecting conduit, or removed a cork, but my brother's position as the first trumpeter was secure. My brother's musical talent was beyond comparison and no one else could do it better.

In July 1961, four months after my brother took up the trumpet, a competition for individuals and groups took place for concert bands nationwide.

The families of the participating students must have made a lot of commotion in the morning, packing delicious lunches and snacks and ironing band uniforms. In my family, the morning hours passed as usual. Actually, no one knew about the contest. My second brother was so taciturn that my neighbors often wondered whether he was a mute, so he left the house without saying a word about the competition.

Toward the evening, the neighborhood children told me, "Your second brother blew a horn and got first place. They say he's received a prize, too."

Only then did I remember that my brother had stashed his band uniform in his bag. My heart soared with joy. I ran home as fast as I could. While running, I remembered the shooting stars. One of them had heard my prayers . . .

Entering the house, huffing and puffing, I saw my brother sitting in the room.

"Brother . . . the horn . . . you got first place?"

In response to my breathless question, my brother, who rarely smiled, grinned, saying, "Yeah."

Overjoyed, I jumped up and down in the room. "My brother got first place!"

Smiling again, he began to take out the prizes from his bag. First came a commendation certificate, then a musical box, and then a doll. My eyes grew wide with wonder.

My brother pressed the doll to me and said, "Now you can throw away that old doll of yours."

I pinched my leg, wondering whether I was dreaming. It was no wonder because the doll I had played with was a doll in name only. My father found it in the trash when I was six; now it was so faded that it was impossible to tell her original colors and she had no eyes, nose, or mouth. That was why I had prayed to the shooting stars to let me have a new doll. I didn't throw away the old doll of mine, though. I couldn't bring myself to play with the new doll, so I put it up at the top of the wardrobe and admired it from afar, while continuing to play with the old one.

That evening, laughter was heard from my house for the first time in a long while, as we admired the commendation certificate and prizes my brother had brought home.

My father, who had always kept his head bowed and didn't speak much, held his head high as he said, "So, you're the best horn player in Japan. I'm so proud of you! I'm so happy that you defeated all the Japanese kids."

My mother concurred in a broken voice, "Why didn't you tell me in the morning that you were going out to a competition? I could have at least fried an egg . . . Did you eat lunch all by yourself again? You should eat well to have strength in your stomach to blow the horn well . . ."

Only my eldest brother was quiet. He kept opening and shutting the musical box. The box held the tune, "The Maiden's Prayer," and sent a snippet of a melody that seemed to convey a girl's heartfelt wish when it was opened and then halted when it was closed, and then the sad music continued from where it had stopped.

Thinking back, his behavior must have come from his regret about his younger brother, who would end up becoming just like him.

The next morning, there was a pounding on our door. Unexpectedly, it was our district's president of the General Association of Korean Residents in Japan. A tall man with big eyes, nose, and mouth, he wildly waved the newspaper clutched in his hand as he said, "Look at this. The second child of this family has caused quite a ruckus." He guffawed. To my father and mother, whose eyes were wide open with question, he showed the picture of my second brother printed in the morning edition of *Kyoto Shimbun*. He then read aloud: "'Musical Genius—Boy Trumpeter. In the national concert music contest held in Kyoto Hall July 7, Bok Seigen (Pak Song-won), seventh grader of Rakunan Junior High School, came in first without dispute . . . The thirteen-year-old boy started learning how to play the trumpet only four months ago. The judges were astonished by his refined performance. A pride of Kyoto, his future looks promising.'"

Stopping here, he asked my mother for a glass of water and gulped it down. "The water's so refreshing. How's that? Is he only the pride of Kyoto? He's the pride of our Korea, isn't he? You have such gifted children. But then, because of that talent, your eldest almost became a ghost under the railway bridge. If I hadn't found him then, the boy would be dead by now. It would be wonderful if you take these gifted boys of yours to our fatherland and bring them up there! I think it would do your family good if you return to our fatherland with the boys." His booming voice shook our entire house, almost lifting up the roof. After pressing the paper into my father's hand, he returned to his office.

After he left, our room seemed to be swirling with fresh air, and Father was deep in thought the entire day, looking intently at the newspaper.

We learned about it later, but my brother had almost not made it to the contest. Several days before the competition, there was a serious discussion at school about who, of eighty students in the band, would be sent. All the students in the band were asked to play their instruments in front of the principal and music teachers. No one came close to my brother's trumpet performance. His name was mentioned among the principal and the music teachers. After the principal said, "He's a dirty Korean, isn't he?" no one dared speak his name, however. There was silence before the music teacher in charge of the band said, "But the famous wrestler Rikidozan is Korean too." Once again, my brother's name was on everybody's lips. "Bok is Korean, but he's a student of a Japanese school, not a Korean school, so the honor will belong to Rakunan, don't you think?"

That was how my brother could enter the solo competition. We heard that a big commotion had taken place during the competition. The seats in Kyoto Hall were overflowing with dozens of bands and over three hundred soloists from all over Japan. The group competition came first. My brother's band shone above all other competitors and won the first prize. The solo contest followed. The sounds of soloists on the saxophone, the horn, the flute, and the clarinet flowed from the stage one by one, and finally the trumpet solos began.

My brother played the Italian folk song, "O Sole Mio." When his performance was over, the audience was silent for a moment, but it soon broke out into applause. He had been as good as the newspaper article described. After he won first place, the teachers, overjoyed, hugged one another and circled round and round, and the principal, grinning from ear to ear, forgetting that he had hesitated because of my brother's ethnicity, thumped my brother on the back.

Years later, watching a foreign singer belting out "O Sole Mio" on TV in Pyongyang during the April Spring Friendship Art Festival, my second brother said, "That Italian folk song likens a lover to the sun, but when I was playing it in the solo competition, I played it with a completely different feeling. I yearned that there would be the 'sun' that would brightly shine on our poor family . . . Maybe my trumpet sounded all the more heartfelt."

After the competition, its outcome was reported in *Mainichi Shimbun* as well, heightening the reputation of the Rakunan Junior High School and my brother. When Rikidozan, the pro-wrestling world champion, came to Kyoto for a match, the Rakunan Junior High band was invited by the Kyoto City Hall to march all over downtown to play welcoming music. That day, my brother left home with more enthusiasm than ever, saying, "I'm going out to play for Rikidozan." Since he was Korean as well, when the wrestler appeared, my brother got to see him in person and played his instrument with every ounce of energy he had until his head spun. For some reason, however, he was in despair when he returned home that night.

"Brother, did you see Rikidozan?" I asked.

He answered in a dispirited tone, "I thought he was Korean, but he was just another Japanese." He didn't want to elaborate.

Probably getting a glimpse of Rikidozan surrounded by a welcoming crowd, he must have thought: he is Rikidozan the Japanese, not Korean, and it's the same with me, the one who's playing the welcoming music. From the next day on, he began to change little by little. His enthusiasm for the trumpet seemed to be flagging. His nightly practices at the riverbank took place less often and he stopped going out to the waterfall, so I no longer had a chance to act as his music stand.

That autumn, my father decided to take his family to our home country.

At the news, the first person to rush over to my family was the music teacher. He said to my parents, "Please entrust your son to me before you leave. Your son is a rare musical talent. I've recently come into an inheritance of a considerable sum. I will take responsibility for sending your son to Tokyo Musashino Music College. Wouldn't it be great to cultivate an Asian as a world-class trumpeter?"

He must have thought that my parents would be impressed by the name Tokyo Musashino Music College, but my father's unexpected reply rendered him speechless. "Even if he becomes the number-one trumpeter in the world, he will be known as Japanese. Will he ever be known as Korean?"

The music teacher could not come up with an answer. Still, he followed us all the way to Niigata, where our homecoming ship would be launched, unable to discard his hopes. On the day of boarding the ship, the Japanese Red Cross officials asked everyone, including children, "Do you really want to go to North Korea? If you change your mind now, you can stay in Japan." They especially asked my second brother several times. This was because of the music teacher's "behind-the-scenes operation."

My brother's answer was one and the same. "I'm going home."

He had little notion of his fatherland at the time because he had gone to Japanese schools all along, but I think that his awareness of being Korean, sprouted in his heart during his not-too-long life overseas, pushed away the music teacher's tenacious temptation.

The Niigata pier was teeming with people who had come to see the passengers off. Among the throng of people stood the music teacher. To my brother boarding the ship, he said, "I really wanted to raise you as a world-class trumpeter. I admit that I hoped to be known as a famous soloist's coach. You made me think about music and one's nation. Make sure to be successful in your home country. You have special talent." I stood there, holding my brother's hand. I was afraid that my brother would be whisked away.

At last, the ship left Niigata port. The land of Japan receded in the distance. The music teacher standing on the pier looked smaller and smaller until he became a mere speck. Eventually even the speck disappeared. Soon, the land of Japan was out of sight.

2

Our life in the fatherland passed peacefully. My first brother went to music college. After several surgeries, he almost completely regained the functions of his injured hand, allowing him to play the trumpet without any impediment. Over the repeated operations, my parents often said, "Receiving such difficult surgeries for free . . . No one could dream of it in any other place than our own fatherland."

My second brother, as a middle school student, went out every evening to the Potong River to play the trumpet. At the time we lived in a five-story apartment building on the riverfront. He hoped to go on to a music college. No one doubted that his dream would come true.

Even in the touch-and-go situation in the aftermath of the incident of the American imperialists' spy ship, the *Pueblo*, my family's stability was not broken. Our Socialist fatherland did not budge at all in the face of the American imperialists' threats, no matter what they were.

In 1969, my second brother graduated from high school and was recommended to go to a music college. Soon, an admission letter arrived. It was a happy occasion.

That evening, however, my house was weighed down by unusual silence. Such a heavy atmosphere was rare in the evening since our arrival in our fatherland. All our family members had gathered. My eldest brother, a trumpeter in a first-rate theater group after his graduation from music college, was holding his brother's admission letter.

He said, "You always wanted to go to music college. What is this sudden talk about joining the People's Army? Don't you see this admission letter right here?"

My taciturn second brother didn't say anything.

After moments of silence, my first brother said, "The indignity you suffered in Japan because of the trumpet stays with me like a knot in my heart. I hoped for you to become a renowned musician to show the world that you made it against all odds. Now the path is wide open, so why are you saying no?"

Of course, I put in my two cents' worth. "Look, brother. You have an admission letter, so why are you doing this to yourself? Don't you think you should show that music teacher who tried to persuade you until the last minute, following us to the ship, hoping to take you away?"

Despite our attempts, the object of our conversation kept silent for a long time. Finally, he blurted out, "I will not change my mind. Everyone in my class filed a petition to be allowed to join the People's Army. We had already agreed to do it at the time of the *Pueblo* incident."

As if endorsing my brother's assertion, the television started reporting on how an EC-121, a large-scale American military reconnaissance plane, had entered our airspace and how our side had shot it down. Immediately, all of us fell silent and watched the news. Even after the report was over, no one spoke.

Finally, my father said, "Son, I think you've made the right decision. What's the use of music if we have no country? You're right. My family should have at least one People's Army soldier, because we have enjoyed only benefits after our return home."

My mother, sitting next to him, concurred, "I agree that you should join the army. Our country comes first."

Indeed the generation that experienced the loss of country thought differently. So, my second brother, fully supported by his parents, joined the People's Army together with his classmates.

While in the army, he rarely wrote letters to us. Even occasional ones were short, merely saying that we shouldn't worry about him because he was in good health and fulfilling his duties well. Thinking of my brother, who was of so few words even in letters, I would mutter to myself, "Oh, how terse you are! But it's amazing that such a curt person could play the trumpet so well." Still, I polished his trumpet until it gleamed, hoping that he would play it again after his discharge. I had no doubt that he would express the life of a soldier through his trumpet when he returned.

One day in May 1972, my brother's long-awaited letter arrived. All his letters are still kept in my parents' home.

". . . Some time ago, as a member of the military band, I participated in a parade held in the Kim Il Sung Square to celebrate our great leader's sixtieth birthday. Looking up to the fatherly leader, who was standing there like the sun, I played the trumpet at the forefront of the ranks in the square. Only then did I finally meet the sun, which I sought so tearfully on the stage of a foreign country. I think I've learned how to play the trumpet for this very day, despite all kinds of humiliations since my childhood. I played my heart out from the beginning of the parade to the end. Father and Mother, I will sing about the great sun all my life. A person who sings about the sun! Please don't be disappointed that I left the city without coming to see you, though you live so nearby. I am a soldier in uniform. My outpost the '3,000-li March' awaits me . . ."

After receiving the letter, I polished his trumpet with even more care. I couldn't forget his words that he would sing about the sun.

At last, my brother was discharged. As he entered back into our home, we saw that he was no longer the boy with a red collar who had joined the army.

"Oh, look at you! I almost couldn't recognize you. I think all the girls will swoon over you!" So happy, I laughed and babbled like a child.

Father and Mother were very proud of him as well. At the time, my eldest brother was not at home because he was performing overseas.

While we talked about all the things that had happened in the intervening years, I blurted out, "Brother, you will take up the trumpet again, right?"

I took out the trumpet, so shiny from my constant polishing, and handed it to him. Though I didn't elaborate, my underlying thought was, "You said you'd sing about the great sun, didn't you?"

My brother, however, stroked it for a long time and put it down without bringing it to his lips.

He said to my parents, "I have decided to enter the stone production sector."

"What?"

To my consternated parents, he handed an assignment letter he had already received.

"Brother, what's going on? How did you get assigned to the stone sector? This is too much!" Furious, I shouted.

But my brother smiled. "I volunteered for it."

I was aghast; I couldn't understand him no matter how I tried.

Regardless of my indignancy, he became a member of the stone production section of a certain general bureau. While working there, he went to a mining college and became an engineer. Thus, my expectation that my brother would become a talented musician came to nothing.

Why did my brother, who had said he wanted to sing about the sun, abandon music and become a stonemason? For the life of me I couldn't understand.

My brother got married, and I was married soon after. Though I was busy with my life at my in-laws' house, I couldn't stop thinking about my second brother and his trumpet, all the more so because I worked in the art sector. Whenever I saw a musician, I couldn't dispel the regret and emptiness I felt about my brother's talent that had been buried under heaps of stone.

My taciturn brother had become even more silent, as if he himself had turned into stone.

On special holidays, I would visit my parents with my journalist husband and children. My first brother and my husband enjoyed a convivial time, talking about the elegant musical world and a journalist's life revolving around people. But as soon as my second brother arrived, the atmosphere would turn awkward with his talk of the mine and stones.

Watching such a brother of mine, I would think: How come it's so hard for him to answer simple questions in a normal situation, but he turns so voluble when it comes to stones? Is he really my brother who started playing music despite every adversity and proved to be a musical boy genius? But what good did it do to ignore his talent?

By now, he was a middle-aged man going on fifty, so the musically gifted child was just a sad memory. When we got together, I was glad to see him but soon felt the same regret. Even these get-togethers, however, came to an end after a while. With the start of the "arduous march" in the mid-1990s, even the shadow of my brother was impossible to catch at home. He was entrenched in his mine and rarely came home.

Some time later, my brother's eldest son was about to join the People's Army. I went to the Pyongyang train station to see him off. Looking at him, wearing a red collar, I remembered my brother more than thirty years ago, when he left for an outpost with the exact same kind of collar.

Thinking about how the years had flown by, I suddenly missed my brother, whom I hadn't seen for a long time. But at the station, there was only his wife.

"Sister, what about my brother?"

"I think he will come soon because I called him at the mine."

My nephew was alternating his eyes between the clock in the station and people around him. I did the same. My brother didn't show up that day, though.

After seeing off my nephew, who left disappointed, I couldn't help blaming my brother. I couldn't fall asleep that night, picturing my nephew's disappointed face as he left without seeing his father. My brother, though of few words, had been thoughtful and affectionate since his childhood. Where did that brother of mine go, the one who had been happier than I when he gave me the doll he had received as a prize? Had he turned into stone himself?

Soon after, I discovered a surprising bit of news in the *Rodong Sinmun*. The government awarded citations to those who had achieved great feats in building monuments, and my brother's name was on the list of recipients. Pak Song-won. It was clearly my brother. According to the newspaper, my brother was awarded a citation from the respected and beloved general Kim Jong Il.

My astonishment was beyond description. My brother received the highest award! I rushed over to my brother's house right away. I wanted to congratulate him and hear what he had to say.

"Sister! It's been a long time. Come in," my brother's wife welcomed me.

"My brother's at home, right? He must have attended the award ceremony yesterday. I learned it from the paper."

"Is he ever at home? He left for his granite mine last night. His own home is no better than an inn now," she said as if nothing was out of the ordinary and managed to laugh. "Even if you get to see your brother, he won't say much, anyway. Sit down and relax. I will bring something out for you." She headed for the kitchen before I had a chance to stop her.

Left alone in the room, I looked around and approached my brother's desk. Piled on the desk were books on stone production and processing. I looked at them for a while. What attractions did stone hold for my brother, a one-time music buff, to steer him to such a different path?

I noticed a thick, faded notebook, its cover worn. Written on it were the words, "Creative Notes," which caught me by surprise. Then my brother hadn't given up music altogether? I opened it, and a yellowed newspaper clipping fell out. "Musical Genius—Boy Trumpeter." The unforgettable article published in *Kyoto Shimbun* so long ago!

I stared at the article for a long time. So my brother hadn't forgotten about those days and still harbored some lingering feelings about music then. What made him opt for a life in a quarry instead of the one with the trumpet? Recorded in the notebook were my brother's impressions about his soldier days. Underneath were musical notations of short melodies, expressing how emotionally overcome he was. I turned one page after another.

XX day XX month in 1973 at Iap Township, Chungsan County. We heard a story that brought tears to our eyes. One day after the war, the sun was setting before a house. The chairman of the township Party was standing there all alone, having lost all his family members because of the American bastards. The fatherly leader couldn't bring himself to leave him there all alone. He entered the house again and spent the night with him. That night, the sun emanated from that gloomy house.

Several musical notations were drawn below. They were scratched out, redrawn, and then crossed out again. After two or three pages of such attempts, he wrote:

It doesn't work. Until now, I've thought that music is the most powerful thing, an emotional language that can express everything. But it's not the case. There's no melody that can express this great, passionate love. Like no artist can draw the sun . . . Even if I create the most solemn melody, it is no better than a letter written by a reed on crumbling sand.

A poem followed:

> *You fragile reed, you crumbling sand,*
> *You fugitive waves, I trust you no more!*

The lines from one of Heinrich Heine's poems. How did it come to be written there? I thought I could fathom the course his heart had taken.

On the next page, he talked about "3,000-li March," about the path of the great leader's love, which he saw everywhere he went in the country.

> *Our march today was arduous. It was a long march into the deepest part of the mountain. Had anyone else walked this path before? We felt as if we were on an untrodden path. We walked like that. When we came upon a hamlet in such deep mountains, it seemed almost mysterious. This hamlet consisted of three houses, the kind that appears in an old tale. A tiny hamlet in no-man's-land, far from the human world. Entering it, we were shocked one more time. A clean wood marker stood, on which letters were engraved: This is where the great leader Comrade Kim Il Sung visited on such-and-such day in October 1949. Ah, did the fatherly leader come all this way, to this deep mountain? While he was so busy with founding the Party, the country, and the army! I have heard so much about the fatherly leader's love, but the shock today was truly great. Ah, Fatherly Leader!*

This was followed by numerous notations—drawn, crossed out, redrawn. Below them was another entry.

> *The great sun, the story of great love! I cannot come up with a suitable trumpet melody. The world of the trumpet, the world of*

music that I've loved so much. But it is too weak to sing about the
mercy of the great sun. It is helpless. Is there any musical melody
that can convey that great love to the people in the world at all?

Stopping here, I fell into deep thought. I realized that I was watching my brother at a crossroads in his life. Something overwhelming,
which I neither had known nor tried to understand, made my heart
pound. I turned the page.

The revolutionary battle site in the northern part of this country,
where one can feel the breath of Mt. Paektu, the sacred moun-
tain of the revolution. Our marching ranks stood under the
grand monument of Samjiyon, rising high into the sky. The
grand monument depicts, in relief, some anti-Japanese guerrillas,
who were following the great leader clad in an anti-Japanese
guerrilla uniform, smudged and torn with gun smoke and the
showers of fire during the bloody battles against the Japanese . . .
This is a grand monument erected by the great General Kim Jong
Il to commemorate the respected and beloved leader's revolution-
ary achievements for 10,000 generations to come. I stood in
front of it for a long time. The more I looked at it, the louder a
solemn, unusual melody seemed to ring out. I touched the granite
base and put my ears to it. At that moment I heard majestic mu-
sic. An ode sung by the stone about the heaven-sent great man . . .
The wind blowing from Mt. Paektu was swirling around the
granite. I put my ear to the granite again. I clearly heard the solemn
music again. It was the majestic song lauding the great man and
the leader's eternal life, infused in the stone by the great General
Kim Jong Il. This is music. This is the pious music I yearned to
hear so much, imbued in the world of stone by the great General
Kim Jong Il. I will live in the world of this music. In the world
of music created by the great general to be handed down forever!

Next came Heinrich Heine's poem "Declaration," part of which I had read earlier.

> *And with a mighty hand, from Norway's forests*
> *I wrench the tallest fir tree*
> *And dip it deep*
> *Into Etna's burning maw, and with this*
> *Fiery-tipped pen of giants*
> *I write on the darkling dome of heaven,*
> *"Agnes I love you!"*
>
> *Every night since then they burn*
> *Up there, the eternal words of flame*
> *And all the children of men to come*
> *Will rejoice to read the heavenly words.*

I seemed to be able to hear the overwhelming melody that echoed in my brother's heart, which I hadn't even known. Letting out an exclamation, I gripped the notebook with both hands and pressed it to my chest. I knew so little about my brother. He had never abandoned music. My brother, who had wished to sing about the sun forever in the parade site, where the fatherly leader was present, was still playing that music. My brother lived in music, bestowed by the great general on the world of stone. He lived in the dignified world of music, played by the monuments for the cause of the leader's eternal life being erected all over our fatherland.

I looked out. Through the window I could see the soaring Juche Idea Tower and the Monument to Party Founding. The granite stones that form the giant bodies and bases. The solemn music played by the stones seemed to reach out to us. The music of eternity.

Ancient people called stone one of the ten longevity symbols. The Incas and Mayans in the distant past created stone cultures with edifices, mammoth monuments, and pyramids, and they remain until now. But they are no more than fossilized relics.

No era, no nation could imbue majestic music in stone. But the stones in our country play solemn music. The legendary song of great and lofty love for the people! This song will go down in history forever as long as the earth exists.

The song rings out from Kumsusan Memorial Palace, that supreme sacred place of Juche, the Juche Idea Tower, the Arch of Triumph, the Monument to Party Founding, and historical monuments all over the country, doesn't it? The Monument to Three Charters for National Reunification at the entrance of Tongil Street, the gateway to Pyongyang, sings the song of reunification for 70 million fellow countrymen.

My brother was the very person who played the music.

He was a true musician!

I would like to end my story by explaining my brother couldn't make it to see off his son when he joined the People's Army. Having heard that his son was leaving, my brother headed for Pyongyang in a truck loaded with raw granite rocks to be used for the fence of the Kumsusan Memorial Palace. The truck climbed over a hill from the mine and reached a wide road when it stopped. My brother looked down and saw a woman with a baby strapped to her back, a few old people, and children standing in the middle of the road hoping to catch a ride.

"Please give us a ride to Kangso," the woman said. "I'm on my way back home from my parents' but as you see, I have a baby."

It was hard to refuse the woman when the sun was setting over the western hill and the sky, orange with an evening glow, was darkening. Interpreting the driver's silence as permission, she approached the car. "Mr. Driver, thank you very much." But she stopped short, with her eyes on the window, which held a sign "construction for Kumsusan Memorial Palace." The woman slowly lowered her body and knelt before the truck and made a low bow. Then the old folks and children knelt and bowed toward the car. When the flustered driver was getting out of the car, the woman said, "Please keep going . . . Please forgive me . . . for stopping a car heading for Kumsusan Memorial Palace, where the fatherly leader rests."

The baby on her back woke up and started crying. The woman seemed to be oblivious because she didn't stand up until the car was out of sight. The old folks and children also kept their heads bowed toward the truck. After a while, my brother put his hand on the arm of the driver.

"Please stop the car."

Caught by surprise, the driver didn't answer.

"I will return to the mine."

"What?" The driver was puzzled. "You're not going to see off your son who's joining the army?"

My brother didn't explain.

That day, he got off the truck and returned to the mine. A woman who shed tears of atonement for delaying the truck heading for Kumsusan Memorial Palace, just for a few minutes, and the old folks, and children . . . They must have heard with their hearts the immortal majestic music ringing out from the stones loaded in the truck, the music imbued by the great general.

FROM *HWANGJINI*

Hong Seok-jung

TRANSLATED FROM THE KOREAN
BY BROTHER ANTHONY OF TAIZÉ

*Hong Seok-jung was born in Seoul in 1941 and moved north
with his family after Korea's liberation from Japan. He is the
grandson of renowned novelist Hong Myeong-hee. Seok-jung
served in the North Korean navy and majored in literature at
Kim Il Sung University. He made his literary debut in 1970
with the short story "Red Flower," and in 1979 became a member of the Joseon Writers Alliance's Central Committee, North
Korea's official literati organization. His most widely read work
is the 1993 epic novel* Northeaster.

*South Korea's nineteenth Manhae Literary Award was be-
stowed on Hong in 2005 for his novel* Hwangjini, *a first in
inter-Korean relations. The heroine whose name serves as the
title to this sometimes ribald novel is a real-life courtesan
(*gisaeng*) who encounters starving masses, corrupt officials,
and a governor "completely immersed in booze and women."
The story is set in the sixteenth century, but several have commented on the parallels to the current political situation in
North Korea, though this will not be apparent from the short
extract translated here (chapter 1, section 15).* Hwangjini *was*

*first published in North Korea by Pyongyang-based Munhak-
yesui (Literature and Arts) Press in 2002.*

Tell me, now, don't you sometimes have moments when you long to get away from other people, sit down in a quiet woodland, and immerse yourself in meditation, sensing the pure, innocent breathing of nature? This evening, here and now, beneath a night sky thick with stars, I am experiencing one such moment.

Come this way . . . quickly.

Leading you, I walk on through the grove behind our house that lies wrapped in mysterious shadows. Somewhere far off a dog is barking. The bell of Bongeun temple outside Gaeseong's Ojeong Gate can be heard ringing in the distance. Stars are playing at hide and seek in the dark green treetops of the forest that blocks the road ahead.

Why, dew is falling. Just sit here for a moment, on this tree stump.

Did you ever stroll through a forest at the height of summer, then kindle a fire with dew-moistened dry twigs? Lightly surround the spark with dried moss, then blow. Even the eye-stinging smoke is fragrant, is it not?

Ah, the fire has taken. The sparks from the blaze begin to dance in the darkness and as your dew-soaked shoes dry out, your inner feelings awake from deep sleep, your mind wanders and you begin to feel restless like a child after a first taste of wine, your lips grow light.

Way back, a full century and several decades more ago, when our country's fortunes were already on the wane, something happened here. At the spot where there now rises a great spindle tree on the way toward our house there used to be a neat little thatched cottage.

One balmy spring day, that known as Cheongmyeong, early in April, a handsome young gentleman of impressive appearance came knocking at its front gate. A moment later there was a sound of steps and from behind the gate a young girl's voice could be heard responding. The gentleman explained the reason for his visit. He was on his way to view the spring flowers from the octagonal pavilion in the nearby flower garden, and he had knocked in the hope of obtaining some water to drink as he was feeling thirsty.

At once the gate swung open. The gentleman had the sudden impression that there was a bright light shining in front of him. A pretty girl in the bloom of youth, some fifteen or sixteen years old, was gazing at him gently. Was her beauty that of a nature spirit, or that of a celestial creature? The girl said nothing but courteously ushered the gentleman inside and served him some fragrant green tea.

But how could such an event end well? As cups changed hands, fingers touched. Starting in surprise as if suddenly burned by a glowing ember, they looked at one another. At times like this, eyes speak, fingers speak. Though their lips were sealed while the flames of affection kindled, what spoke was a mysterious love.

The young nobleman's heart was beating hard. The hand holding the tea cup trembled. Hardly daring, he plucked up the courage to glance at the young woman. Through bashfully lowered eyelids, a pair of brightly shining eyes expressive of an inner refinement were gazing intently at his face. He was entranced. He blinked. He lowered his gaze. Just as after looking at the sun, even though he deliberately did not look in her direction, her beauty continued to glow brightly in his eyes.

In confusion, he murmured:

"Perhaps I am dreaming? I feel as though I have climbed Mount Cheontae and come across a celestial nymph. Please tell me who is the master of the house."

The young gentleman fumbled for words, while the girl stood with her back against an ornamental peach tree smiling gently, as if embarrassed. Eyes like jewels, lips like cherries, teeth like pomegranate seeds, delightful dimples . . .

The young man's whole body was ablaze.

"In Buddhist teaching, don't they say that if just the sleeves of a man and woman touch, that indicates karma inherited from past lives, a predestined bond leading to marriage? Might it not be that our meeting like this today is the result of some such fate from a previous existence?"

Still, while the blush on the girl's face grew deeper, she simply bowed her head and kept silent. The youth had no choice but to quit the house with unfaltering steps. As he headed on toward Manwoldae he looked back and saw that the girl was leaning against one of the pillars of the gate, watching him vanish into the distance with a dispirited air.

From that day, the young gentleman grew almost mad thinking about her. He only had to open his eyes for her lovely face to loom vividly before him, and if he closed his eyes her enchanting figure grew even clearer. If he opened a book, her delicate eyes glimmered between the lines; if he went walking, her pretty laugh haunted his every step.

The young man was in the midst of studies destined to bring him the top position in the following year's government service exam. But now that he had lost his heart at the sight of the girl, what was to be done?

He resolutely took control of himself. He strove to conquer the temptation to go racing back to the girl's home and stuck to his studies.

Days, months passed, until it was early April the following year. All the various spring flowers were in full bloom, the melodious birds were making lovely songs in quest of a mate, and he could endure it no longer. Casting his books aside, he went running straight to the girl's house.

But its gate was shut tight. Disappointed, he could not bring himself to leave it after a brief lament and a long drawn sigh, but loitered until nightfall, when he expressed his feelings of regret in a poem that he fixed to the gate before returning home.

> *One spring day last year inside these walls*
> *you and the peach-blossom contended in beauty.*
> *Where are you today? No way at all to find you*
> *and the peach blossom laughs alone in the spring breeze.*

Returning home, the youth remained lying down from that day onward. His head was completely filled with thoughts of the girl, he was unable to read anything, unable to sleep, unable to eat. So-called love sickness is to that degree cruel and fearful.

With his last reserves of strength he finally rose and went out. Walking with the help of a staff, he headed for the girl's home. He intended at least to inquire as to the whereabouts of the vanished girl.

To his amazement, the gate stood wide open. A sound of weeping came from inside the house. Seized by some kind of ominous presentiment, he called for the owner and a sorrowful old man emerged. He gazed piercingly at the youth's face, promptly seized his hand, and asked:

"Could it have been you who ten days ago went away after fixing a poem to our gate?"

"Yes, that was me."

The old man burst into tears.

"Wretched fellow, no matter how heartless you are, you should have shown some propriety; where have you come from now? Could you not have come back even just one day earlier? You are one day too late, and so I have lost my only daughter, my only child."

Tears poured down his cheeks as he spoke. Directly after Cheongmyeong day last spring, his daughter's mood had suddenly changed, she seemed sunk in melancholy as if she had lost something important. Sometimes, she would arise deep at night and walk up and down the garden sighing and weeping; sometimes she would go out before the gate and gaze absently toward Mount Songak, but the old man had simply thought it was because she was missing her recently deceased mother.

Then ten days previously, he had gone with his daughter to the family's burial ground and on their return the following day, a poem written on a sheet of paper had been fixed to the gate. His daughter had no sooner read the poem than she fainted, startled out of her wits as if struck by some kind of thunderbolt. From that moment she refused all food and drink, and lay sick; multiple kinds of medicine had no effect and finally she had quit this world the previous night.

On hearing his words, the youth had the impression that the heavens had fallen. He felt as though he was being torn to shreds. He hurried into the room where she was laid out, fell onto the body of the girl, who was lying there beautiful as though she had just fallen asleep, and began to pour out his lament.

"Ah, you heartless heavens! If your soul refuses to return, how can I remain alone here in this world? Rather I will follow after you. I will enter the world beyond so that we can unite our severed bond of fate!"

His tears rained down onto her face. And an amazing miracle occurred. A flush returned into her face that had been white as paper, the breath that had hitherto been held back by her tightly clenched lips emerged again. And at last she opened her eyes . . .

This singular love story is told of Kim Gyeong-jo and the lady Yang, his wife; he was an official under the Goryeo dynasty's loyalist scholar Po-eun Jeong Mong-ju, and lost his life together with him, slain at Seonjuk bridge in Gaeseong.

Perhaps you are laughing? You find the story of the dead girl coming back to life preposterous? But it is not that kind of detail that interests me. No matter how much is true and how much is dream, they were happy. And if they were happy, it was on account of the intense, burning love that came blazing up in both their hearts simultaneously.

Supposing a flame of ardent love had only blazed up in the heart of one of them, and the other could only respond with pity to the expectation of requited love, how unfortunate and unhappy that would have been. It would be as cruel as giving dry food to someone intensely thirsty and longing for water. Although it would be a crueler torment still to be the person compelled without choice to offer dry food to someone dying of thirst.

Kim Gyeong-jo was such an outstanding person that he paid no attention to Po-eun's exhortations but followed the demands of devotion and honor, staying with him to the very end at Seonjuk bridge. While I was writing the tale of their love just now with envious feelings, I could not help thinking of the lady Yang learning of her husband's end.

What do you think? Perhaps you feel that obviously, confronted with her husband's bloody, club-battered body, she must have killed herself on the spot? Well no, not quite so. Hanging herself was not the kind of death that would have been proper for such a woman. She must rather have taken a sharp knife, plunged it deep into her heart, and bathed her beloved husband's body in her lifeblood.

The Milky Way is nearing the horizon. The first cockcrows are ringing out in the azure dawn. I hear dewdrops forming on the leaves of trees.

The sound of a voice calling me back is drawing closer. It is time for me to go home.

But you give signs of wishing to stay here in the forest, not turning your steps to accompany me. Sincerely, I long to go on forever sharing with you tales of the agony of sweet love, of heart-throbbing sighs of love, of the torments of overflowing love, the death of happy love . . . but Hanyang city is a hundred and several dozen leagues away, the ridges of Samgak Mountain lie far off.

Yearn though we may, no other meeting
than that found in dreams is possible.
While I seek for you thus, my love,
I beg you, seek for me.

Long dream paths
traveled every night,
in one brief moment's dream
we meet along the way.

THE FIFTH PHOTOGRAPH

Lim Hwa-won

TRANSLATED FROM THE KOREAN
BY YU YOUNG-NAN

The North Korean authorities teach their citizens that American capitalists maneuvered to imbue erosive capitalist trends in the Soviet people, successfully bringing down the Soviet Union in the early 1990s. The North Korean regime is convinced that the "U.S. imperialists" are determined to implant a fantasy about an affluent capitalist society in North Koreans, while isolating and crushing the regime. In the following short story, published in the North Korean literary magazine Choson Munhak *(Korean Literature) in 2001, the author echoes the official stance: the only way to withstand the capitalist pressure is to learn from the tragic Soviet experience, remain faithful to revolutionary ideals, and defend the Great Leader Kim Jong Il to the death with military might. Biographical information on the author is not available.*

It was an unexpected reunion.

"Hello, how are you, Mrs. Jin Ok!"

Calling this out to me, a stocky foreigner rushed over from a corner of the theater. At first, I didn't recognize him. I assumed he was a Russian because he was speaking Russian.

Soon I located him in my memory. When exactly had I come across this man in Moscow on my way home from Syria? Who would have dreamed that I'd see that unforgettable youth in the closing ceremony of the April Spring Friendship Art Festival? Back then, he had said he was twenty-seven, so now he should be thirty-five.

Everything was vivid in my mind as if it had happened only yesterday, probably because I had been shocked so much at the time.

"I recognized you right away," he said. "Your beauty hasn't changed at all. It's great to see how you've defied the power of the years." His blue eyes revealed how happy he was to see me.

"Don't joke with a woman who's over forty and fading fast . . ."

I discovered that he was a journalist. He said that he'd come to Pyongyang to cover the spring festival, but was to return home the next day.

"I assume you're still working hard as a researcher at the Academy of Sciences Light Industry Branch, Mrs. Jin Ok."

"You're right."

"I really hoped to see you again, but I wasn't sure you'd be . . ." He threw an empty smile, curling up his lips.

"Don't be silly . . ."

The audience was ebbing out of the theater, and we could hardly stay longer to continue with our conversation. I had never dreamed an unexpected future reunion was in store when I said goodbye to Seryozha in Moscow.

That night, I couldn't fall asleep for a long time. The incident of eight years ago unfolded before my eyes, stabbing my heart afresh.

1

On Moscow's Sadovaya Street, autumn leaves were falling in great numbers. There seemed to be something going on in a small park off the street by the way several people had gathered.

Passing the street in a car, my mouth fell open when my eyes caught red fist-sized letters on a white piece of fabric, unfolded like a placard.

"Director, look over there!"

At my exclamation, the director, whose hair was half gray, turned his eyes in the direction of my finger, pushing up his thick glasses.

Family History of Fools, Product of Socialism.

The director clucked his tongue in disapproval.

"Let's go and see. I wonder what it's all about . . ."

The driver parked in front of a four-story building near the small park. The building had an antiquated look.

The placard that had startled us was fixed by two poles on either side of the back of a bench on which a pretty, sharp-nosed young blond sat, one leg folded over the other. Her arrogance was palpable.

"Miss, can I touch the pictures?" A tall man, with a tape recorder hanging from his shoulder, asked in halting, awkward Russian.

Only then did my eyes catch what looked like a biscuit tin resting next to the woman. Four photos were inside, each bearing a stamp-sized piece of paper fixed with a paper clip: "No. 1," "No. 2," "No. 3," and "No. 4."

"Please take a look at the backs of the photos, too," advised the young woman, who was tapping her foot in the air. Nodding her head curtly, she smiled.

That was an odd smile. Could one even call it a smile? It would have been more fitting to say that she snickered. Just as when water is dropped in the sand, her smile was so fleeting that if you missed the exact moment of its occurrence, it would be difficult to claim that it even happened.

When the tall man cautiously picked up a photo, others reached out toward the biscuit tin. The four photographs slowly made their way around the bench, from one hand to the next. No. 1 and No. 2, palm-sized black-and-white photographs, showed a person each, and looked rather old, while No. 3 and No. 4, twice as big and in color, featured a person and a group of three respectively.

I was able to study the photos being passed around.

The subject of the most faded black-and-white photograph, No. 1, was a middle-aged man sporting a black leather jacket and a round star-studded cap pressed low on his forehead. On his waist hung a Mauser pistol. Judging by the inscription on the back, "October 20, 1919, leaving for the southern front," it was clearly taken during the Civil War.

No. 2 showed a middle-aged officer in a fur coat. This man looked quite different from the person in No. 1. It was taken during the Soviet-German war, judging by the explanation on the back, "November 6, 1941, leaving for the Kalinin front."

With curiosity, I carefully examined the color photos marked with the numbers 3 and 4.

No. 3 depicted a solider with a diamond-shaped epaulet. He looked very young. On the back was an inscription, "Honor. September 16, 1955."

No. 4 showed three people: a middle-aged man in a suit, a young man in a brown shirt, and a young woman with a flower in her hair. Since it was taken with a date-showing camera, one didn't have to check the back to see when it was taken. The date was July 23, 1986. On the back were the words, "Happy Occasion."

Amazingly, all four photos had the same background, a building's front door framed by two cylindrical pillars.

I had no idea why this Russian woman was letting strangers paw her pictures.

A plump woman wearing sunglasses asked something of the young woman. Since it was neither in Russian nor in English, I couldn't understand it. The director, who spoke German, told me that the majority of spectators were German tourists.

The young Russian woman, probably to indicate that she didn't understand, shrugged, and that same smile flickered on her face. It was indeed a strange smile, now that I glimpsed it again. I got the impression that she was a cold-hearted, eccentric person.

The tall man played the interpreter with his halting Russian.

"This lady asks if No. 1 and No. 2, who went to the front, returned alive."

"Both kicked the bucket."

"That's too bad."

The young woman stood up abruptly, took out a bunch of handbill-sized papers from the biscuit tin, and waved them. I caught sight of the typewritten Russian word "Information" on top.

"All the details are explained in this sheet. What I'd like to add is that all the people in the photos are related. They are members of the Sinzov family. No. 2 is No. 1's son, and No. 3 is No. 2's son. And No. 4 shows No. 3's son and daughter with their father."

In my eyes, the young soldier in No. 3 and the middle-aged man in No. 4 looked completely different, which could be explained by the intervening 30 years. In a word, the four photos contained a pictorial genealogy of the Sinzov family, whose members staked their destiny with that of their fatherland.

The young woman, for some reason, seemed to harbor frightening hostility toward the characters in the photos. Otherwise, how could she state so crassly that they had "kicked the bucket"?

The tall man grinned as he put a tape in his tape recorder. He asked, "Who is the young woman in No. 4? I have a feeling that she looks like you, Miss."

What he said made sense. The cute face with a flower in her hair—it certainly looked like the young woman.

"It doesn't matter. What matters is why the young woman, a descendant of an old Bolshevik family, wants to get rid of her family photos, putting them up for sale." The spectators murmured.

I was so flabbergasted that I closed my eyes. How could she sell the pictures of her family, including one that featured herself?

Suddenly, the young woman stared at me. Was it because an Asian woman stood out in the crowd, or did she read my thoughts from the darkness of my brown irises? I didn't avert my gaze but returned hers intently. She finally bowed her head.

An aged woman in zebra-striped knitwear looked at the Russian woman with disapproval and approached the tall man to whisper something. He interpreted for her.

"This woman thinks you're out of your mind. She says you will be punished if you insult your ancestors."

Some of the tourists nodded their heads in agreement.

At this rebuke, the face of the young woman turned frosty like a sheet of ice. Her two eyes, which sparkled like jewels, exuded the coldness of a lake that is surrounded by thick ice but not yet completely frozen over.

"I hear that there's a German phrase for a dim-witted woman. I've memorized it to give advice to such German women when I happen to meet them. 'Lange Haare, kurzer Verstand!' "

Giggles rose from the tourists. I asked the director what the phrase meant. He whispered into my ear, "Though hair is long, understanding is short."

The zebra lady glared at the young woman. Ignoring her, the

young woman took out a cigarette from her purse and put it in her mouth. She looked confident that she could sell her goods without a solicitous smile.

The tall man flicked his lighter for her and spoke with a grin. "I admit that your goods are valuable."

"You're wise."

"I'm tall, but I'm of the tribe that doesn't wear its hair long."

The young woman jumped onto the bench, and, with her boots firmly planted, pointed at the antiquated four-story building on the other side of the park, two cylindrical pillars decorating its front door, with her hand grasping a bunch of information sheets. It was the very building in front of which we had parked our car.

"You see that house over there? The four photographs were taken before that front door during the heyday of the Communist Party, because it was supposed to be meaningful. The Sinzov family held onto them as if they were great treasures. Now, with Communism bankrupt, these treasures are sold in front of that very building as products of useless memory. What else can better show the irony of the years?"

The woman's gloating face was glowing like an autumn crape myrtle.

The director tapped my shoulder and tilted his head to signal that we should leave. I, too, had had enough. My heart was heavy.

2

Our delegation of the Academy of Sciences Light Industry Branch planned to visit several Russian light industry bases in two groups during our several days' stay in Moscow. The inspection site that day for the director and myself was a factory located on the outskirts of Moscow.

A series of unpleasant incidents occurred one after another. Returning from the factory, our car broke down. We were held up for several hours until it was fixed. Then, soon after we entered downtown, we came upon a traffic accident.

A young man, carrying a thin bag at his side, was traversing a wide avenue with an unsteady gait. A large cargo truck raced toward him but he seemed oblivious. The truck, in the face of this unexpected situation, veered, ran down the youth, and then drove away.

Our car was right behind the truck, and we became unwitting witnesses to the horrible scene. Bringing our car to a screeching stop, we ran to the young man. He had been thrown to one side of the street, which was strewn with fallen leaves, and he was unconscious. Fortunately, he was still alive, his breath reeking of alcohol.

We carried him to our car and rushed to a nearby hospital. The doctor on overnight duty, who sported a thin mustache, admitted the accident victim.

We forgot to drop off his bag at the hospital because we were in a state of such confusion. It was only the next morning that we spotted his bag on the ledge behind the backseat. It was an old affair, and nothing was inside. We decided to take it to him when we had a moment free.

We left the bag where it was for two days as we moved from one place to the next until the afternoon before our departure to our homeland. After completing the day's itinerary, we returned to our embassy residence. I yanked my bag from the back ledge as I got out, and the man's empty bag tumbled down onto the seat. A piece of paper peeked out from the worn bag's side pocket. Without thinking, I pulled it out. It was a palm-sized piece of paper. I couldn't believe my eyes.

Before me was one of the photos that I had imagined would be in the hands of some German as a keepsake of his Moscow trip, or if he had already returned to his country he could have sent it to a publisher that might be interested in the collapse of Soviet Socialism—No. 1, featuring a middle-aged man in a leather jacket. I felt as if I were in the middle of an unbelievable detective story.

Intact on the back of the photo was the inscription, "October 20, 1919, leaving for the southern front."

The rest of the pictures—No. 2, No. 3, and No. 4—were in the bag's thin pocket.

The director and the driver were also astonished at the sight of the pictures.

How did the young man, who was drunk enough to get hit by a truck, have them in his bag? Was he one of the German tourists? But at the next moment, I discovered the startling likeness between the owner of the bag and the man in a short-sleeved shirt in No. 4. Though the picture had been taken six years before, I had no problem identifying the two men as one and the same.

Then the owner of the bag had to be the brother of the young woman who had tried to sell the photos in the small park on Sadovaya Street. How was such a coincidence possible?

Leaving behind the director, who had some business to take care of at the embassy, I got in the car and visited the hospital with the driver. In daylight, I saw that the hospital was a three-story building. The doctor in charge of the bag's owner was the mustached one who had been on duty the other night.

"He has regained consciousness. He just received a slight concussion. The problem is he'd been drinking like crazy." Expressing his displeasure about his patient, the doctor guided me and the driver to the back garden of the hospital. It was a cozy place with some white birches.

At the back of the garden, a young man with his head bandaged sat on a bench all alone, absentmindedly gazing at the birches dropping their leaves. The doctor took us there.

"These are the guests from Pyongyang who saved your life the other night. Pay your respects!"

At the doctor's words, the patient turned his head toward us. His eyes were bloodshot.

"How are you?" As soon as I greeted him, he stood up quickly, but he was too flustered to greet me in return. His eyes were fixed on the bag in my hand.

"Then, I'll take my leave to let you talk," said the doctor before he left.

The young man impatiently stretched out his hand. "Give me back my bag!"

With the bag in his hand, he lifted the pocket cover to check the photos. Only after verifying the presence of all four photos did he breathe a sigh of relief and thank us repeatedly. We exchanged names.

He introduced himself as Sergey Ivanovich Sinzov, and asked us to call him Seryozha. He was a graduate of Moscow State University. Before the collapse of Communism, he had worked for the Municipal Moscow Committee of the Young Communist League. He lived on Gorky Street.

Seryozha's eyes, nose, and mouth had a striking resemblance to the young woman I had seen several days before. At first glance, it was clear that they were siblings.

"We were surprised to find these photos in your bag," I said.

Seryozha looked confused. "Why was that?"

"I have seen them before. Three days before your accident, in a small park off Sadovaya Street, a young woman . . ."

Before I had finished talking, Seryozha covered his face with his hands and started crying. I regretted saying something unnecessary.

"That was . . . my sister. Her name is Katya," stammered Seryozha in tears.

"I guessed she was your sister. By the way, is he your great grandfather?" I changed the subject, carefully picking up No. 1.

His respectful gaze caressed the photo. "Yes. His name was Vadim . . . He was a longtime Bolshevik. During the Socialist revolution, my great grandfather participated in the historic battle that captured the Kremlin. After the victory of the revolution, the Party dispatched my great grandfather to a cavalry regiment as a political committee member. But the gunshot wound he received during the Kremlin battle worsened, so he had to have his leg amputated at the knee. He had to wear a prosthesis, but he never dismounted his war horse."

Around that time, Seryozha continued, his father's cavalry regiment was engaged in a difficult battle against Denikin's White Army on the southern front. He led his regiment on the front lines braving the rain of fire. He died as he charged into Novorossiysk on the Black Sea coast, the last stronghold of Denikin's White Army.

Before his departure to the front, he had a souvenir picture taken in front of the building with two cylindrical pillars, which had been a private bank during the Czarist era. This bank building on Sadovaya Street held Vadim's most precious memory. The place, which had been the underground Bolshevik Party's hideout, was where the Party had deliberated on, and decided to accept, his membership. While taking the photo before going off to war in front of the unforgettable building, he again affirmed the vow he had made at the time he joined the Party. This was how No. 1 was taken.

Vadim's son Timofei wore a military uniform, following in his father's footsteps. He had gone to a military academy as well. In the summer of 1940, soon after he was promoted to colonel, however, he was imprisoned on the false accusation of being a German spy. He had no resentment toward the Party at all, though. It was his conviction that he would shout "Soviet Communist Party, Hurrah!" even if he had to die on the charge of being a spy.

The accusation fabricated by extremist elements was ultimately cleared as the German Fascist Army was sweeping toward Moscow, the heart of the Soviet fatherland.

Timofei, upon his reinstatement, participated in the Red Army's parade held in Moscow's Red Square to celebrate the anniversary of the victory of the October Revolution, and immediately took off to the front with the ranks of parading troops. He was killed while commanding a division on the Kalinin front.

Before he went to war, Timofei had a picture taken in front of the old bank building, as his father had done. When a journalist following his division saw Vadim's photo in Timofei's possession on his way to the battlefield, he kindly volunteered to take a picture of Timofei, saying, "Look! Bolsheviks go to war from generation to generation! Comrade Commander, you can't just go to war. Let's go to the place where your father took the photo." That was how No. 2 was taken.

The two photos became important family treasures for the Sinzovs. More followed.

Seryozha's father Ivan served in the military in the Moscow Military District, and after his discharge he worked at construction sites for some time. Then he went to the Party School and started working at a Moscow district Party as first secretary. He had already joined the Party during his military service.

Ivan regarded the Party membership as the biggest honor of his life. When he earned this honor, he had his picture taken in front of the old bank building to commemorate a new launch for his Socialist Soviet fatherland, and forged his resolve to devote his life to the glory of his country as his grandfather and father had done. The photo in question was No. 3, which had the inscription "Honor."

No. 4, which bore the words "Happy Occasion" on the back, was a family photo taken to celebrate Seryozha's induction into the Party. Ivan had a celebratory photo taken with his arms around Seryozha and Katya in front of the old building, which moved him deeply. He said in a satisfied voice, "We have another family treasure now. It is a happy occasion. When our Katya grows up, you will come here and take a meaningful launch photo, won't you, my dear?" Katya stood on her toes and kissed her brother on the cheek, with a big smile on her face.

3

"But Katya's life didn't turn out as our father had wished. It's not easy to speak ill of my sister . . ." Seryozha sighed.

He continued, "My father became a widower two years after he became first secretary of the district Party. My mother died of leukemia. My father had no intention of getting married again. Katya valiantly looked after him, though she was only in middle school. Like our mother, she had a good heart and she was diligent. Yet she had something else that she didn't inherit from our mother. It was her artistic talent. Since childhood, she had enjoyed drawing. But after she entered Moscow Art College, her personality changed beyond recognition."

As a college student Katya had a busy life. The discotheque played a central role. What she hated most were the Communist Youth League meetings, which would be held from time to time after school. By this time discipline had loosened up, and attendance was not a must. She loved this lax atmosphere. Sometimes, she skipped school altogether to go to the discotheque.

Before she realized it, Katya, a pretty blond, embodied popularity itself on the dance floor. Young men competed with each other to dance with her. Katya's happiness was at its peak.

However, her happiness was eclipsed because of Galya, a freckle-faced classmate. Every time she went to the discotheque, Galya donned a different outfit, showing off her youthful charm. The dresses she wore were foreign-made and in the latest fashion. It was no wonder she looked so gorgeous. Her freckles were of no matter. As the saying goes, the clothes make the woman!

Galya's father Matrenko was the organization director of the district Party where Katya's father worked. In other words, his position was lower than that of Ivan.

Katya couldn't understand. Matrenko's salary must have been

smaller than that of her father, so where did Galya get all the money to buy expensive, trendy dresses? Compared to Galya, she was no better than a dowdy country girl.

One evening, Katya visited Galya's house and she almost had a heart attack. The entire house was luxuriously furnished with foreign goods. Milk and pastries, offered by Galya's mother, seemed to be the only Russian products they had at home. Outside, laborers hired by Matrenko were busy renovating a garage under bright light. Galya said that her father paid them wages in foreign hard currency.

Grinning, Galya said, "Well, our life is based on Marx's materialism. Materials come first, and next comes consciousness . . . Hah, I'm just joking. By the way, I'd love to see your house. I'm sure Comrade First Secretary's house is really swanky."

Katya felt she was making fun of her.

District Organization Director Matrenko's pocketbook was much bigger than his income, and he even had laborers for hire. Socially, it was not something to be proud of, especially because he was a Party functionary.

It was inconceivable that Galya, who hadn't exactly been born yesterday, didn't know this. Yet, she freely bragged about her family's finances in front of Katya. She didn't seem to care that her friend's father held a higher position than that of her own father.

After returning home in humiliation that evening, Katya learned something that made her wallow in disappointment. A manager of a furniture factory under the jurisdiction of the district secretly had sent a luxurious massage chair to the first secretary's house, but Katya's father sent it back right then and there.

Bursting into tears, Katya expressed her resentment to her father for the first time in her life. "Father, what have you done for our family? You'd never understand how humiliated I feel, even though I'm a first secretary's daughter. Do you have any idea how other people live?"

Ivan stared at his daughter in shock. "I didn't expect this. What's wrong with our way of life? Why do you feel inferior? Katya, I don't know what you mean by 'other people,' but to me they don't seem to be living the way they're supposed to. Come to your senses! You're a Party functionary's daughter."

Katya didn't pay any attention to her father's words. She snorted to herself, thinking, "Isn't Matrenko a Party functionary, too?"

Katya's complaint was due to her disillusionment with the changing Soviet society, where capitalist phenomena spread widely to production and nonproduction units, guidance and execution units, and where all sorts of corruption and abuse of loopholes in regulations, reduced honest labor to a contemptible endeavor.

Katya abhorred people who flaunted their material satiety, accumulating wealth with un-Socialist corruptive trickery, but she didn't hate their ideology. It was in some sense a hatred that was unrelated to ideology, but closer to jealousy of those who ate well and lived well with an unearned income. Such hatred was dangerous, for it was likely to push her down the very road of unjust acquisition of wealth.

Where does my family fall short of Matrenko's, making us unable to live like them? she thought. This was the key to Katya's discontent. Needless to say, the concept of entitlement—her father was the district Party's first secretary—was lurking behind it.

A pitiful person who was struggling all by himself in the sea, hanging onto the pieces of plywood called principles amid the violent waves of the capitalist trend—this was what Katya thought of her father. If her opinion of her father was such, she should have made efforts to see why he had to struggle so desperately, but she had no interest in doing so. The daughter, who was his own flesh and blood, didn't have any intention of understanding her father's biggest worry—that all types of capitalist ideological currents were ruining this huge country, the Soviet Union. This saddened Ivan.

"Katya, why are you behaving like this? You wouldn't do this if you thought of your great grandfather and grandfather, who sacrificed their lives for Socialism. I'm so concerned . . ."

Katya found her father to be absurd. While people like Matrenko grasped that "material comes first" and exhibited a conspicuous lifestyle, her father, a Don Quixote, was trying to protect outdated "consciousness" with so few possessions in his name.

Katya didn't feel good about making life difficult for her poor widowed father. She didn't complain to her father just for her own sake, though. When the luxurious massage chair had been sent back, what had come to her mind first was her father's bad back.

Seryozha said, "Anyway, our Katya complained constantly. She complained about her clothes, about our house, about our car. Katya turned into a girl who was full of discontent. Both Father and I tried to talk some sense into her, but she turned a deaf ear to our advice. A little later, she started harboring an odd dream. The dream was . . ." Seryozha smacked his lips in displeasure before he continued. "It was a dream brought by a foreigner."

A young American engineer named McCunly, living in Moscow, was involved in a joint venture with a Soviet shoe factory. Katya got to know this handsome man who had an intelligent and gentle nature.

McCunly spoke Russian like a native, but his dance moves were so awkward that they incited giggles on the dance floor. Although he seemed to have a lot of money, he was always dressed in a modest checkered overcoat. When Katya asked whether he had better outfits, he whispered, "Ekaterina Ivanova, I am a straightforward person. I have a feeling that you're the same. We can say the checkers in my coat symbolize our two straightforward lives being intertwined, do you not agree?" He flashed a smile. He was an interesting man. He always addressed Katya as "Ekaterina Ivanova" and spoke very formally to her.

Soon after they met, McCunly gave Katya presents—a pair of expensive American shoes and blue jeans.

"Thank you, but why are you so nice to me?"

In the face of Katya's curious question, McCunly blushed and hesitated a while before he called her "Katya!" for the first time since they had met. He embraced her so tightly that she had a hard time breathing. He said in a low voice, "I'm not married yet!"

Katya doubted her ears. It was clearly a confession of love. Her heart pounding, she let him have her lips for their first kiss.

Katya loved McCunly no end. She then came to love the idea of New York, his home, the city of skyscrapers. She scoffed at Gorky, the symbolic owner of her street, for having called New York the "City of the Yellow Devil." New York, the wealthy, dazzling city! The mere thought of it made her heart race. She hated staying in Moscow's Gorky Street, that nondescript place.

Until then, Seryozha was in the dark about his sister's close relationship with McCunly. He only knew that an American named McCunly danced with his sister from time to time.

One day, out of the blue, Katya brought McCunly home. Seryozha's impression of him was that he looked very respectful and gentle.

McCunly showed an unusual interest in the photos of the Sinzov family hung on the wall and expressed his admiration. When he learned that Vadim, wearing his artificial leg, had had a photo taken before he rushed to the front to die so bravely, he took out a handkerchief, dabbed his eyes, and lowered his head in silence to pray for him.

He said, "They really are family treasures. Though I'm a citizen from a country on the other side of the ocean, I have a deep understanding of the Russian Revolution. I would like to pay my deepest respects." He had the talent of convincing people of his sincerity, speaking in a low, serious voice. Such was his charisma.

After examining the family photos several times, McCunly sat down with Seryozha. Katya brought them coffee.

After taking a sip, McCunly suddenly asked, "Sergey Ivanovich, who inflicted the wound on your great grandfather during the Kremlin battle?"

Seryozha shrugged. "How would I know?"

"Who was the man who killed him during the Novorossiysk battle?"

"What good would it do even if we had the answer?"

Suddenly McCunly gripped the coffee cup until his knuckles turned white.

"You must know. You should seek revenge. You're too soft-hearted."

"Revenge?" Seryozha had no reply to the unexpected vehemence, so he just spun his cup round and round.

"Do you think I'm too cruel? Then do you think Edmond Dantes' revenge in *The Count of Monte Cristo* cruel, too?" A spark flashed from McCunly's eyes, which had been gentle only moments before. This murderous intensity could make even "The Hound of the Baskervilles" shudder.

Seryozha laughed. "Then are you saying this because you have someone to take revenge on, like Baron Danglars, Fernand Mondego, and J. F. Villefort?"

"Of course, I do! Oh, I'm sorry to shock you with this frightening talk. I shattered a pleasant memory of the Sinzov family."

His eyes grew softer, but his face was still bunched up. Seryozha couldn't bring himself to look at that face.

"I'd better be on my way. I have organized a shoe exhibition in Zagorsk. It's time for me to head over there." McCunly stood up.

"Zagorsk? That's where my great grandfather came from."

McCunly's face brightened immediately. "Ah, is that so? I will pray for him when I'm there. I very much enjoyed this visit. Thank you for your hospitality."

Katya rushed out of the kitchen, where she had been cooking, and held onto McCunly, who was politely bowing to Seryozha. The couple's embrace lasted too long.

After McCunly left, Seryozha thought about him for the longest time. He could say that overall the man gave off a good impression, but he couldn't forget the murderous light that had shot out of his eyes. McCunly was far from a gentle person. His heart was smoldering with a terrible vindictiveness. Of course, it was of no importance to Seryozha who the object of his vengeance was, but he couldn't help but pay attention to McCunly because he seemed to be so close to Katya.

There had been other young women who grew close to foreigners in Moscow, but most of the time these relationships brought misfortune to the women. Seryozha, a functionary of the Municipal Communist Youth League, knew many such cases. A female typist of a factory that produced state-of-the-art electronic goods for military purposes fell into the evil hands of a foreign spy. She was caught while systematically smuggling out classified documents and then was prosecuted and received legal punishment.

Then what kind of a person was McCunly? Seryozha's mind drew a blank. He felt an inexplicable anxiety. That evening, Katya, her face flushed with excitement, confessed to her brother that she was in love with McCunly.

Seryozha jumped up. "What? How can you have a love affair with a foreigner you know so little about? Are you out of your mind?"

Katya lost her temper. "What's wrong with it? Don't you know that Gorky said there are no borders in love?"

Gorky, who elicited Katya's disdain for having said that New York was the "City of the Yellow Devil," also said something else that suited her needs.

Seryozha abruptly stopped talking. Sitting on the hospital bench, he seemed lost in thought. A birch leaf fell in his lap. Gazing at the yellowish leaf, he let out a deep sigh.

Seryozha continued to fill us in. "A little later, Katya discovered that she was pregnant. McCunly talked her into getting an abortion, saying that they shouldn't have a child until they were married. I couldn't tell this to our father, because he would have been crushed. To make matters worse, misfortune fell upon my family. My father had an ideological confrontation with Matrenko, a revisionist and the district Party organization director.

"Do you know who Matrenko was? He was a terrible, greedy bureaucrat. Tyrannically wielding the Party's power, he used the organization as a means of accumulating wealth by unjustified means. Pocketing bribes—that was the ultimate goal of his Party work. More seriously, Matrenko didn't hesitate to commit crimes of treason. He took enormous kickbacks in return for unilaterally giving advantageous investment conditions to foreign companies. Applauding Gorbachev's 'glasnost' and 'perestroika,' the ever-smart Matrenko transformed the Party into an organ of money. He was keeping with the times. You know, my country was in the throes of capitalization.

"The struggle with Matrenko was far from easy. Although he was under my father, he had strong connections with the municipal and provincial Party. He considered my father beneath him. That was why his daughter openly made fun of our Katya and looked down on her.

"My father was ultimately defeated in his confrontation against Matrenko, and he was expelled from the Party. Matrenko, wearing the victor's laurels, was promoted to the seat of the first secretary of the district Party and swaggered into my father's office.

"My father collapsed with a brain hemorrhage, and only managed to communicate with his children by writing on their palms. While my father was struggling with death, the country's sick Socialism and Party were also walking down the path toward their demise.

"The day when Yeltsin announced a decree disbanding the Communist Party's monopoly, my father looked as if he wanted to say something urgent to us. His facial muscles were paralyzed, so he couldn't show his emotions at all, but painful tears kept flowing from his eyes, soaking his pillow. I stretched out my palm to my father. He shook his head. Now Katya extended her palm. He nodded, stroked her palm, and then slowly drew one letter after another.

" 'Soviet Communist Party Hurr . . .' My father couldn't finish his laborious drawing. His tearful eyes bulged . . ."

Wiping tears with the back of his hand, Seryozha continued with his story.

Ivan dedicated the last moments of his life to defending Socialism and the Party using the silent slogan, "Soviet Communist Party Hurrah!" as his final weapon. Katya knew well enough why her father wrote that slogan on her palm. It was her father's last heartfelt words left behind for her.

After burying their father in a cemetery, Katya returned home and vacantly looked at her dead father's picture on the desk.

She murmured, "I love you, Father. Please forgive me. Your undutiful daughter can't even follow your last wish. What did you get, Father, by embracing the Communist Party so conscientiously? There is no Communist Party in the world now, which you can uphold with 'hurrah!' If anything, there remains only a group of people like that damned Matrenko. It's a good thing that Communism collapsed. Yes, it is!"

Seryozha, sitting next to her, heard his sister, and almost jumped out of his seat. How could Katya utter such harsh words? Though Seryozha cried out, "Katya!" she ignored him. She filled a large glass to the brim with vodka and tossed it down. Then another glass . . . Making a fist, she suddenly shouted, "My father was a fool! A fool!"

Seryozha couldn't stand it any longer; he held her wrist and squeezed it.

Katya smirked and slurred, "Hey, Brother. It was just a slip of the tongue . . . Take your hands off me . . . I'll talk nicely now."

He didn't want to be the one confronting a drunkard, so he sat back.

Now waving her finger at the family photos on the wall, she muttered. "Brother! Who is that colonel . . . wearing the fur? He's Timofei, who was stupid enough to think of shouting hurrah at the moment of his death . . . though he was about to die in jail . . . thanks to the Communist Party. Right? That foolish grandfather of ours raised our father to be a fool. Oh, Brother, please don't look at me that way . . . It's frightening . . . Now, listen. It's interesting . . . Now, that political committee member of the cavalry regiment . . . in the leather jacket! He was crippled . . . but took a stupid photo before he went to war . . . he rushed to the front line and then got killed, that Vadim . . . That stupid great grandfather of ours raised our grandfather to be a fool . . ."

She ticked off the fools, muttering, "Fool No. 1, Vadim . . . Fool No. 2, Timofei . . . Fool No. 3, Ivan . . ."

Seryozha couldn't fathom how Katya had ended up like this. If this story was told to writers, they would shake their heads and say—it certainly makes no sense, it doesn't fit the logic of character development, it is too dramatic a change.

If McCunly hadn't visited at that moment, Seryozha would have beaten the daylights out of his sister. McCunly blocked Seryozha, who was charging toward Katya, and said in a pleading tone. "Sergey Ivanovich, why are you doing this to your sister? You've lost your parents and now there're just two of you in the world. Calm down! Please!"

Seryozha's heart was broken.

Katya writhed, hugging her brother. "Brother, please forgive me . . ."

The next day, Seryozha went out to the street and spotted Katya among the crowd of demonstrators marching with a banner supporting the dismantlement of the Communist Party. Seryozha fought his way through the marchers and tried to drag her out.

Katya shook his hand off and spat out, "You're Fool No. 4!"

Seryozha was so shaken that he didn't know what to say. What they should have objected to was change in the Party and society, but stupidly Katya was against the Party and Socialism. What a pathetic fool she was! Katya herself was the one who had changed.

Right before his eyes, the waves of demonstrators marched forward. They were a group of people buoyed by the fantasy that their lives would be wonderful after the Soviet Union succumbed to capitalism, endlessly longing for capitalist society where "gold rain" would shower down.

Right then, Seryozha caught sight of McCunly. Wearing a checkered overcoat as usual, he was walking alongside the marchers, searching for someone in the crowd. Was he looking for Katya? If so, it was a good thing. McCunly might not want Katya to join this kind of demonstration. Hadn't he professed that he had a deep understanding of the Russian Revolution?

Harboring hopes, Seryozha followed him slowly. Unexpectedly, though, he did the opposite of what Seryozha hoped. As soon as he spotted Katya among the ranks, he threw a kiss with his hand, with a big smile on his face. Katya reciprocated with a wave of her hand . . .

Seryozha spat on the street and turned around. McCunly! He hadn't known McCunly was a sleazy playboy who changed his actions depending on the situation to attract women, with no social or political integrity whatsoever.

Seryozha continued with his story. "McCunly left for New York without telling Katya. A year passed but there's no news from him. He toyed with Katya and then threw her away like an old shoe. Katya sank into despair. But whom could she blame? She was the one who ruined her own life."

Seryozha grew so calm that it looked almost puzzling to me. It was probably because he had given up everything about his sister . . . Dark ashes of agony must have been piled high at the bottom of his heart.

He gave me a closer look. "By the way, Mrs. Jin Ok, did you study here?"

"What do you mean?"

"I'm asking because your Russian is so good. Your pronunciation is impeccable."

"No. I just graduated from Kim Il Sung University."

"Ah, I see."

My thoughts were still on Katya. "So how is Katya doing now?"

"She takes an opposite stand to whatever I think or do. Her personality has warped beyond recognition since our father's death and McCunly's betrayal. Even her smile is bizarre . . ."

I pictured Katya's odd fleeting smile. So, unhappiness was lurking behind that grimace.

"Katya must be cursing McCunly now," I observed.

Seryozha snorted. "I would be happier if she did. She fantasizes he'll reappear and whisk her away to New York. When she glimpses a checkered overcoat in the street, she bursts into tears and weeps with abandon. She still keeps a portrait of McCunly she herself drew on her bedside stand, so what more is there to say? And she took our family photos and tried to sell them on the street . . . She's crazy."

Seryozha had been able to recover the photos thanks to a friend who worked with him at the Communist Youth League. The friend happened to pass by Sadovaya Street and wrested the photos from Katya while she was bargaining with foreign buyers (it must have happened just after we left the scene).

Seryozha had decided to erase Katya forever from his mind. But tears blinded him. With his heart empty, feeling that the world had come to an end, he drank late into the night at his friend's house. On his way home in his completely drunken state, he was hit by the truck . . .

Seryozha was working at a construction site, as his father had done as a young man. He confessed that life was difficult because not much work was available these days.

I asked him whether Katya had come to see him at the hospital.

Seryozha clapped his hands. "Ah, now I remember. You left a deep impression on our Katya. When she met your eyes, she felt you were like her elder sister. A scary sister, a sad sister, an affectionate sister . . ."

"What a complicated sister! When did she come?"

"Only two hours ago . . . She came with a bottle of booze . . . We drank together. And then we held onto each other and cried together . . ." He blinked his eyes and tears tumbled down.

My heart ached with pity for the brother and sister. "I'm glad that you've made up."

"Made up? She still doesn't get it."

We said a sad good-bye to Seryozha.

Before I left, I said by way of farewell, "I just hope that Russian families like yours don't have to experience so much unhappiness. Please take good care of those photos. And guide Katya well so that she does not insult the remarkable heritage of your family."

The day after my unexpected encounter with Seryozha, I had the opportunity to see him again at Pyongyang Airport. My institute's researchers, who would stop by in Moscow on their business trip, were leaving on the same plane. I was expected to say good-bye to them at the airport.

One thing bothered me. I had not prepared any gift for Seryozha, but fortunately I had something for Katya.

I had a traditional Korean painting at home, a birthday gift from an artist friend of mine that I'd received two days before. It depicted the Taedong River at dawn, with a flock of birds flying against a reddish morning glow. This was a beautiful painting, showing off the skilled techniques of a People's Artist. I thought I could ask for my friend's understanding later. I could have given it to Seryozha, of course, but Katya had studied art, hadn't she?

When I had run into Seryozha at the theater, I didn't forget to ask him how Katya was. But Seryozha didn't say much, except, "She's still around," and quickly changed the subject. I thought he behaved that way because he didn't get along well with his sister.

Since she was "still around," Katya would receive my gift. How happy she would be! The next day, I met Seryozha in the airport's waiting room. As we sat side by side on a sofa, Seryozha said, "Mrs. Jin Ok, it has just occurred to me that I know nothing about your family."

I told him that my husband was a military officer, that he often visited other regions on business, that he was actually on a business trip at the moment, that I had two twin sons, and that both of them were in the military, following in their father's footsteps. I also re-counted a moving story: A while ago my sons had the honor of meeting the respected and beloved General Kim Jong Il during his on-the-spot guidance to People's Army units.

"Congratulations, Mrs. Jin Ok!" Seryozha grabbed my hand and raised it high above my head.

I continued. "At home, I have a daughter still in high school. Her name is Sun-hui. She's a great violin player."

"Then is she planning to go on studying music in college?"

"No. She will graduate next year, but she says she will join the army like her brothers."

"I'd love to meet her some day."

There was an announcement that boarding would begin soon.

Seryozha, with a regretful expression, stood up. "Mrs. Jin Ok.

I will come back for the fifty-fifth anniversary of the founding of the Korean Workers Party."

I remembered that the day before he had shouted something to me at the theater, pointing to the slogan billboard. He must have said the same thing.

I hurriedly removed the wrapping paper from the painting and showed it to him. He gazed at it in fascination. Rubbing his palms together, he exclaimed, "What a beautiful painting!" He seemed to think the artwork was for him.

Rewrapping the painting with the paper, I said, "I'm sorry. I will have something for you next time . . . Please give it to Katya."

"Katya?" Seryozha croaked. Dark clouds passed over his face. "What's there for me to hide from you?" he said, "Our Katya is not in Moscow, not in Russia."

"What?"

"Do you remember McCunly, the American I told you about eight years ago? He showed up in Moscow and lured our Katya away. Even without my knowledge . . . I hadn't heard anything from her for several years. But just a few days before I came to Pyongyang, I received a letter from her, which was a great surprise. But, oh, I can't go on. I'm heartbroken. Good-bye, Mrs. Jin Ok!"

As he turned around after a hurried farewell to me, his face glistened with tears. What kind of life did Katya lead to make him act that way? Because of her, our farewell was as sad as it had been eight years earlier.

Soon after Seryozha's departure, I unexpectedly received a letter from him. Many sheets of paper were inside the thick envelope. They began,

My dear brother! How you must worry about me, your wretched sister. But I'm no better than an insect, and I don't deserve your concern. I just would like to recount a story McCunly has told me . . .

Realizing that it was the letter from Katya that Seryozha had mentioned, I continued reading with great curiosity.

You realize that Zagorsk was the family seat of a count named Zhahar. You must have forgotten his name: Provka. Before the October Revolution, he served the army as a captain, and afterward he fought with General Denikin and then left Russia, shedding bitter tears.

Since he had a considerable amount of money and other valuables, he didn't have to worry about his livelihood. He had lost a lot, however. A big factory, a bank, a mansion, a summer house, and a comfortable life he enjoyed there . . . According to McCunly, he lost them all to an unreasonable plunderer, the Socialist revolution.

You must remember who used to own the four-story building on Sadovaya Street, the backdrop of our precious family photos. It was Zhahar's bank, wasn't it?

Count Zhahar's family, pledging revenge, lived in a foreign country, but its members, from generation to generation, steadfastly carried out the long-distance struggle sponsored by Americans to bring down the Soviet regime. Well, the struggle was not exactly all long-distance. When World War II broke out, Tikhon, Provka's son, who was with the American Ordnance Corps, went over to the German side on the North African front, and passionately petitioned to be sent to Vlasov's Russian Corps. So, as a staff officer of the Russian Corps, Tikhon personally fought as a member of the German Army against the Red Army. Using the

expression we learned at school, he was a class enemy of our Sin-
zov family.

When our great grandfather was young, he was a gardener at
Provka's family mansion, the butt of all sorts of ridicule and
scorn. Only when I heard about it did I remember what Father
had told us. Our great grandfather grew up as a revolutionary in
such an environment and used Zhahar's bank as a hideout for
the underground Bolshevik Party.

As a captain in the military, Provka attempted to capture our
great grandfather, who moved from one place to the next in se-
cret, but he didn't succeed. He came face to face with our great
grandfather during the Kremlin battle, but his bullet didn't pen-
etrate our great grandfather's heart; instead it veered toward his
knee. McCunly said that God had given another great chance
during the Novorossiysk battle.

Reading this letter, you must be wondering how would Mc-
Cunly, an American, know all this? I had the same thought. He
mockingly said, "I've told you already that I have a deep under-
standing of the Russian Revolution. I will tell you the reason . . ."

Oh, Brother, please brace yourself. McCunly—he is Provka's
great grandson!

My eyes stayed fixed upon the page. McCunly, whom Seryozha
considered a "sleazy playboy"! He had concealed his identity! It was
frightening. The letter continued:

McCunly went on. "To be frank, I just wanted to have a little
fun with you and then move on. I think your brother will
understand because he's a man, too. Unexpectedly, though, I
learned that you were a descendant of the Sinzovs, my family's
mortal enemy. In my house in New York, we have the photos of
the factory, the bank, the mansion, and the summer house that

Count Zhahar owned. At first we didn't have a photo of the bank building, so we had someone take a picture for us. It was when the building was in the Soviet government's possession, and a red flag was flying over the roof. My family vowed that we would not erase the flag from the photo. It stoked our desire for vengeance.

"The photo hanging on the wall of your home—from the picture taken in front of that bank building I got to know the faces of our mortal enemies. How can I describe the jubilation and hatred erupting in my heart at the moment?

"I told you that I was praying for Vadim, but do you know whom I remembered with tears? My great grandfather Provka, who couldn't close his eyes at the time of his death, so grieved was he about his life in a foreign country, and my grandfather Tikhon, who was captured by partisan bastards and ended his life without realizing his life's ambition.

"To confirm my suspicion about the Sinzovs, I asked your brother one question after another. I mentioned that I was going to a shoe fair in Zagorsk to verify that Vadim had been from there.

"I made up my mind to take revenge—with flair at that. I set my plan in two stages. The first was to make you turn your back on Socialism, Katya. We can say that my family had a similar experience. But it was a bitter failure . . ."

According to McCunly, while his grandfather Tikhon served in the Russian Corps, he received an order from General Vlasov to convert a Soviet prisoner-of-war, who was imprisoned on Row A of the special section in the Sachsenhausen concentration camp. Do you know who that prisoner was? Would you believe it? It was Yakov, the eldest son of Stalin.

Tikhon told Yakov: Your heartless father coldly turned down the generous German offer that you be exchanged for General Paulus. You're discarded. Make up your mind. What will you do? Yakov shouted, "Traitor!" and slapped Tikhon in the face.

They had tried to convert Yakov several times before Tikhon joined the Russian Corps, but had failed.

"So at that time, my family came up with a motto that the Bolshevik idea must be crushed with violence. In the Khrushchev era when Socialism turned mushy like a tomato whose stem was about to fall off, however, we revised this motto, following the example of the Americans. In keeping with Khrushchev's revision of Marxism-Leninism. This was based on the new conclusion that the Red Flag could be easily transformed into a three-colored flag with the skillful use of the West's ideological culture and money.

"Of course, you're nothing compared to Yakov. But still you were an interesting target. A descendant of the Bolshevik, our mortal enemy.

"I exerted influence on you in many ways. You must realize it all by now. At the time, you were like a sponge, so you sucked in everything I dumped out. Finally, you grew to hate your Bolshevik ancestors, not to mention Socialism. What an exciting development it was!

"I'm sure that fool Sergey had lots of questions about the shocking transformation of your personality. He will get it if he hears everything.

"Even after my departure from Moscow, I followed your every move. I had someone watch you. I heard that you put out the photos in front of our old bank building and spewed venom about your Bolshevik ancestors. I couldn't have been happier.

"You did your part in breaking down the Soviet Union, didn't you? My second plan was to crush your humanity . . ."

It was some time ago when McCunly babbled this. He coaxed me out of Moscow and threw me into a pit of despair, and then disappeared. He suddenly showed up several years later.

Brother, do you know where I am now? I'm in a brothel in

Munich. I couldn't put up with this disgrace at first, so I thought of killing myself. But now, everything seems to be a dream of long, long ago, so I can calmly talk about it all to you. What's there for me to do if it's my fate?

I lost a leg in a car accident. This inconveniences my making a living. When McCunly saw me, he said, "What happened to your leg? You're like Vadim now. You may suspect that I played tricks behind your back, but that couldn't be farther from the truth. I was happy enough to turn a Bolshevik descendant into a hooker. I wouldn't have gone to such lengths! This Edmond Dantes of New York is not cruel." He even stroked my hair.

I slapped him on the cheek. But this retaliation was too late. Rubbing his cheek, he babbled on arrogantly. "My ancestors were defeated by yours, but in our generation, we beat you! We have never forgotten the past, but the Bolsheviks were pathetic. They forgot so easily. That was the key to our victory! I will victoriously enter Russia, the land of my ancestors. Tell this to Sergey. If he has a hard time eking out a living, he's welcome to come and see me. If I'm pressed, I might hire him as a gardener in my mansion, like Vadim!"

The letter gave me much food for thought. More than anything else, I thought I would tell my daughter about what was written in it. Katya ended her letter like this:

Do you remember how I insulted our ancestors as fools? I called you that, too. But who was the real fool? I don't know how many tears I've shed by now, but what good will it do even if my tears formed an ocean? I just hope that no fool like me appears ever again in our Sinzov family.

Yours, Katya

In the envelope was a letter in Seryozha's handwriting.

Dear Mrs. Jin Ok,

You have paid kind attention to our Katya. This letter from Katya was brought by a friend at the newspaper where I work (he was the person who had wrested from Katya our family photos for sale), who happened to bump into Katya during a business trip to Munich. After reading Katya's letter, you may be disappointed in her. But please don't just blame Katya. Have pity on her!

As you know, Mrs. Jin Ok, our great grandfather, grandfather, and father were the warriors who staunchly defended Socialism. But why do we see someone like Katya in our generation? Because of imperialists and class enemies? It looks like that's not really the answer.

The imperialists and class enemies existed in the past as well. My Bolshevik ancestors lived at difficult times when they had no choice but to aim their guns at the enemies and fight, shedding blood. But none like Katya appeared.

Why was that? I have noticed that the Korean people frequently use the expression, "Socialist ideological encampment." It is indeed a meaningful expression. The encampment . . . the encampment. How solid is that encampment in Korea, where Great General Kim Jong Il is upheld! I strongly sensed it from your children, Mrs. Jin Ok.

During the Paris International Exposition after World War I, Russia, pathetically, could only afford to exhibit the sparse Deco. Only 40 years afterward, however, it put forth a model of Vostok, the first manned spaceflight in the world, showing off the Socialist fatherland's mighty national power.

Then why has my country become like this? It is because the Socialist ideological encampment has broken down. I think that is exactly why our Katya's life was ruined. The country where the Revolution's traitors swept away all revolutionary principles and ideological education, the society where Western-style liberalization and un-Socialistic corruptions and irregularities encroach on people's mentality, dumped such a fate on Katya.

Katya says that McCunly couldn't hide his glee as he described her as a contributor to the destruction of Socialism. If I may add something, she is also a sacrificial lamb of those who destroyed Socialism.

I cannot help cursing those sinful periods of Gorbachev and Yeltsin. When you take a look at Katya's photo, you will painfully realize the situation she finds herself in. Of course, this is not what she sent. My friend cut it out from a magazine in a hotel room in Munich.

Mrs. Jin Ok, you have given me that beautiful painting, telling me to give it to Katya when she shows up. But my heart is torn at the thought that she can never be like one of those birds that fly to the Taedong River.

I will stop here because I cannot control my tears.

Yours, Seryozha

After reading his letter, I couldn't fall asleep that night. Katya—I suddenly remembered Katya in Tolstoy's novel *Resurrection*. The humiliating fate of a prostitute was forced upon her during Imperial Russia. It was a frustratingly vicious cycle. What happened in Russia all those years to take Seryozha's sister back to Katya before the time of Leo Tolstoy's *Resurrection*? My eyes kept wandering to Katya's photo sent by Seryozha.

Thick make-up, fit for a theater actress. Long blond hair cascading down to her shoulders. Katya was sitting on a stool, wearing a loose pink spring coat. Her white flesh under her neck showed, giving an impression that she was wearing nothing underneath. Resting in her arms is a pair of purple crutches decorated with roses. Her lower part was deliberately faded with exposed light. Katya was smiling. The photographer captured the moment she was throwing an odd smile, but it couldn't hide the mist of agony and sorrow etched forever in her eyes. The caption read: "A Russian hooker with one leg missing . . . Sharply emanating magnetism, pity gathering like thawing snow . . . Doubled popularity!" I couldn't stand the pain in my heart, so I cut the caption out.

Katya in such awful circumstances! My whole body shook as if I had a chill. I don't know the details as to how she had fallen so low as to become a prostitute, and about how she had lost her leg. But her fate was a result of discarding Socialism, tricked by the class enemy, the Revolution's enemy, because she was born in the wrong era. I pitied her so much that tears welled up in my eyes. A strange sound drifted out of the other room. I quietly opened the door and found Sun-hui weeping, with Katya's photo turned facedown on her desk, the fifth photo of the Sinzov family that I had seen.

Several days later, the *Rodong Sinmun* printed an article summarizing impressions of a trip to Pyongyang from the Russian newspaper *Zhelaniye*, under the title "The Great Birthplace of 'Pyongyang Declaration' Enlightens Our Past, Illuminates Our Future." The byline read "Sergey Ivanovich Sinzov."

FALLING PERSIMMONS

Byungu Chon

TRANSLATED FROM THE KOREAN BY
WON-CHUNG KIM AND CHRISTOPHER MERRILL

This poem was published in Choson Munhak *in 1992.
Its message of reunification is extravagantly portrayed through
the image of the persimmon, the poet's happy memories con-
trasting with the dire reality of his divided land. He hopes
that the Korean sense of unity will eventually serve as a basis
for reunification, despite the political differences. No further
information on the author is available.*

Persimmons fall
thump, thump,
where the demarcation line cuts
across the weedy hill, above the Kwansan ferry.

The owner's gone;
only the house remains.
For many years, the persimmons have ripened
in solitude and fallen mercilessly on the earth.

If I stretched out my arm, I could pick
the ripe red persimmons.
But the barbed wire fence along the demarcation line
cuts my heart, keeps me from taking even a step.

O, persimmon tree!
you also suffer from division.
I wonder when the day will come
for the owner to return, climb your green boughs,
and harvest you in happiness.

The girls in this village used to marry
before the feasting table
on which were heaped delicious persimmons
then cross the Imjin River, bound for Paju.
Now wrinkles have furrowed
faces once as red as persimmons.

Where have they gone—the girls of yesterday?
I search for them across the river—in vain.
The persimmons I touch in dream
thump in my heart.

Calling for the owner, for unification,
the persimmons
cut into this land
thump, thump.

Syria

For decades Syria represented an enigma to the West, a literal "black hole" where any attempts at understanding its economical, cultural, and political environment were thwarted due to the researcher's inability to decipher the codes of subversion that dictate day-to-day operations in modern-day Syria. The United States' infamous dubbing of Syria as a "rogue" state in the early 1990s, and the subsequent placement of Syria on the State Department's blacklist along with other mostly Arab countries (Iran, Iraq, Libya, and Sudan) allegedly sponsoring terrorism, did not help matters much and increased the schism of misunderstanding of both the country and its people.

Not unlike other Arab countries surrounding it, Syria's literary production has been greatly intertwined with its political background. Historically, Syria's literature suffered from the harsh censorship of Ottoman rule in the mid-nineteenth and early twentieth centuries, a fact that forced many Syrian writers to leave their country either for America (later producing *Adab al-Mahjar*, or emigration literature), or to Egypt, where they contributed a great deal to the rise of *al-nahda*, or the renaissance of Arabic literature. The period between the two world wars, 1918–46, brought about the French occupation of Syria and along with it the flourishing of the romantic trend in literature, influenced by a desire to break away from traditional molds of artistic expression so dominant in Arabic poetics, particularly in poetry. However, the annexation of Palestine in 1948 and the subsequent establishment of the state of Israel marked a period where romanticism gave way to *Adab al-Iltizam*, or the literature of political commitment. Thus the 1950s witnessed the eruption of the social realism trend in Syrian literature of which Hanna Minah, Syria's most prominent novelist and one of the writers represented in this section, is a major proponent. Minah believes that literature should be written for the people and should derive its legitimacy from addressing the problems of the people, and not that of the ivory tower of art for art's sake. Thus, political engagement remained the driving force behind literature produced in this period and came to the forefront in the literature produced after the 1967 Arab-Israeli war that marked the Arabs' defeat and the loss of the Golan Heights, the West Bank, the Gaza Strip, the Sinai Peninsula, and all of Jerusalem to Israel. As a result, *Adab al-naksah*, the literature of defeat, came to investigate the external and internal causes of defeat and offer solace and solutions to the populace and leadership alike.

The last four decades mark what is probably the most enigmatic period of Syrian literature. During this period, the Ba'athist party took power in 1963 and it subsequently declared martial law, which has yet to be lifted. The police state that ensued had to secure its power and authoritarian dominance by creating a strict censorship apparatus that controlled all modes of expression, newspapers, books, media, and film. It prevented Syrian researchers residing abroad, for example, from ever tackling any research topics pertinent to Syrian culture or politics. Most importantly, it gave itself the right to confiscate or destroy literally and symbolically any works or authors deemed to be a threat to national security.

In the face of threats of persecution or imprisonment, most of Syria's writers had to make a choice between living a life of artistic freedom in exile—as do Nizar Kabbani, Ghada al-Samman, Hamida Na'na', Salim Barakat, and prominent poet, critic, and novelist 'Ali Ahmad Sa'id (Adonis)—or resorting to subversive modes of expression that seemingly comply with the demands of the authoritarian police state while undermining and questioning the legitimacy of its rule through subtle literary techniques and new genres. Ironically, the explosion of innovative literary genres, particularly in the novel and the short story, may be attributed to the strict censorship system that forces writers to resort to alternative ways of safely expressing dissent and criticism of the status quo. Among these genres is the historical novel, which boasts Nabil Sulayman, Fawwaz Haddad, Khyri al-Dhahabi, and Nihad Siris among its major proponents. In this genre, writers dissect the problems of the past because they do not like the way it has been written about, and also because they fear censorship for discussing political issues of the present. A subgenre of this form is the folk narrative of which Nihad Siris is the main figure. Magical realism is another way to critique the present from behind the masks of ghosts and mystical figures, as does Salim Barakat's critique of the status of the Kurdish minority in Syria in the following pages. Furthermore, the autobiographical novelists including Hanna Mina, Ghada al-Samman, and Hamida Na'na's experiment with interfacing the story of a nation with that of the individual to help remind the reader of bygone eras of more personal freedom and tolerance in Syrian history. Other genres offer writers even more artistic freedom, such as science fiction, in which Nuhad Sharif and Talib Umran took refuge in futuristic utopias.

The challenge to understanding the hidden critical messages

within most of these genres resides in what Mohja Kahf calls understanding "the poetics of Syrian silence." She finds similarities in the different ways in which silent and pregnant moments are reflected in contemporary Syrian literature. She contends that "the nostalgic, moist-eyed silences of Ulfat Idilbi's narrative could not be more different from the chilling, cynical silences in Zakaria Tamer's stories. The impassioned lacunae in Nizar Kabbani's poetry proclaim exactly what it is they are not saying explicitly, while the poet Muhammad al-Maghut's silence is sardonic, sneering both at the authorities and at himself, at the futility and absurdity of the human situation under authoritarian rule."*

Contemporary Syrian literature has been a constant battle between the axis of the internal evil represented by the dominance of the authoritarian state and the external evil represented by the way in which its citizens and practitioners are perceived by the West and the dominant superpowers. Perhaps this explains the status of the double absence that has endured over the years, for it mirrors the life of its artist, as Adonis asserts, who "lives between two exiles: the internal one and the external one. To paraphrase Sartre, he lives between two hells: the I and the Other."†

Hanadi Al-Samman

* Mohja Kahf, "The Silences of Contemporary Syrian Literature: Is There a Syrian Literature?" *World Literature Today* 75, no. 2 (Spring 2001): 225–36, cf. 231.
†Adonis, *The Pages of Day and Night*, trans. Samuel Hazo (Marlboro, VT: The Marlboro Press, 1994), xiv.

ON THE SACKS

Hanna Mina

TRANSLATED FROM THE ARABIC
BY HANADI AL-SAMMAN

To the dear little one, "W. A.," who asked me: "How
and when I started to write?"

—Hanna Mina

Hanna Mina is considered one of Syria's most prominent nov-
elists. He was born in 1924 in Latakia. He has worked in a va-
riety of occupations, as stevedore, barber, and journalist. He has
been imprisoned for his political activities, and has spent time
in exile. His earlier novels focus on social realism and class con-
flict. In his later works, Mina turns to a more symbolic analysis
of class differences, and later to the autobiographical novel. The
employment of symbols in the language of his later works reflects
his shift in vision from the obvious realism to a more refined
writing style. He is particularly well-known for his depictions
of the Mandate period and the period of political upheaval im-
mediately following independence, and for his novels of mar-
itime life. Two of his novels have been translated into English:
Fragments of Memory *and* Sun on a Cloudy Day.

"On the Sacks" is an autobiographical coming-of-age

*narrative that documents a mode of life prevalent in Syria in the
early twentieth century. Originally published in the story collection* Al-Abnusah al-Bayda *(White Ebony) in 1976, it is set in
the port of Al-Suwaydiya in the Iskandarun province, which
was captured by the French and annexed to Turkey despite the
fact that the majority of its population come from Syrian Arab
descent. On November 24, 2005, the eighty-one-year-old Mina
was awarded the prestigious Arab Writer's Prize for his lifelong
literary achievements, spanning over fifty years.*

My dad did not return tonight, either. He had gone to sell pastries in Iskandarun's villages. In the morning, I had seen him
hoisting the copper plate, full of yellowish snakelike cookies, fixing
it on his head, atop the head cloth, while making the sign of the
cross and invoking his parents' blessings. He was lifting the dessert
stand to hang it on his shoulder, putting the empty basket on his elbow. Then he departed, accompanied by the prayers of my
mother—who was always afraid of some unknown entity—and by
the prayers of my sisters and myself, the youngest, asking for a successful sale of his desserts and for him to come back loaded with
bread and food . . .

At dawn, my mother was already up mending our clothes, crying
while singing a sad tune. I saw her from the window, so I entered.
She had opened a box to take some clothes out, and, seeing that I
was not there, she took out a toddler's dress for a two-year-old girl,
my departed little sister who died recently, and started to smell it
and kiss it. She was talking to her as if my sister was still wearing the
dress before she died. I overheard her say, "Darling! Why did you
depart so quickly? Are you angry at your mother? Don't you miss
her? Won't you come back? Am I not to see you ever again? Is this

dress, and this doll (she had sewn the doll for my sister from cloth) all that remains of you then?"

I snuck into the room and sat behind her. I cried as well. I was, like her, in need of these tears. She overheard my sobs and turned to me, alarmed. I tried to wipe her tears, she smiled nervously to hide them. "Sweetie," she said, "why did you come back so soon? Go and play with your friends." She hugged and kissed me. She cradled my head to her bosom. I buried my head in her neck and smelled, then, the perfume of motherhood emanating from her warm neck due to her tension and tears. I felt her tears on my cheek, and her hand playing with the chestnut locks that crown my head. Then, she lifted my face to her and looked into my eyes, which were red—I could not control myself and did not want the tears to flow over my cheek again—while pulling out half a piaster from her pocket. She said, "Go and buy a pretzel . . . And do not cry, men do not cry."

I asked her, "What about women?"

She said, "Women too." Seeing me quite unconvinced, she added, "Women . . . sometimes!"

At noon, she brought us *frifirah*, which is cracked wheat with onions, and sent my sister to borrow some oil from the neighbors. She boiled an egg and placed it in front of me . . . We were five around the straw plate: my mother, three sisters, and me. The fourth sister left us a while ago. I did not know her, but from a rumor I learned that some accident had befallen her. She was a maid in one of the rich homes; then she eloped with a man and married him. It seemed that she went against the family's wishes, so they ostracized her and avoided mentioning her in the house. One day, I happened to see a cart driving to and fro on the main road in our neighborhood. The cart stopped and from it descended a lady who proceeded to speak with some kids who pointed to me, at which point she ran, hugged and kissed me, and stuffed some money inside my pocket. The cart disappeared then, and I ran toward the house and recounted what had happened to my mother. Immediately, she ran toward the street and waited for a long time at the spot that I specified to her, but the cart did not appear again. Heartbroken, she returned and cried secretly that night. Then, she took the money and bought candles and incense with it. Upon noticing my astonishment, she explained, "This is not your money!"

I protested, "But I did not steal it!"

She replied, "This is charity and I do not want you to accept charity from anyone." She then asked me not to tell my father so as to avoid his rebuke, and not to mention this incident to anyone else.

Thus I grew up with only my three sisters. Around the straw plate, I saw how they were looking at the egg placed in front of me. They were used to my privileged treatment as the only brother, and I could have eaten that egg without any scruples. However, my youngest sister, who died years after that incident, could not help but touch the peeled egg with her finger. At which point my mother interfered and cut her a small portion of it.

When evening fell, we glued our eyes to the road. My mom impatiently left our dull neighborhood for the main road and did not come back till after sunset. I was kneeling on the tablecloth watching her from the window and awaiting her return with my father. So when I saw her return alone, I was frightened and rolled myself into a ball. She entered the house, lit the faint gas lantern, closed the door, and sat on the straw mat with my sisters around her.

Oftentimes, upon his return, Dad would clear his throat or cough. He knew that on the nights he arrived late we were all ears, anxiously listening to any sign of his safe return. His cough was, perhaps, a good omen calming our frightened hearts. When we were sure that it was his cough, we would run to the door, happy for his return but saddened to see his disappointment at the copper plate with its stale desserts. At a moment like this, I would grieve in silence.

His agony would pour into my heart like melted lead, like my mother's tears over my lost sister and the other dead one, like the smoke of our gas lantern when its only globe exploded, like my younger sisters' glances at my mother in those nights when we would sleep without supper.

As if to encourage herself, my mother said, "He will come back despite his delay. In the summer he visits distant villages, then he waits until the weather cools down."

At which point my older sister asked, "Why the distant villages? Isn't he afraid?"

Mother answered, "So that he can sell his desserts, my daughter. There is no money in the neighboring villages where the peasants are poor like us. Oftentimes salesmen do not reach the mountains . . . only your father can get there where they know him and buy from him."

My sister inquired once more, "And he would return at night all by himself? How, at night, does he know the road? You often told us in your stories that the mountains are full of genies, monsters, and highway robbers!"

Annoyed, my mom scolded her, "Keep quiet, we do not even think such thoughts!"

As silence prevailed, heightening our anxiety, I imagined that I heard the sound of footsteps. So I tried to listen with all of my senses. I put my ear on the windowsill; my movement stirred some attention, but the footsteps were just an illusion. So we kept quiet and allowed our eyes to travel the mountain roads, following the race, and imagining our beloved father in the valleys at times, and in the hills at others, stumbling between the thorns and the rocks, surrounded by darkness and wolves howling, holding his plate, his stand, his basket, alone, tired, dusty, and afraid just like us.

Mother suggested that we pray, and this meant that she had given up on his return tonight. We knew the rituals for the absentee prayer and rushed to perform it with enthusiasm. I stood up with my sisters all in one row in front of the Virgin Mary icon with our mother behind us, and we recited "Our Father Who Art in Heaven." Then my mother and my older sister recited as much as they knew from "I Believe in One God," while we kept quiet. Then we repeated with mother the following prayers: May God protect our father and return him safely to us . . . may God protect him from all misfortunes, keep him away from evil and from bad people, and from anything that may fly, crawl, or hurt people, may God facilitate the sale of his goods. For reasons we do not know, Mother often suggested that we repeat a certain prayer three times, so we did. Then she took the Virgin's picture and brought it close to my lips, so I kissed it with all my heart while she was reciting this prayer:

My Virgin Lady! Do not expose the head of this poor maid, and do not let this little one live as an orphan, protect us under your wings, and intervene with your beloved Son for us, Amen.

Then she passed the icon around to all of my sisters, kissed it, returned it to its place, and kneeled in front of it; so we did the same. She got up and uncovered her head announcing the end of the prayer, for it seemed that there was nothing left but to succumb to sleep.

However, this time she announced that she would roast some chickpeas for us which she kept in a container on the kitchen shelf. Her announcement stirred some energy in us, and she went out with my sister, brought some wood, and made the fire while reminding us not to fall asleep yet. Since the chickpeas were of the hard kind, she poured some water on them after roasting them, and covered them so that they could soften. Then she distributed a handful to each of us, keeping a portion of it for tomorrow. So that we wouldn't use up all of our gas, she spread the mattress on the floor and suggested that we sit on it and eat our chickpeas in the dark. Thus, she extended her hand, brought the lantern close to her, and blew out its flame. Then she mumbled a special incantation for the occasion: The light has vanished, and the enemy has disappeared. In the darkness we did not hear anything but the crunching of the chickpeas between molars. After that, each of us laid in our place, as close as possible to Mother, and we fell asleep dreaming of a miracle to happen, of hearing our father's footsteps or his cough before we were overcome by slumber.

That night, before I fell asleep, I decided to do something for Mother and the whole family. I thought of working as a day laborer somewhere, but I was small of stature, skinny with yellow cheeks. I have never stolen anything, although I had eaten from what my playmates stole in the past. My mother instructed me not to steal, and said that Virgin Mary would punish me if I did. Perhaps I did not have enough courage to do it anyway, but my young, poor, dirty, vagrant friends, who were soiled with our neighborhood mud and dust, would steal things from the harbor and storehouses. They would sell them and buy food and candy and offer me some, so I would accept it when I was hungry. We were all barefoot in the summer, and wore half-soled shoes in the winter. My friends would protect me from harm and from the attacks of others. They acknowledged me, I do not know why, as a gifted kid among them. This was due, perhaps, to my success at school, to the fact that I was my parents' only son, and that I was kind and tutored them in their studies.

The Falfat brothers liked me. They were mischievous thieves, strong, and courageous at neighborhood fights. The youngest among them was in my class. He was generous and smart, and works now as a butcher in Beirut. He was the one who led the kids to work at the beach that particular summer. He suddenly declared that he did not want to steal but to work. He said that he had arranged with the workers' supervisor for any willing kid among us to work in the storehouses. He claimed that work was a piece of cake! The shores of Iskandarun, the main port to Syria at that time, were full of huge grain storehouses. And since the sea had no port, the ships had to lay anchor far out in the sea. Thus wooden bridges were created, no one is sure by whom, in order to connect the storehouses by rail. Small, flat metal carts sat atop these rails, on which sacks of grain and merchandise were placed. Our role was to push these carts with their contents from the storehouses to the wooden bridges and vice versa.

The workers used to take care of this task, but here came a man who was willing to employ minors instead of the workers. So the minors went to work, and after a couple of hours the men attacked them. So, they ran and dispersed. It was at that time that my friend's talents for perseverance and mischief were revealed, and they became the reason for his ascendancy to leadership. He convinced some minors to derail the carts by stoning them. And since there is no shortage of pebbles at the beach, a war ensued and my friend emerged as its deserved leader. Blood flew as a testimonial from one of the boys' heads. The supervisor put an end to things by standing up to the men who hit his youngest workers. A terrible fight ensued, atop the burning sands. As a result a man fell, so the *Yazirly* (this was the title of the supervisor then) carried him like a sack of lentils and dumped him in the storehouse corner. A discussion followed, at the end of which the supervisor agreed to employ minors in his storehouses, so they accepted and allowed the minors to work.

My working friends used to tell me these stories, so I offered to go and work with them. They agreed on one condition—that my mom approved. But she refused, citing my poor health. I was disappointed at being unemployed and was left to wait, in grief and loneliness, for the return of my friends in the evening so that they could tell me what transpired during their day at work.

I woke up early, and as soon as I opened my eyes, I searched for Father only to discover that he had not returned that night. I entered the kitchen and poured some chickpeas into my pocket and announced to my mom that I was going to work. Then I ran so that I wouldn't hear her entreaties or see her tears . . .

I caught up with my two friends at their home and informed them of my intention to work. I told them that my father had not returned yet and we did not have any food, and pleaded with them to help me. The youngest replied with his usual generosity and determination, "Come with us and do not be afraid. I will not let you work hard . . . just put your hand at the cart's bar and do not push . . . I will be with you."

His older brother was skeptical that I would be allowed to work, due to my skinny frame and young age. So the youngest brother promised to ask Yazirly or force him to accept my employment. He had the utmost confidence in himself—a confidence that increased after the stoning incident. He always considered me one of his gang, of which he is both the leader and the protector. Perhaps, in terms of leadership, he wanted to be Yazirly's rival even if it meant instigating a new stoning fight.

At sunrise, we reached the storehouses. At that time, work began with sunrise and ended with sunset. I was afraid of rejection, and on the way I was secretly praying to the Virgin Mary. The closer we got to the storehouses, the more apprehensive and anxious I became. And when I saw Yazirly my heart raced, and my paleness deepened.

Yazirly received us with a hail of insults, threatening to fire those who were not working hard enough and threatening to dump the troublemakers into the sea. A worker interfered in the conversation, and Yazirly admonished him, saying, "Son of a bitch, keep your mouth shut or I will have your tongue cut . . . Nobody interferes!" Everyone was silent . . . then he screamed, "Back to work . . . what are you waiting for?" The kids went to hold carts in foursomes, and the men pulled the hooks out and moved toward the rough sacks that were as high as the ceiling.

The storehouse, oftentimes called *Anbar*, was extremely wide. It had a thick iron door that slid, upon opening and closing, over an iron track on the floor. The depths of the *Anbar* had caverns and turns, and along the width of its back walls were windows with thick rusty bars. The windows were almost obscured by spiderwebs behind which all kinds of insects, dust, and straw were stuck so they could not open or close. Perhaps they were like that from the moment they were constructed. The light barely penetrated these windows. And because stacks of sacks had blocked all the windows, the cavernous grottos of the *Anbar* seemed dark. The floor and the walls emanated a moldy, salty, suffocating odor: the stench of dead rats and urine. Meanwhile there stood Yazirly, the ruler of this cavernous kingdom and the one who controls all the workers in it. His legs stood apart, the seam of his dusty black pants rounded between them. On his waist hung a hook, even though he did not carry sacks like the rest of the men.

As soon as he was done giving orders, he turned to my friend and me. His tan copper face, the burgundy *tarboosh* resting on his wide forehead, and his bulging eyes, purple thick lips, and tall bulky figure scared me at first. Awaiting my sentence, I kept my eyes to the floor while my friend started thus: "He came to work with us!"

Immediately, I heard Yazirly's hoarse, sarcastic voice saying, "We do not hire sparrows here."

The next minute his hand was holding me by the collar and lifting me up in the air. I did not scream, but horror left my tongue tied. I expected him to throw me to the floor, but he kept me hanging in his hand and walked toward the door where he threw me outside on the sand, like a dead cat. Then he screamed at my friend, "Run to your work!"

As far as I was concerned, this was the end of everything. One night, I had overheard my mother praying and reproaching her Christ: "Why then do you punish us sinners, O Lord? Why did you desert us?" At that moment, I felt like he had abandoned me despite all my prayers. Under the pressure of pain, defeat, and annihilation my childhood sentiments reproached Him with harsher words. At once, my rancor erupted at heaven, the universe, my frail body, my weakness, my mother's tears and prayers. An untamable anger at life swept my soul, and I saw in my mind's eye heaps of pebbles like an ever-spreading oil stain. And my friend's deed that I heard about seemed the best and most useful of actions. So, I tightened my fist over an imaginary stone that I wanted to throw at Yazirly's face in order to bloody it.

My friend's voice sounded even bolder than I expected: "I won't work if he does not work as well."

Yazirly screamed, "To hell with you, son of—!"

And he grabbed him, but my friend escaped out to the sands and turned back and cursed him in the same manner. I imagined that Yazirly would follow him to the end of the earth, step on him, and tear him apart with his teeth. I found myself running senselessly in order to escape him and to stand behind him at a good distance. Yazirly stood up at the entrance of the storehouse, hands on his waist, shouting, "If you ever step on this area, or if I ever lay my hand on you, then we will get even, you son of . . ."

My friend shouted back indifferently, "And if I ever allow any of the kids to work with you, then I will be a son of . . . you . . ."

After that, I do not recall the insults that they exchanged, for, in this regard, I was certain that my friend would excel him. He had informed me that he had practiced the art of insults for a whole day. He placed his brother in one out-of-order caboose at a train station, and he sat in another, then they traded insults till the evening. After that incident, whenever we would pass two women fighting, or a fight among people, he would stop and listen attentively; then when we resumed walking he would say, "These are lightweight insults, not worthy of being mentioned." Or he would continue to walk with disgust, saying: "This is a refined fight, one that does not involve obscenities as if the feuding parties were raised in a nunnery!"

Truth be told, though, he never employed obscenities in his speech, for he was used to striking with his hand, not his words. However, his hobby was listening in on women's fights, for if one of them came up with something innovative in her cursing, he would immediately back her up. When I asked him the reason, his answer was surprising: "He who curses is often weak."

"Then why are you collecting this repertoire of insults?" I asked.

He said, "It is just a hobby and it may benefit me someday!"

That day had come! I envied my friend and spat out some insults of my own secretly. Suddenly, however, Yazirly changed his position, for he saw that the kids had stopped the carts and gathered around us, and that the workers had left work and formed a ring around him. Perhaps he realized that this was a losing battle or felt that his argument with this boy was undermining his authority. It might have been that he simply admired my friend, so he forgave him in the same manner that my friend forgave a kid who used a novel word to curse him. The important thing is that he asked him to come to the storehouse to work it out! "Hold your mustaches and I will come," my friend bargained.

When the workers laughed and applauded, trembling Yazirly rebuked them but still held the tip of his mustache and said, "Son of a bitch . . . come over here before my anger erupts anew."

My friend went to him, and he held him from his ears, but one of the workers yelled, "Remember, you placed your hand on your mustache!"

Yazirly said, "I will forgive him if he kisses my hand"—then indulgently—"and if he swallows his curses."

Then my friend retracted his curses, and the reconciliation happened at the hands of an older worker who declared: "Offenses uttered during a fight are not offenses at all!"

My friend marched to the cart and I followed him . . . by placing my hand on the iron bar, I entered the world of business and said farewell to education. That was the last encounter with schooling for me, at the age of twelve.

Joy engulfed me. My friend became larger in my eyes, and without any suggestion or request from me, the boys elevated him to the rank of a leader. In recognition of his favor and in order to be deserving of his trust, I started pushing the cart forcefully. The deep blue sea extended like a valley as far as the eye could see, and across the grainy sands that swallowed our little feet stretched the metal track, straight from the storehouse to the scaffold. The white crests of the waves were falling on the doughlike sandy shores and the sun blazed in a crystal sky, quickly drying wet things.

On the track of the scaffold there was an incline a bit higher than the sand's level, and the loaded cart needed a stronger shove then. My friend pointed out, "Be careful, this may cause a hernia." However, on the way back to the storehouse with empty carts, the kids were pushing hard and jumping on the carts that cross the sands due to the forceful descent from the incline. I truly liked this game, but my friend forbade me from carrying on with it because the cart might derail due to the tracks shifting in the sand. Then the cart would fall upside down, causing bruises and broken bones. I asked, "Then why do they play this game?"

He said, "You will know in a little while!"

He was two years older than me, and in one stroke, he became older than me by many years. At school, I used to be the head of the class and older students respected me, but this was not school and I had to pay my dues. It was the body's strength, not the mind's, that counted. I was often enraged at my frail body, particularly when I lost a fight with a boy younger than me. Deep sorrow would engulf me as I realized that he'd won due to his good nutrition, so I consoled myself with that fact, was saddened, and kept it to myself. At that time, I used to think that poverty was a shame, so I tried in vain to hide my poverty.

The feelings of rage and weakness due to malnutrition returned to me only hours after I started my job. I did not take my friend's advice. I hated cheating so I pushed with all my power. My strength was weak, inexperienced, so it dwindled with each step. I started to pant and tried to hide it as much as I could. I avoided Yazirly's stares so as not to expose myself and embarrass my friend. In the few minutes between loading and unloading the metal cart, I chewed a few chickpeas, my only provision, in an attempt to regain my strength. Despite that, I failed miserably.

Did my friend notice? Did he reveal my agony and see my fearful glance and my weakness being exposed in front of Yazirly, the boys, and him? Perhaps . . . to relieve me, he suggested that I ride the empty cart back to the storehouse. I refused vehemently due to my embarrassment. He then suggested for us to ride together and descend with the cart like all the others. So we did, but the cart would travel only a quarter of a distance that way before stopping. Then we would have to get down and push it. Our feet sank into the sands that grew warmer with the advent of the July day, then turned into burning ashes by noon.

He who lives in the oven of hardship is the only one capable of understanding suffering.

We were walking and pushing a cart that weighed a ton or more on the sand that felt like live coals, under the burning sun, with humid, smoldering atmosphere, and dry throats. Whenever I felt faint, my brain would start sending out imploring messages: One more step . . . another one . . . pull your right foot from the sand . . . pull the left one . . . once more for the right one . . . and again for the left.

Well! I dragged my foot, holding on to all my will and determination and dreaming of a break at noon. I closed my eyes to stop my head from spinning, and allowed myself to cheat a little. I stopped pushing hard and tried to push only when the cart reached the scaffold. I avoided the hot sand only to find the iron bars even hotter. I thought about stopping mid-way; my head was humming, my stomach was queasy, my glances clouded and tired. Meanwhile the sands were moving like waves in a mirage. Just like a man standing on top of a mountain short of oxygen, I felt I was suffocating. The mere idea of sitting at the foot of a shady wall seemed to me the ultimate of all wishes . . . Oh, how I wished that I could return to our dusty house with its broken threshold that we used to spray with water at summertime. I wished that I could lie down inhaling the smell of earth and moisture! I thought: Oh, my kind mother! If I were to place my head on your chest, then I would cry till I filled the empty food cask with my tears. You, Mother, are the only one that I am not ashamed of exposing my tears to; for you understand my cries. And you, heaven, how far you seem to be! With Christ, the Virgin Mary, and my little sister; and me joining them, transported by clouds. I want to go to her. She made the right decision by leaving us, and perhaps she is playing under a tree. I wish that she would see me coming, I wish that I would see her sitting on her small chair with her little doll in her lap just as I have known her among us!

We crossed to the sea, and back to the storehouse. The cart was full again and the pushing started. I was not pushing, though, I had stopped a long time ago . . . I was placing my hand on the sacks and dragging . . . I bit my lips and dragged myself. Secretively, I would hold on to the tip of a sack. Nothing stirred my interest or desire anymore, not the sea, nor the house, nor my mother's face, nor heaven, nor even my little sister. My father and sister were no longer part of my memories. Everything was severed. I was detached from

time and existence. The factory of imagination and sensation outside of the self was out of order. Just me and the sands and nothing
else. Then the hand that was holding the sack became loose, so I fell
on the sands and stayed there.

I tried to take a step, then another, then a third . . . suddenly existence seemed to fade . . . and the sky started to spin at a horrifying
speed. It seemed to me that the sky was a blue dome rotating on an
invisible axle. When its spinning increased it became smaller and
turned into what resembled a plate, then the tip of a drinking vessel,
then a button, and finally it became a flicker of light that was extin-
guished. A total darkness prevailed.

When I opened my eyes, my friend was in front of me and Yazirly
behind him. I did not object to Yazirly's presence, it was all the same
to me. I just wanted to be left where I was. My friend squatted and
patted my cheek. He called me by my name but I did not answer.
When I regained consciousness, there was a cracked onion in front
of my nose; my clothes were wet and Yazirly's palm supported my
head. Despite my fatigue, I felt comfortable sitting in the shade of
the storehouse. The desire for sleep tickled my eyelids. Then Yazirly
lifted me from my armpit, and seated me on an empty sack. He pre-
sented me with a soft drink and brought it close to my mouth.
When our eyes met, I could not believe that he was the same person;
he was a different person altogether—one who does not hit children
as I had imagined. The palm that had lifted me only to throw me
outside was now holding my head. In the yellowish, protruding eyes
there was compassion and love, and the brown-colored skin was no
longer strange and scary.

My friend left me in order to return to work. It seemed that he was
in agreement with Yazirly. While resting, I learned that Yazirly did not

say a word about the morning fight, and when I fell on the burning sands and blood flew from my nose, the kids yelled: "He died!"

Everyone in the storehouse ran with Yazirly ahead of them. He picked me up from the sand, cradled me in his strong arms, and returned to the storehouse with the men and the kids behind him. Work stopped at the highest crux, and at times like these, and for any reason, Yazirly would low like a bull and would angrily pull his hook and start hitting. Then he would appease his anger by hitting the floor with his hook till he made a hole in it. Suddenly, silence would prevail and work would continue as usual.

Yazirly placed me in the storehouse and poured a whole cask of water on me. He rubbed the arteries of my hands between the thumb and the index finger, then placed an onion that he crushed with his heavy palm in front of my nose, and wiped away my blood with his handkerchief. Thus, his first aid measures brought me back to consciousness. This whole thing happened so fast, and in the same manner, he yelled at the onlookers: "Go to your work!"

So, they dispersed, except my friend, who stayed behind for a little while, silent and perhaps ashamed and expecting to be rebuked any minute now. He expected Yazirly to make fun of him and of the sparrow that he had insisted on employing with them. However, he did not do it, and in the end he ordered my friend to go back to work, so the latter obeyed. He then placed me on the empty sack where, crushed from tiredness and shame, I stayed at the mercy of the workers and the boys' glances.

I was not exactly sure how long I stayed, for I regained my consciousness gradually but not my will to work. I wished to be left alone. I never thought of my condition or of anything else. I was a small, discarded mass of flesh that breathed, with black eyes under long chestnut hair, a round head on top of a skinny neck, pointed at the occiput and bent down at the shoulder in a careless, relaxed posture, incapable of making any movement. My glances roamed the space through the storehouse door like a sickly camel. My glances traveled to our alley, followed my mother and sisters at home, and my absent father in his agonizing wandering in the villages while holding the desserts that were dried out by the sun, dusty, and covered by flies. My glances returned from their journey to face defeat; dreams of work had vanished and the idea of returning home had become shameful.

The strange thing is that I did not think of killing myself, nor of death and meeting my little sister in heaven, nor of returning to the alley and crying on my mother's chest. I felt the same sensation of gentle sadness like autumn leaves, the sensation that often overcame us when my father would come home disappointed. He would come back sad and heartbroken as if he had committed a sin. At those times, silence would prevail and each one of us would respect the sorrows of the other. If it was evening then, I would sneak out and walk alone, avoiding my playmates and painfully thinking of the situation in which I left my family. Then, I would sleep without asking for anything.

This morning I defied the nature of habitual and depressing things in our patient family, and I left for work. I revived, perhaps, a hope within my wishful sisters of the advent of the day when I would work and help my father put the pebble in the cask of water as in Mother's stories. And here I was, in a humiliating struggle, adding with my defeat another new thread, as Dad would say, to the rope that fate had spun for us. I decided not to go back home. Even if I returned to our neighborhood, I would await darkness and tiptoe to the park and sleep under the trunk of a tree. It would be best if I left in search of work and provisions. And as soon as I got them and my pockets were full of money, I would eagerly return to my mother and pour all that I had in her lap and offer my sisters cookies and candy. So let me get up and stealthily walk out of this place.

It does not matter where and till when . . . perhaps there, where the sky connects with the earth. I wonder what lies behind their merging! Does the universe end? The teacher told us at school that, No, earth is round and that we often return to the same point that we depart from. I was depressed. I thought that I could cross that distance in one day, and be done with this world, particularly since I wanted a distant journey—one that wouldn't bring me back to the departure point. I wanted to walk, walk, and pierce that connecting screening far at the horizon in order to see what was behind it. Perhaps, as in fairy tales, a fairy would adopt me and open up treasures for me. Or perhaps I would reach a city whose people were waiting to make a prince out of a foreign newcomer. Perchance I might meet that lady in the cart who kissed me and gave me money. Even if I did not see her, or find food or shelter, walking aimlessly in this manner was my only consolation and exit out of this predicament.

I left the sack and moved toward the door. No one was looking at me or cared about me. I waited until Yazirly moved to the back of the storehouse in order to make my exit. However, an accident happened that prevented me from launching my imaginary trip around the earth.

The pallet sacks that were transported from the storehouse to the sea were stamped with big Latin letters. These letters were stenciled on tin sheets. Yazirly would choose one of those sheets according to a piece of paper that had all the brands printed on it in the office, and then a worker would stain this sheet with ink in order to draw a letter or letters on the sack. Fortunately for me, but not for the worker, one of these sheets was lost and work ceased. Yazirly searched all the sheets, all the corners, and he did not find it. He was agitated, cursed, and ordered the loading to stop, but the sheet was still lost. He was holding the paper and hitting it: This is the brand . . . the ship will not accept the merchandise without it! I approached him cautiously, looked, and found the letters very clear. There was the letter "n" among them, so I said in an inaudible voice, "I will write it!"

He turned his head toward me; once more I saw viciousness and disdain in his eyes. However, he turned quickly and asked, "Do you read and write?"

Afraid, I said, "Yes."

As usual, he screamed, "I am asking you, do you write and read in a foreign language, not in Arabic?"

I said, "In a foreign language too!"

In order to prove that to him, I took the brush and drew the required letters on the floor. When I raised my head, I had regained my self-esteem through the amazement of the eyes around me. Immediately, life's sweet sap flowed into my blood. So I carried the ink bucket and the brush with a shiver combining strength, happiness, and embarrassment; all these conflicting feelings in the face of a sudden and violent change.

I had to work fast in order to allow the stopped carts to deliver their load. Yazirly was watching me lest I made any mistakes. He was comparing the letters on the paper with those on the sacks. It seems that this time, I passed the first practical exam in my life successfully. And among the workers' remarks and the kids' comments, all in my favor, the sparrow was ascending the stacks of sacks with a squirrel's agility, leaving behind him his first letters on surfaces other than school notebooks. Now, he was writing on the sacks with ink in front of men who had never learned the road to school and never held a pencil in their lives except to sharpen it. He was writing in front of boys raised in alleys who opened their mouths as they watched his hand marking the letters in shiny black ink.

Finally my friend's cart arrived. By then, I was at the top of the stacks, close to the ceiling. From his place on the ground he shouted, "You, what are you doing up there?"

Proudly I answered, "Writing, as you see!"

Then Yazirly said, "Your sparrow is a schoolboy then! . . . Why didn't you tell me this morning?"

My friend smiled and ran to me. He was in my class and was capable of writing just like me, although with less perfection and agility. Still he refused to boast and did not want to undermine the importance of my work. Perhaps he looked at it as his own victory. Or perhaps his child's heart did not know envy. He was happy and satisfied when he left me, but, alas, he did not notice my excessive and overwhelming feeling of superiority. In this delusive pride, I was regaining my self-confidence and avenging my weakness and failure due to the shame inflicted on me earlier.

The whistle of the ship came from the depths of the harbor. The sailors and porters were familiar with the whistle signals. Not only could they interpret them, but they knew which ship generated them. Yazirly started to urge us, saying, "The ship is requesting the merchandise!" Then, in an experienced and proud porter's move, he took off his jacket and pricked his hook in one of the sacks. Thus he lifted it onto his back, threw it in the cart, and moved on to the second one. He was screaming, "Men, where is your zeal?" His sack would fall sideways in the cart, so he would not need to straighten it or arrange it with his hook. After the ability to lift large sacks that weighed over a hundred kilograms, this was another mark of a true skill. One of the porters who was known for lifting two hundred kilograms' worth of used clothes sacks and ascending to the wooden bridge with them said:

"Do not display your manhood, Yazirly . . . we are working with all of our energy. You have men here!"

"Men are in the other storehouses . . . I am not saying that you are women, but you are old men."

"If you were truly the son of your father, you would have been fair."

Yazirly stopped, stared at him, then spat: "I am the son of . . . because I work with a son of . . . like you?"

From the other corner, another porter interjected, "If you do not like our work, you can fire us . . . there are a thousand employers out there."

"Of course . . . It is summer now . . . in the wintertime your tone will change, you will kiss shoe soles . . ."

"Kissing soles," a one-eyed porter said, "is not one of our attributes . . . you know your men. You would have been a beggar without them . . ."

Yazirly screamed at him, "Shut up or I will pierce your healthy eye, you one-eyed liar."

The one-eyed porter pulled his hook and descended from the sacks, "If you aren't a woman, let us see you do it . . ."

"Indeed, I will be a woman if I do not do it . . ."

I was shaken and confused to the point that I spilled some ink on the sack. I could not believe that there are people in this world who get into fights and curse each other that easily and without any reason. I did not understand the hidden meaning of the slanderous words, and how eager people are to fight. So in horror and amazement, I followed the movement of the hooks, brandished like spears, and noticed that Yazirly's eyes were protruding even more. The one-eyed man's healthy eye was fixed, unblinking. Men descended from the sacks, held the fighting parties, and pushed them away from each other. Yazirly accepted the intervention and then screamed, "Enough! Go back to work and we will get even in the evening . . ."

The porter who often carried the used clothes sacks jumped and squatted on the floor, screaming as he threw down his felt cap, causing a cloud of dust, "As for me, I will not go back . . . I am getting drunk tonight!"

"It is up to you," Yazirly said. "After work do what you want . . ."

"You will advance my payment then?"

"In your dreams . . ."

"Would you loan me the money before payday?"

"In your dreams as well."

"I swear to God that I will not move until I know my destiny . . . I am your guest tonight, Yazirly."

"Gladly, come tonight to the bar and drink till you drop dead."

"I do not frequent bars."

Voices were raised:

"He wants his share before working."

"Yes . . . I want it before working."

"This will depend on the quality of your work."

"A word of honor, Yazirly?"

"This is Yazirly's word . . . come on . . . Make up the lost time for me . . . help me . . . can't you hear the ship's whistle?"

The porter who was squatting got up, leaving his felt cap on the floor. He made a joyful shrill sound and twirled like a clown. Then, he thrust Yazirly aside, separated his feet, and picked up the sack. Immediately, bursts of laughter resounded . . . As I was working I watched him in order to learn the reason for the laughter. He was snatching the sacks like a dog. He would lift the sack between his arms, leaning a part of it on his chest, then he would walk and throw it on the cart. Encouragingly, Yazirly screamed,

"Well done . . . you are a hero."

One of the porters complained, "We are doing our best as well!"

"Yes, you are, I can attest to that."

"You inspect us harshly upon leaving . . ."

"Because you are greedy . . . Look . . ."

I looked around and saw a gray-haired porter, who had a high-pitched voice and a laugh that resembled the cackling of a chicken, return from the outside. The porters resumed their laughter, and the one-eyed porter said, "He did it!"

"Yes . . . I did it . . . like everybody else."

Yazirly screamed, "You deceitful old man . . . where did you hide the wheat?"

The old man swore he was innocent. Yazirly left him and went outside; after a while he returned with a headdress wrapped around a tin can half full of wheat. He untied and emptied its contents on the pile of sacks torn as a result of loading the carts.

At midday, I was entrenched in my job. With my friend leading the way, we went to the sea and took a dip. I offered him some of my chickpeas and he accepted. I also ate from his provisions. I merrily returned to my job. I loved the storehouse, its men, their curses, fights, and the stench. While I was drawing the letter, I started imagining the path back home and the words that I would narrate to my mother and sisters. Only one worry ruined my happiness: that I would return and not find Father home. After work, in the evening, Yazirly insisted on searching the men. They had thrown their vests on their shoulders in preparation for leaving. Yazirly said, "The heat can burn the bird's tail and you are wearing jackets . . . in formal attire! Come close to me."

The jackets had deep linen pockets in their lining and it appeared that Yazirly guessed right, for they were full of wheat, lentils, and all other kinds of grains. The pants had pockets as well, so he ordered them: "Empty what you have on the ground . . ."

The old man yelled, "You see! You are back to being a stern zealot . . . I only have a handful of wheat (*salika*) from the sweepings for the kids."

"I will leave one handful, even two and three . . . but anything more than that will have to be returned. If there is a difference in the weight, I will be bankrupt. Empty your pockets."

They started to turn their pockets inside out . . . Then they came closer to him, so he examined them one by one. I noticed that he was examining some of them in a pro forma way, ignoring the small amounts. Laughter exploded when it was the old man's turn. He was walking as if he had a hernia . . . in the bottom of his pants was a *ratl* of wheat. Yazirly stretched his hand to touch it, but as soon as he did the old man screamed.

"Oh . . . my hernia! You killed me, you son of a bitch."

Then he ran toward the door and exited with the porters behind him. I laughed for the first time that day from the bottom of my heart. When I started to leave, Yazirly asked me to stay a bit longer: "Do not go . . . I have some business with you; wait a little bit."

He said it and dismissed the children, my friend among them. Then he disappeared in the depths of the storehouse, checking doors and merchandise while I was astonished at his diligence and trustworthiness, his cruel and kind nature all at once. When he was done, he took me to the light by the door and took out a small notebook from his chest and ordered: "Write what I say to you: one entry for Jawad dated today . . . underneath it five kilograms of lentils. One entry dated today to the bald one . . . underneath it ten kilograms of wheat . . . entry . . ."

When I wrote what he asked, he returned the notebook to his chest and gave me three piasters along with this remark: "This is in addition to your salary . . . Don't say anything to anybody . . . Understand?" Then he frowned and dismissed me.

My hands were stained with ink, and just in case the ink was not visible enough, I stained them even more before leaving work. I entered our neighborhood with relaxed arms on both sides, and open palms, so that everyone could see them. At home, the good news was that Dad was back! My mom kissed me and cried from delight. After I told her everything, except for the story of the entries, I gave her the three piasters. She kneeled in front of the Virgin Mary icon, and vowed a votive offering to her. Then she frequented all the neighbors' homes, saying: "Did you hear the news? My son has a position . . . he is a clerk, may your kids follow suit."

At the end of the first week, salaries were paid to the men and the children by a clerk sent by the merchant who owned the storehouse. Yazirly asked me to tarry a bit, as it was his habit every night, and after clarifying the prices of each category for me, he ordered, "State the prices of each entry . . . each with its individual name!"

So I did. He shook his head and cursed, then said, "What is the total?"

I tallied all the entries for him and their prices. He resumed his cursing and shook his head.

"They were robbing me, sons of bitches, me who cannot read or write . . . Now, however, business should be in order. I have a clerk, thank God. Come tomorrow to the coffeehouse, I will be waiting for you."

So I went and he gave me some money as a bonus . . . In the following days, he asked me after I recorded the new entries, "Why don't you wear a jacket like all the others? Wear a jacket, and tell your mother to enlarge its pockets . . . Winter days are upon us, and a little bit of *salika* is necessary."

And in order to make things easier for me, and to avoid bad opinions of him, he pointed to a heap of wheat at the corner.

"He who gathers honey, should be allowed to lick his fingers . . . Here we don't lick our fingers . . . I won't allow it . . . but this is only sweepings . . . we have to sweep the floor. It is the grounds offering; you don't owe me any favor."

I did not believe his words. For at times, one of the sacks would break and at other times they would tear them deliberately. Plus I did not see his entries . . . I recorded them but did not see them. However, I doubted that they came from the sweepings . . . Most likely they come from the honey. I did not even think of the sin of licking honey off of one's fingers. Had I said anything about it to the others, they would have laughed at me, or perhaps even hit me.

However, while I was searching the storehouse, I found booklets published by Mohammad Babli al-Halabi and his sons from Egypt or Aleppo. There was a name written on them and one of the booklets had lost its cover. I took out a booklet with drawings on it and started reading the first story of *The Thousand and One Nights*. Then, whenever I could get a chance, I would circle around the boxes to lick my fingers as well . . . Yazirly saw me and approached me, smiling. "Take what you want . . . These sweepings are for mice only . . . No one else cares for them."

As long as I worked with him, I surely discovered that no one else cared for these sweepings but the writer of the entries and the storehouse rats.

After this incident, Yazirly suddenly went to jail. I was extremely sad for him. The porters were sorry too and discussed his situation. As far as he was concerned, they were divided into two camps. I only understood what exactly happened from my friend. "Yazirly pounced on his female neighbor when she was completely naked, in her birthday suit."

In quest of more exciting details, I asked him, "Without a single piece of clothing?"

"I told you, naked . . . exactly in her birthday suit . . ."

"And how did he see her naked?"

"She was bathing . . . sitting in her large tub with her chest, breasts, and white back . . . have you never seen a naked woman before in your life?" Rubbing his palms, "Oh! How I wish to see a naked woman just like him!"

"Shame on you! What would you do with her?"

"Shame!" He shoved my chest gently. "You are still young . . . Go and kneel in front of Virgin Mary."

That night, I did not kneel in front of the Virgin. I wanted to prove that I am an adult, and I slept thinking of the naked woman, sitting in the tub, with white complexion, bare shoulders, chest, and back . . . I came to forgive Yazirly for seeing her, but still wondered how he managed to see her. What gave him the audacity to barge into her house? I also wondered why he took that risk that got him into jail? Why for a woman? And what did he do after he walked in on her?

However, Yazirly's imprisonment did not last. He got out on a bail posted by the merchant and resumed his work in the storehouse. And I also resumed recording the entries. His arguments and screams at the workers continued too. Oftentimes, his anger at some insinuations in these fights would antagonize him and turn him into a madman.

I liked him because I found in him a fearless man. On Sunday, I went to his house and found the used clothes porter in his house. They were drinking *Arak*. The porter was sitting in front of him slapping his head with delight, while Yazirly was singing and threatening those who falsely testified against him. Placing both of his palms on his ears and bending closer to his friend, he was shouting. "When the lion fell, the base one said: hurray! May the perjurer be cursed with blindness!"

Then the immigration from the province happened and we separated . . . I did not see him or hear from him for twenty years. Then late one afternoon, while I was in a Damascus street with some of my friends, I saw him at a school's gate. Poverty and old age were visible on him. In front of him there was a little round table from which he was selling candy to the children. I got closer and saluted him, after I introduced myself, and he greeted me too. One of my friends who knew our story said to him, "Hannâ is famous today: a writer!"

He smiled with a bit of grief and remembrance, he bowed his head and said, "Yes . . . I know him . . . he started writing at my place! On the sacks!"

Translator's Note: this translation is dedicated to the memory of Najdat Hasna-Chaker, and grateful acknowledgment is made to William Hutchins for his invaluable assistance.

FROM *JURISTS OF DARKNESS*

Salim Barakat

TRANSLATED FROM THE ARABIC
BY MARILYN BOOTH

*Salim Barakat, born in 1951 in northern Syria, is a Kurdish-Syrian novelist and poet, currently living in Sweden. His first published text, the "unfinished memoir" al-Jundub al-hadidi (*The Iron Grasshopper*), appeared in 1980, while he was living in Syria. The widely acclaimed* Fuqaha' al-zalam *(*Jurists of Darkness, 1985*) was his first novel, appearing after he moved to Cyprus in the early 1980s, where he co-edited the Palestinian Writers Union journal* al-Karmil. *He has published many volumes of fiction and poetry; his work has been translated into European languages, but only excerpts and poems have appeared in English. He has been the recipient of the Swedish PEN Tucholsky Award, given to writers living in exile or under threat.*

Mullah Binav, son of Kujari, worked hard to maintain his usual stately poise. He smiled but without allowing his lips

to part over his strong, large teeth, and then recited Surat al-Fatiha*
in a low murmur.

Some of the men who were clustered around the seated mullah
launched into elaborate and drawn-out flattery but he paid them no
attention. His only response was to rise to his feet calmly and roll
out a small carpet. He prayed two sequences, bending and prostrat-
ing and repeating the ritual words of prayer, and it became very
clear that he was taking longer than necessary to complete his religious duty. The mumbled words of thanks and expressions of
praise around him died down. He folded and then rolled up the rug,
put his feet into his plastic sandals, and went out into the walled
courtyard.

It was a large space: the reception area whence Mullah Binav
headed took up the north side. To the east a series of abutting rooms
each opened onto the courtyard. On the southwest edge was the enclosure, and next to it was a small space set aside for the oven,
roofed over with bare, undulating tin.

Leaving behind him a trail of yellow marks in the gauzy
patch of snow, Binav made for one of the rooms. Two meters
from the enclosure he came to a stop suddenly and swerved to the
right. A small bird was knocking itself repeatedly against the inside wall of the trap that held it. Binav leaned down and picked it
up gently. Ziwan, his son, yelled as he ran toward his father,
"Papa, this is the second one today." The mullah loosened the jaws
of the trap and the bird wobbled off. His astonished son's mouth
fell open.

The father hurried to speak first. "May our actions be good ones,
son. I will make it up to you." He threw the boy a coin that was
heavy enough to sink into the snow. Delighted, the child fished it

---

* The Qur'an's short opening chapter is recited customarily not only before prayer
but also when concluding a contract and on other solemn occasions.

out, still nested in a fistful of grass yanked from beneath the white layer. The father returned to his path, entering one of the rooms and coming out immediately with a long knife in one hand. He headed for the pen.

The first lamb burst from the enclosure's entrance to collapse in the snow. A second one followed and then a third, a fourth, all at a run, only to fall as soon as they emerged. Staggering to its feet, each animal turned crazily in place and dropped once again, spraying a crimson shower across the white snow and leaving tiny lakes of red from which a light steam rose. As Mullah Binav came out of the enclosure with his red-darkened knife, two men hurried over to take it from him. They bent over the lambs to skin them.

Somewhere in the direction of the rooms a woman ululated. Mullah Binav's hand shot up, gesturing for silence, and she stopped. "Everyone has sons, I'm not the first," he said to her as he walked toward the reception room.

At the threshold he removed his shoes. The men made room for him next to the blazing oil burner and he squatted down. He turned to his left, to his right, his face suggesting contentment and ease, his head nodding as if in response to proffered greetings: a subtle thank-you. He reached for an engraved silver tobacco box which he handed immediately to his neighbor. When it came back he handed it to another figure who crouched opposite him, behind the heater, his extended arm lightly tracing a circuitous path above the carpet.

Now the tin tobacco boxes were flying back and forth among the seated men. As soon as one man pushed his own box toward someone else, that person responded by handing over his own tin. Thinly rolled cigarettes, and others that were thicker, of near-transparent paper and moist leaves: large fingers busy sealing them with unerring skill.

"What will you name him, *Sayyiduna* Mullah?" someone asked.

"Bikas," came the answer immediately, as if he had prepared the name long since. Though the name came as a surprise, the startled questioner tried to turn it into a compliment.

"Why do you call him 'the one,' *Sayyiduna*, when your children are many—and praise be to God?"

"Each of us has only his sheep and his house; and his wheat, which deceives him sometimes, and leaves him exposed," answered the mullah. Swallowing this answer, the questioner bent over his cigarette, licking it, moistening the paper to seal the edges tightly.

The women were going in and out of the doors to the contiguous rooms east of the courtyard. They were all absorbed in tasks: white swaddling and bowls of bread, meat and broth moved briskly with them in joy that melted and spread like the snow dissolving beneath the footprints that tracked the spaces between each door. The interval stretching between those rooms and the enclosure remained an untouched patch of white, and it was there that the children had placed their traps, burying them carefully so that only the tiniest edges of torn bread poked out. Birds swarmed and circled above, before flying at the columnar shapes visible beneath the diaphanous surfaces. The birds were nervous, even fearful, since two of them swooping across those visible bits of moist bread had been brought down.

Had they given the scene slightly closer examination they would have seen that there was no cause for fear. After all, and at the most cautious of estimates, it requires an hour at most for bread submerged in snow to go completely soft and fall apart. Any beak would easily snatch it crumb by crumb without engaging the trap's spring. This was what ordinarily happened when the children left their traps in the snow for any length of time. The birds would swallow the bread without causing the trap's jaws to snap shut, at which the children would nibble on their fingers in annoyance, shouting from behind the windowpanes that looked out upon the courtyard.

"Break his neck, stupid!" But the trap would go on being an idiot, and a silent and still one, too. Yet they could not replace the bread every few minutes, since their footprints across the snow were likely to keep the birds away entirely. So, hoping for success, they would wait until the tracks they had made disappeared and the camouflage was at its most perfect. It was always a matter of very delicate timing, though, because the falling snow might well pile up too high to be useful.

Grains of wheat were the more common bait for these traps. But the snow covered them up so rapidly and easily, in less than a minute of snowfall. That is why the children had replaced the wheat with largish pieces of bread that would be visible for a longer time. But now, here was the weak link in this strategy!

Time. Aah. Bait had its own timing, and Mullah Binav had his time for reflection. The clock said it was nine-thirty in the morning. A few last, lazy flakes of snow fell unhurriedly. There was no wind. Here and there a starling clung to the electric wiring strung across the courtyard, ruffling its feathers until its neck seemed lost in mottled blackness. A dog stood on its hind legs outside the wooden gate that opened onto the courtyard, staring in through the cracks at the neglected remnants of sheep innards and skin.

Mullah Binav's neighbors were the first to show up. His wife had gone into labor at dawn. Since the previous evening the Assyrian woman had been waiting for a summons, and early this morning she had arrived with her husband. This man was the only "city type" among the men. The *madani*: that's what they called anyone who wore trousers and a vest. Mullah Binav offered his guest a chair next to the oil stove, while the others, all of them, sat on the worked carpet, wrapped in heavy cloaks edged in fur. Mullah Binav held out his silver box but the Assyrian excused himself with the comment that he was not skilled at rolling cigarettes, and in any case he preferred ready-made cigarettes with filters.

The near and the distant: they would be arriving soon. These were the thoughts in Mullah Binav's mind, and they were disquieting ones. He wasn't concerned about the inhabitants of this small town who were sure to show up, for they would not cost him more than he could afford. What did worry him, when things were as they were now, was the thought of those who would come from the villages to spend whole days as his guests. The previous summer had broken his back. The wheat had not risen higher than a foot off the ground and so they had not harvested it but rather had left it for the livestock. He felt his sense of self-respect being torn away, leaving him vulnerable and constricted. These days, he was forced to keep in mind how many sheep had been slaughtered and how many he could afford to slaughter from now on. How many sacks of flour would do for those about to arrive? How many mats would be irreparably soiled by feet soaked in a wet mixture of snow and mud that seeped into every shoe? The air of grave self-respect with which he faced the world was the result of an unremitting reserve which allowed no show of mirth; but now his bearing was truly uncompromising, an attempt to preserve whatever he still had left to him.

In the past he had not paid much mind to what went on inside his home; even when present, he was not really there. Three-fourths of his day was spent in the merchants' quarter, the market where one little chamber sat next to another and all were called "offices." Each had a few cane chairs around a table across which samples of grain could be spilled; the compartments were roofed with cement punctuated by high narrow windows sealed in with thick glass. The other quarter of his day was spent at home, but that fraction was interminable, comprising the evening and part of the night. Not with the family and its needs and concerns; no, rather he sat with the visitors who came to round out the day's conversations about their commercial affairs.

In summer, naturally, there was more to be done. What he didn't manage to conclude in the market he would take care of in the courtyard of his home. The front gate stayed open and the truck drivers came and went. Loads of grain arrived directly from harvesting to be put immediately into the truck beds. Porters arrived and left, some to take the places of others while those who remained were paid their tips. Samples of grain came mounded in men's colored kerchiefs so that the best could be selected. Sometimes men from the transport customs stealthily mingled with the crowd to get their shares in exchange for "facilitating" business.

In the fall it was different. There was the search—a long and hard task—for leasable land which had already proven its fertility. That was followed by the search for plows and uncontaminated seeds. In winter there was the rain to be collected. In spring all eyes were glued to the wheat markets and equally to the sudden and unexpected hailstorms. And there was all the rest of it, all the way to commitments which had to be made to harvester owners and the harvesting teams that had to be chosen, from the cook to the driver of the provisions truck.

But now that Mullah Binav was seeing the expanse of his affairs shrivel to so little, he seemed to find his voice, or himself, only when confronting the household: "Why are those dirty shoes of yours stepping onto the rug, boy?" And when the frightened lad gave no response the mullah slapped him. "Who let the stove go, who didn't refill the kerosene?" Hearing no answer, perhaps, he would give the stove a kick that caused it to teeter ominously and the smoke to seep through the disturbed joints in the big pipes which mounted to the roof. "Close the door behind you, donkey. Cold air is blowing in." "Stop that demented boy's screaming!" "I can smell the burghul burning. Aren't you paying attention, woman?" "Donkeys, a whole family of donkeys!"

There was an undefined anger he was deflecting onto those who bore no blame; he was aware of that in the calmer moments which settled on him when he was hunched over the folios in which he kept his accounts, the page edges worn from so much fingering. In a gentle affection discolored by mute regret at his behavior he would gaze around him at the faces which did not breathe if he did not, and did not smile as long as his expression remained solemn. He did not smile in any case but rather returned his gaze to his notebooks, filled with column after column of numbers written in pencil.

All those matters were over and done; what remained were the pale gray-silver numbers. "Who is party to this account?" he would ask himself sometimes, in a mutter, pondering for moments before answering his own question. "Aah." The record books were of graduated sizes: small, spiral-bound, for his pocket; mid-sized, of blue graph paper; and the rest were large with thick, heavy covers, so embossed with the traces of fingers that the color had changed. Mullah Binav was concentrating on some matter: a thing that had escaped his mind to become pure numbers. Who knows.

Who knows, and anyway, this morning was not like other mornings. Number five in the sequence of his offspring had come to him. A boy, whose naming had taken place already, at least in his father's head: Bikas. The mullah was surely feeling some pleasure at this new gift from God, but the snow was making it hard to act decisively and positively. To get up and sit down, to say good-bye and to welcome, opening the doors each time to blazing, stinging granules from outside—these were not matters that summoned any joy. As daylight spread, moment by moment, the routine task grew more immense, interrupted by minor fits of coughing due to his constant shuttling between the fiery stove and the ice-cold entrance.

At seven minutes past ten, precisely—that is, at the moment when Mullah Binav looked for the first time at the pocket watch suspended by a silver chain from one button of his vest—his eldest son Kirzu came to him, beckoning from the door as if to request that he come near enough to hear the boy speak. Binav ignored him, going on with what he was saying to one of the men seated with him. When the boy persisted in his silent gestures the father called out loudly and sternly to him as was his usual way with people. "Come over here, don't stand there at the door looking like a big desert rat! Now we are all cold because of you."

The boy had leaned his upper half into the room, leaving his feet outside so as not to step on the carpet. Now he had to remove his shoes. It took some vigorous knocking of the shoes against the threshold to extract his feet. The plastic shoes were probably tight. He slunk in timidly, squatted next to his father, and said something into the mullah's ear behind the white piece of cloth that came down over his ears and neck. Binav looked at him dubiously but quickly wiped the doubt off his face with a leaden smile as he glanced around at his seated companions. But they were engaged in some conversation or other and did not notice the rapidly shifting expressions on his face. He gestured to the boy to leave and Kirzu went out. Mullah Binav sat for moments, looking perplexed and confused, before getting to his feet and following the boy's footsteps.

Outside he saw the women heading for a room that was not the room sheltering his wife, where she must be with her newborn. He saw his sister, who had given her day to him, standing in the door, directing them gently. "Into that room, yes, there, please." Barina was not holding up well; her face gave signs of a nervousness held in check which seemed on the point of escaping from one moment to the next. When she caught sight of him coming toward her she stared at him, from a distance, without blinking, seized by an image flashing across her pupils like a sparrow hawk. Mullah Binav stared at her in turn, trying to confirm the boy's words before she spoke.

He came close enough that his nose was practically brushing his sister's. The lazy white flakes which fell on their eyelashes gently but insistently did not close either one's eyelids. When he put out his hand to the doorknob her eyes flickered to his fist, to the slow movement that would cause it to tremble in a moment. He pushed on the door, still looking at his sister over his shoulder. He shut the door behind him and looked across the room. His wife lay on a mattress that lay on the carpet. Next to her on the mattress was his new son, swaddled to the crown of his head. Larger than a newborn baby. That is what he thought at first glance—a mere first impression. But his first impression was not wrong. He took off his shoes at the edge of the rug and stepped over to the mattress. His wife gave him a fatigued and oddly anxious look.

He knelt next to the mattress, pulling the edges of his heavy *abaya* over his thighs. "How are you?" he asked her. Her feeble, exhausted stare did not change, but her lower lip suddenly trembled, and then trembled again, and he turned his eyes away, studying the blanket close to her side. He put out his hand calmly to the top of the bundle and pulled it down to reveal thick black hair. He pulled it further and saw a rosy forehead, puckering a little. The mullah's eyes widened and his hand shook. He frowned and muttered something inaudible, and then pulled the cover further down until the face was completely revealed.

News was seeping from the closed room at whose door stood the mullah's sister, and a worried heaviness was making its way onto the faces of the visitors. Greetings and congratulations, now, gave way to a sort of intrusive insistence. Is it true, Mullah? And before the questioner could complete his question the mullah would answer: "God's gift, neighbor. It's God's gift."

Every half hour the mullah found himself making for the closed room, yet emerging gloomier each time. He asked his sister to stop letting in visitors, to gradually usher out those who were there, and then to lock the gates so that no one else could come in. When she gave him a look of astonishment—as if to ask him, "How can we keep all of them away?"—he answered, walking away, "We are no longer here. Let them know that we are not here now."

The indolent snow, a sparkle drifting down from a milky sky, was erasing the human traces minute by minute. The sparrows were still there, still clinging to their wire which connected the poles above the courtyard. The birds, alone, had not yet abandoned that space of quiet. The mullah's six-year-old son faced his father and asked permission to put the traps out again. For moments his father stared at him, his mind not focused on responding to the boy, who broke the silence again.

"Is it really true that the birds are prisoners, way up there?" The mullah twisted his lower lip and lifted his eyebrows.

"That's what they say. On their legs are invisible chains. That's why, when they move, it's with a jump."

"Who tied them, Papa?"

"God, my son. They must have done something wrong that meant they deserved to be tied up."

Noon came. The newborn was between seven and eight hours old. The mullah entered the room and didn't come out. His sister was pacing back and forth in front of the door, blowing on her icy hands, and surely coming to a standstill now and then to listen at the door. Then she resumed her restrictive passage, coming and going, paying no attention to the knocking that could be heard now and again from the gate into the courtyard.

The fire was still going beneath the large pot near the oven. A thick vapor was rising, mixed with the smoke from the damp dung which they used for fuel. An old woman stirred the contents of the pot with a long stick before huddling beside the fire to warm herself. A feast without the people, who had come in the morning, to vanish before the lambs were tender. Not far from that faded welcome for visitors—guests for whom the gate was not opened—the mullah's son bent over the layer of white, covering his cold traps with snow.

"Where did he see all of this, by God's right?" the mullah asked her when his sister asked him what the situation was inside the room and what was happening there. He added, "He knows that I stayed asleep and woke only at the dawn prayer, since I was awake most of the night. Do you believe that?"

"How is she?" asked his sister.

"In a daze."

"What do we do now?"

His head dropping, he answered, "Who can counter his fate? But what frightens me is the question of where it will stop."

The mullah went over, through the snow in the courtyard, to the old woman whose sole concern seemed to be stirring the food in the pot with her stick. His son shouted from the corner of the animal pen which he had taken as an observation post from which to watch the traps. "Watch out, Father, you just stepped on a trap." But the mullah paid no attention to the light crunch of the trap under his feat. He glanced down then went on his way.

"How are the lambs?" he asked the woman, and she gave him a wrinkled smile. "Warm, now, and that's much better than the frost in the pen." "And the fire?" he muttered. This wasn't a question that required an answer; he was simply attempting to keep away the specter of a different question that was so nearly impossible to answer. Like her, he huddled down next to the pot and unrolled his hands to the blaze of those yellow tongues of flame licking the stone supports before they receded.

"Brother." His thoughts were distracted, there in front of the fire, which had transformed the clots of ice on his cloak to threads of water that soon disappeared into the black weave. "Brother!" He heard only his sister's second summons. Still crouching, he turned. She wasn't looking at him but rather toward the door, and he understood immediately that the moment he had anticipated was here.

A youth, rosy-skinned, his hair thick and black, an incipient beard showing in patches across his face, was looking out from the door, shading his eyes with his hand against the gleam of the snow and ice. With his other hand he held together a thick blanket enveloping his body. Short but well-developed, he looked perhaps twenty-seven years old, or even thirty. The mullah rose heavily, slowly, to stand facing him.

"The snow will hurt your eyes, son."

The young man's eyes narrowed to slits as he answered. "I must see many things with my eyes that I only sense now, Father." He was silent, his eyes traveling across the courtyard. "Where are my brothers?"

The mullah turned to his sister and nodded. The woman headed for an adjacent room. Before she could return, the mullah and his son were disappearing inside the mother's room, to sit beside her on the mattress.

A moment later his four sons came in. Children all, the youngest was four and the oldest ten. The mullah's sister was leading them to the most proper place to sit, around the stove. They all appeared overcome by embarrassment. Suddenly, loudly, the youngest one spoke. "I want to get big like Bikas."

The oldest of them chided his brother. "Quiet." The oldest understood instinctively, and through the bewilderment turning to submission on their father's face, that it was no laughing matter.

The father could find no appropriate words of introduction to bring together his four sons on the one hand and this newborn on the other—this newborn who bounded across several years in the space of every hour. What example could offer him guidance? What act of nature could he resort to for help, if they were all to understand, in the face of this leap across years? The only resemblance that came to mind lay in what he knew about a prophet who had spoken as an adult when he was still a baby in the cradle. Filled with confusion, his eyes moved from his wife's face against her pillow to his sister's face. When no strategy came to him, he spoke simply, hardly above a whisper. "Boys, this is your brother Bikas. And those lads, they are your brothers, Bikas." As the mullah's words flashed like tiny cavities on a tin plate, the youth came forward, shuffling on his knees, to where his brothers sat around the stove. He smiled and the younger boys' eyes widened. He put out his pink hand to his smallest brother's head and ruffled and patted his hair, as the little boy dipped his head in an attempt to shake off that hand.

The oldest son, Kirzu, showed none of the aversion to his strange brother that the littlest boy had shown. He pulled himself across the carpet, still seated, to address Bikas. "Hello, brother." He put out his hand. This step on the part of the mullah's first son prepared the way for breaking the apprehensive atmosphere, in the warmth brought by the blaze of the stove. The other three whispered, "Hello, Bikas." And then it was as if the father and mother forgot the strangeness of the situation they were in; the boys' sensible gesture seduced them and they quickly and fervently urged them all to "embrace each other. These are your brothers, this is your brother. What shame, you are whispering as if you're strangers. Raise your voices! Yes, like that."

The boys began to dispel the discomfort and air of formality that the parents had not yet rid themselves of in their hearts. For, a mere two hours after his birth, this Bikas had taken on the demeanor of paternal concern. They saw him a newborn, yet he seemed to contain within himself a father's behavior, yet they could see him before their eyes growing to a point beyond all of that, forcing a perplexed awe to dominate their emotions.

All the parents could do was to watch. Things were taking their own course outside of any direction or control on anyone's part. Ziwan, the setter of traps, directing his words to his brother Bikas, said "Do you like to hunt sparrows?"

"Sparrows?" Bikas inquired. "Ah, sparrows. Birds. I hunted down many of them before I arrived." With a smile, he gazed at his brother who was taken aback by the response, then spoke again to drive the obvious confusion from his little brother's head. "We didn't snare them using bread, like you. We put the traps in among the leaves and we used fruit as bait." He turned to the oldest, Kirzu, leaving the bird-trap specialist to the questions rushing into his head.

"Why don't you ask me how it is that I grow this fast?"

Kirzu opened his mouth as if suddenly he had found a question to ask but Bikas didn't leave him time to go on, turning around to face the parents in whose eyes glistened that very question.

"A curse," he muttered. "How can I explain to you something over which I have no control. I am as astonished as you are. Each hour I see you as if you are different people, growing with me year after year, a dizziness that shakes my fixed understanding of things I knew from you before I came." He was silent for a moment. "My uncertainty is two uncertainties: it's your uncertainty, your helplessness with me, and it's my uncertainty with you. Let's face this together, then—and there is only a little time left. Look, I might be forty by afternoon, and fifty by evening. And nighttime? I don't know. There are things I have to do with you, Father—the cycle is a cycle whether it is completed in one day or in twenty thousand days. It will be hard and cruel for you to explain that to them, those people standing behind the doors, waiting for a definite answer. It is a severe trial for you, a test, so prepare for that, just that, and forget your uncertainty about me."

He patted the littlest one of his siblings on his thigh to make him turn his way.

"Do you have a notebook? *I* do," said the little one. "Ohhh," said Bikas. "A notebook! All the notebooks my father has are mine."

The little one frowned. "No. Those are Papa's notebooks."

Bikas fidgeted; the legitimate questions of these little ones might well go on and on. "Father, I need to discuss a matter with you that's really bothering me. It's urgent." He looked at his mother. "And with you, too."

"Khati," shouted the father. His sister appeared in the door so

rapidly that it seemed she must have been listening from the doorway all the time.

"Yes?"

"Take the little ones and feed them, sister," said the mullah, and
added, "It's gotten late and they haven't eaten yet." His sister walked
over to the smallest and took his hand, and pushed the others before
her like romping lambs.

Bikas crawled over to his mother's bed, exactly as he had shuffled
over to the stove. "Listen to me," he said to the two of them, knowing that they would be listening all the way to their fingertips. "I
want to get married."

He was silent, trying to read their lips, which trembled slightly,
and their faces which remained empty of expression. And then, as if
meaning to further bind them with a magic that would immobilize
them still more, so as to strip flesh from bone in a rubbery convul-
sion, he added, "It is all a test, a trial."

"Trial . . ." muttered the father, as if the word were meaningless.
The mother sank her shoulders into the pillow that supported her,
becoming a gray piece of the gray mattress.

"It is a trial you will forget when it is over," said Bikas. "But I will
not find the time that would let me forget. I want to get married,
and that demand comes before I even ask you about clothes to
wear." As he spoke, the father's eyes were fixed on a blue square in
the carpet that made an implacable bulge. One of its corners was all
but invisible beneath the mattress. He had begun to arrange the
sides of the square in his mind, moving around from a horizontal
line to a corner then to a vertical line, up and down, without saying
a word. The phantom of the blue square overpowered language,
turning language into a huge blue space that covered the courtyard,
a blue nightmare space rather than a series of carefully designed letters. An eloquent span of blue that beseiged the mullah's history,
and the history of his ancestors, that put them all into a blue void

that held no still point, no path. A mute space in a square whose corners were melting away, erased to return no more, he and his wife, there but for this galling silence.

"He'll marry," whispered the mother. The father came to, repeating it. "He'll marry." It seemed that neither of them understood the meaning of that word "marry," though Bikas did, for now he was smiling in this unreal gloom. "Yes," he said firmly. "You know my uncles well, of course, and you will be able to choose one of their daughters."

"Your uncles," repeated the father, twice. "Uh." He slipped into the chasm of the blue square in the carpet. "Your uncles?" And then he burst out, "Are you joking? Tell me you're joking. They will not believe what we have to say. We have not believed it yet, and who will give his daughter for the sake of a lie, Bikas?"

"You must try, father. There isn't much time left."

"Whose time, strange creature that you are? Who is going to care if there is time left or not? And why must I listen to this urging of yours which will only make the ordeal harder? We have protected and governed ourselves by God's truth, and now you are finishing us off."

"No," answered Bikas. "It is already fixed, and you will do it, father."

The mullah rose from his knees, saying menacingly, "And who fixed it?"

"You will understand that afterward, Papa."

"I don't want to understand anything afterward, nor now, either. I'm not concerned about understanding this trial—may your Lord understand it."

His wife pulled at his sleeve as if she were rebuking him for speech unsuitable for a person of his stature. He snatched the sleeve away, muttering "Why me?" and pointing at his own chest. "If I am the one chosen for this trial, I am not equal to it. People have limits, and my limits are no wider than this courtyard in which your brother traps the birds. Listen . . ." His heartbeat was growing louder and his *abaya* shook, as if his whole body had become a pumping heart, the heart of a terrified soul. "It appears to me as if you know everything, so lead us to a way out." He sat back against the childbirth mattress, submitting himself bitterly to the next words of this creature whose eyes were encased in tiny wrinkles that grew deeper even as he spoke.

Libya

Against claims that Libya has had a limited body of literature, classicists may be quick to note that ancient Greek lyric poet Callimachus and the exquisite prose stylist Sinesius were Libyan. But students of Libyan history and literature will note a vast time gap between those ancient luminaries and the writers of today. Lacking important metropolitan centers to match Cairo, Baghdad, Beirut, and Damascus, Libya has historically made a limited contribution to Arab literature. A vast desert land inhabited mostly by shepherds and oasis-dwellers, Libya encountered modernity later than its Arab sisters. Italian colonialism in the first decade of the twentieth century and, later, World War II delayed the country's literary and cultural incorporation of the Arab renaissance that was taking place in Egypt and the Levant. The literature that sustained the population was a form of oral poetry, a good portion of which is still remembered and recited (and later inscribed). The poem "Ma bi marad ghair marad al-Eghaila" ("I have no illness except the illness of Ighaila") is in this tradition and remains the best literary document of the population's suffering under Italian colonialism, when tens of thousands of people died in concentration camps in the desert.

In 1951 Libya gained independence, the first African nation to do so. The establishment of free education and the discovery of oil propelled the country into its own sense of identity. By the late 1960s, a period when dozens of newspapers were published, the country began to have a distinguished literary flavor with the works of prose writers Sadeq al-Neihum, Khalifa al-Fakhri, and Kamel al-Maghur. Libyan poets Muhammad al-Shaltami and Ali Al-Regeie had gained acclaim among Arab readership and were writing a modern type of committed verse that was aesthetically compatible with the best poetry in the rest of the Arab world. Most writers at the time identified themselves with Arab nationalist and socialist progressive movements which swept the region, and which the regime of King Idris generally tolerated. In 1969 a coup d'état led by Colonel Muammar Qaddafi brought a group of young military officers to power who identified with Egypt's Gamel Abdel-Nasser's brand of Arabism. Though the new regime seemed to embody the values of the vast majority of the intelligentsia, it was at the hands of this new regime that the brief golden age of Libyan literature ended. In the mid-1970s Qaddafi's government nationalized all newspapers and established a single publishing house committed to publishing only works that toed the government's political line. During the 1980s a considerable number of the country's writers either lived abroad or languished in jail.

Since the early 1990s, after the declaration of a general amnesty for political prisoners, the country's literary output has grown considerably. Two of Libya's premier novelists, Ibrahim Al-Kouni and Ahmad Al-Faqih, both of whom live outside Libya, have distinguished themselves as among the best in the Arab world. The late Sadeq al-Neihum, living in Geneva, wrote compelling works on the history of Islam and Islam's potential contribution to the modern world. With some independent and semi-independent publishing allowed since the amnesty, writers inside Libya have been active in publishing in all literary genres.

According to Human Rights Watch and Amnesty International, Libya has some of the most severe constrictions on freedom of expression in the world. None of the country's periodicals is independent, and all are subject to censorship. Books are regularly banned. In 2004 new bylaws of the government-sanctioned writers' union mandated the expulsion of all previous political prisoners from the union. This last move by the regime had come after the country's writers engaged in vociferous calls for reform in local publications and on the Internet.

Writers who were expelled remain active and continue to publish and make their works widely available. It is important to note that most writers have also acquired a disciplined sense of self-censorship. They express the urgent need for reform and a reexamination of the regime's past policies and directives, but refrain from critiquing Qaddafi or his family directly. Many writers, aware that reform is a vast cultural project, have focused on producing literary works that do not have an overt political subtext. For many writers the challenge of Islamic fundamentalism, which enjoys wide and salient public support, has proven the need for the expression of humanist ideas to promote individual rights and freedom of thought.

Libya's designation as a pariah state and a supporter of terrorism is widely seen as a result of Qaddafi's polices and not an expression of national will or character. While support for Palestinians and opposition to U.S. policies in the region are strong throughout Libya's population, it is also clear to most that Qaddafi's contributions to these causes have been inconsistent, ineffective, and generally geared to serve his political survival. The same can be said of the regime's dismantling of its weapons of mass destruction programs in 2003. In the 1980s the regime had insisted that writers produce works to support its pronounced causes and ideology. The vast majority of writers have shirked these duties, and since then the regime has found it more beneficial to let literature be. And writers, for their part, have avoided direct engagements with the regime.

As such, Libyan writers have begun to fashion an eclectic literature influenced by local lore, North African and Eastern Mediterranean Arab literatures, and world literature at large. There had never been a "Libyan" school of literature before, but the country is now producing a group of unique and inimitable voices. The following selections attempt to sample some of these writers, with works by the late Kamel al-Maghur as well as the new voice of Ashur Etwebi.

Khaled Mattawa

THE SOLDIERS' PLUMES

Kamel al-Maghur

TRANSLATED FROM THE ARABIC
BY KHALED MATTAWA

*Kamel al-Maghur (1935–2002) was a lawyer by training,
having received his degree in 1957 from the University of
Cairo in Egypt, where he also received most of his secondary
education. Al-Maghur's writings began to appear in the early
1960s; within a few years, he had established himself as one of
the best and most daring writers in Libya. His stories were collected in two volumes,* 14 Stories from My City *and* Lynched
Yesterdays. *However, by the end of the 1960s, al-Maghur
ceased writing, having become thoroughly engrossed in his
law practice and later assuming government positions. In
Colonel Muammar Qaddafi's government, he served as foreign minister, minister of petroleum affairs, and ambassador
to the UN, France, and China. He also headed the OPEC
ministerial meetings and was in charge of the OPEC secre-
tariat. His last duty was leading the Libyan defense team in
the Lockerbie affair. The last few years of his life saw al-
Maghur reappear in print with the publication of several
books:* Four Centuries of Hegemony, Regarding People
and Culture, Stories of the White City, *and the memoir*

Stations. *He passed away in January 2002. The selection below is from* Stations. *Recalling events early in his childhood
during World War II, al-Maghur paints a picture of his
neighborhood at that time, first during the Italian occupation
and later as German troops arrived at the beginning of the
war. Al-Maghur's portrait here also recounts the Allied occupation of the city with the arrival of British, American, and
French Senegalese troops to his neighborhood. In this passage,
al-Maghur manages almost to relive those experiences, and to
demonstrate the near-heroic act of recollection with vividness
and exactitude while at the same time acknowledging the cor-
rosive workings of time.*

The soldiers' green plumes intermingle; they resemble the feathers of the birds they come from. It is difficult to separate them.
Times mingle, eras intertwine. The feet of the soldiers stomp the
paved streets, but never step into the alleyways. There is no reason
for those plumed soldiers to enter Maktaa al-Hajar alley or Beeb alley, no reason for the German soldiers to have a place inside the
souk even though there is no wall to bar them. And there is no mis-
sion for the red-hatted soldiers, the British MPs, to accomplish in
Dunoon or Al-Fawaqi Streets. Only local police and night-watch
volunteers can make their way here.

The soldiers intermingle and, within the mind, times get mixed
up. Some people take up a place in memory that does not suit their
place in chronology. They appear on paper sometimes in their own
times, or before them or after them. Nonetheless, they remain individual.

Bishka is a word that stands for the pureblood Italian soldier in
the Italian army and for no one else. The Italian is *Roomy*, or

Mikaeli, or *Senior*. Sometimes he is Boss. And the Italian woman is *Roomia*, or *Maria*, or *Seniora*. For the foreigners, the Arab is Ali; the Arab woman is Fatima or Mabruka. I have never seen a *Mikaeli* who is one-eyed or blind, and I have never seen a Maria who is crippled or who limps. No Italian ever begged in the neighborhood, and no Italian woman lived by washing other people's clothes or mopping their floors. I have never seen them barefoot or naked, while among us there were the barefoot, the naked, and the blind, some of them sheikhs who memorized the Qur'an and chanted hymns.

Aunt Zaina cleans only the houses of Italians, no Arabs, no Jews or Maltese. The Jews of the neighborhood are as poor as the Jews of other neighborhoods. They are like us, or so they appeared. The Maltese speak something that sounds like Arabic, herd goats, and sell palm wine. Their women clean and mop their own houses. I doubt they were cleaner than us. For despite poverty and the dearth of water, one, even if he is a drinker who frequents a tavern, still has to do his ablutions several times a day. No one can sell palm wine or herd goats and not wash. The reek of palm wine or the potent odor of goat hair would cling to him otherwise.

As one cannot separate the soldiers' plumes from bird feathers, it is impossible to separate the events of the neighborhood from the mind of a young boy who left there when he was ten or so. Time mixes the soldiers of Senegal with the soldiers from Abyssinia, roaming the neighborhood, whipping the residents with their tall frames and the brandings slashed on their cheeks. They avenge the Italian and French occupation of their countries on the residents of our neighborhood. A period of time that seems indiscernible to me now separates them from the plumed soldiers. They tore the residents apart, and the residents tore away their plumes. The residents compared them with the fairy tale's green-feathered bird who killed his mother and ate her for food. They carry their rifles, frighten children, and terrorize adults, speaking with their whips, speaking with foreigners in their languages, and stare down women with strong-eyed lust.

The Italian soldiers, their revenge, and the revenge to their revenge are now a cycle that spins, taking turn from heart to heart. Because hearts do not turn to stone, and a whip can let out the steam of contempt. The German soldiers deal with others with tipped noses. Whether soldiers or officers, they receive little respect from the residents of our neighborhood. People solicit them for white bread, or the remains of rotten cheese, a few cigarettes, or cigarette butts. Sometimes their kindness is repaid with a Fatima, or Aisha, or Mabruka, or other women.

Even the prostitutes they fancy are strange. The residents of the neighborhood marvel at the postcards the soldiers send to their friends beyond the horizon. A pretty half-naked girl, her shyness slashed by a tattoo gored into her face, half-wrapped in a colorful red sash that highlights the brownness of her skin, the blackness of her eyes, and the whiteness of her teeth. The neighborhood cannot recognize these girls as a reflection of its women. Aunt Zaina does not wear a heap of thin silver bracelets, nor do two wide earrings dangle from her ears. If she did, her arms would be chopped off or her ears sliced away from her head by thieves. Zaina does not wash clothes and sweep houses wearing that wide rippling sash tied elegantly at her shoulder-tips like a dancer. Zaina puts a pair of pants between her legs, like a man's, but shorter. She gathers her bosom with an apron, if she can afford such a thing. She may have never worn a dress, but walks about in a long rag sold to her by Jewish peddlers whom she pays no money. She may pay them with eggs or barley or some dates, if she has a relative from the country that brings her such things, or if she has a hen or two in her house. She saves the eggs in preparation for a visit by that strange visitor. She meets him without her regular modesty toward men. She calls out, "That Jew, shame on him," her head raised, uncovered. She enters the courtyard, haggles with him head-to-head, as if he were a woman neighbor. Zaina saves her coins and barters for her living, and most of what she barters away is the motions of her hands rubbing dirt out of clothes and the straining of her arms as she wrestles with a floor. She has two children, the younger one taken by the soldiers, the featherless soldiers of the American air force, who make a big deal of him. The neighborhood recalls him only to forget him soon after. The place lives for a while in his mind and is soon forgotten. He forgets about Zaina as soon as he is recruited, barely ten years old then. He prances the streets wearing a pair of shiny shoes, prattling in a strange language he learned quickly, as if it were his mother's tongue. Soon afterward his gradual disappearance begins, until the soldiers take him once and for all, and he leaves nothing behind except a faint memory, and his mother Zaina.

A piece of land faces our house, surrounded by a fence. This is where Bujaila lives in a ramshackle hut. Even children call him just that, Bujaila, without the deference of "Uncle" or "Mister." For he does not wear the respectable long shirt, the bloated trousers, or the vest. He neither shaves his head nor covers it. He speaks Italian, and no one knows how he makes a living. From early morning, he pores over a heap of junked motorcycles left behind by the Germans and Italians, attempting to make something unusual. As night gets on, one of his machines tears through the silence, so loud and noticeable then even the women, hidden behind doors, stick their heads out to see his mechanical horse rumbling through the neighborhood streets.

This is also the time of Saghir, not like the other young men. Yellow-gold hair slides down the back of his head like the Christians, and he combs it the way women comb theirs. He carries a lute, but no one knows where he played it, or what he played, for no one has ever heard a note out of him. His yellowed clothes match the color of his hair. Definitely there are eyes peering from behind shuttered doors to look at him, so entranced with himself. Saghir disappears one day. Years pass and he returns without his yellow hair, his head bald. He still professes music, composes and sings, and still there is no one to listen to his songs. And afterward no eyes peer at him as he passes by.

The neighborhood is a nest full of birds that depart as soon as they grow wings, as soon as they develop a feature that distinguishes them from the rest. They land elsewhere, maybe on the streets of the big city that surround the neighborhood, or in Italy, or Tunisia, that green country, visited by merchants who return with things rarely found in our city.

Tunisia has a different ring in my ear. My father travels there regularly, like other merchants. I imagine it by the things he brings with him: a sweet that is never sold in our neighborhood stores, squares of white sugar unlike our brown sugar that resembles wheat dust. Pieces of fabric he distributes among my sisters and mother, some of them silk, solid or patterned colors, and they almost choke with happiness. At the end of the night we sometimes overhear his stories, told to his friends about the journey, the road, the wrap-arounds the Tunisian women wear that differ from the ones worn here, and the blond ones who resemble the Roomy women and who stroll the streets with their heads uncovered.

Some of the men in our neighborhood leave and live in Egypt for some time. And how far Egypt then seemed to the people of the neighborhood! Only one or two make it all the way there, maybe three. The neighborhood awaits their return, to see them wearing fezzes, or turbaned like the scholars of Al-Azhar, to come and drench us with their knowledge. Egypt of Al-Azhar, Egypt of fava beans and those small chunks called falafel, those balls made of beans, herbs, and spices, eaten in the morning and enjoyed the way we enjoyed the rare taste of kefta meatballs. Those and so many other strange things. Those returning from Egypt will also have something to say about spectral creatures wrapped up in black fabric, wearing nose rings, who bargained with merchants and whose haunches were rounded like the stumps of palm trees that cannot wait to bear fruit. The returning merchants sometimes talk about the women outside Cairo's city walls, peasant women whose black hair flows like silk, who have delicate noses and eyes that seem to harbor magic. They speak also of the Tunisian women's faces that carry the aroma of the moon. They speak of Zaitouna and Al-Azhar, those seats of Islamic knowledge, the stories filling up the night as late as the nights enjoyed by those who loiter in taverns. People head in and sip on what they learn. Al-Azhar, that abode of learning where my brother studies; he will later return to fill the neighborhood, even the whole city, with knowledge, shedding light wherever he goes.

During the war, the neighborhood loses contact with its sons in Egypt, and the road to Tunis is closed. The city becomes an Italian island in a sea of Allies. We are cut off from knowledge, from the white sugar lumps. There are tobacco and flour shortages. The nights tremble with the buzzing of aircraft, the flames of bombs. And Radio London. Lies told by the Italian soldiers who now crowd the neighborhood circle the streets. The Germans strut around us in their well-made shoes. The neighborhood waits for Mussolini's feet to land in Egypt, riding his white steed, brandishing the sword of Islam.

Nothing can defeat the Italians' strength and the Germans' might. They take the sons of the neighborhood into the army. They light with them the first fires of Sidi Barrani and Alamain. The news broadcast from London is telling lies, for how could the Allies win while these green plumes still block the neighborhood's horizon and still sing of victory? These planes raiding the neighborhood are nothing but desperate measures taken by the English. So everyone believes, until a night of doom that shakes the city, drags its residents away from the harbor and surroundings. A night in which Allied barges pour their fire onto the city, silencing the spirits of men, tearing the bodies of women and children.

No night is more remembered by old and young. The women run out of their houses bareheaded, the men search for shelter. Only old people, and the handicapped, remain in the neighborhood, all able bodies departing, those who have places to go and those who have beasts to ride. I now have nothing at all except a child's imagination to aid me, an imagination of meetings and farewells.

The neighborhood does not say farewell to the Italian soldiers. They leave suddenly and without resistance. The locals who had joined the Italian army say nothing of cities and battles, for they had gone to neither. They were pushed like sheep to the butcher's knife. The first rows fell to Allied bullets and died. The rows that followed surrendered. The British urged them to join them, to enroll into the Libyan army they started up in Egypt, a fifth column against the Italians. They told them they could go home to their families. They had no food to give them, and they had no need for guards to protect the desert. Among the prisoners of war, I have a cousin, an aunt's son. He returns from Egypt the way he left, no turban or fez on his head. Sidi Barrani was the end of his road, and he brings no learning back with him; he did not enter Al-Azhar, and he returns only with the gratitude of those returning from war. He walks about the neighborhood proud to have been a prisoner of war, looking for work.

Some of the neighborhood's men return unlike the other prisoners of war. They were Allied soldiers hidden on this side of the front, among us. They say they were the Allies' men. The neighborhood was always like that, always followed someone else's lead. They say they were local informants installed in the city who revealed to the English what their airplanes could not discover. They hid in houses, tucked away like rats. Others hid in the farms on the outskirts.

No one knows what information they gathered, or how they managed to send it to the English. But everyone quickly knows them when the English arrive. They appear the way young chicks rise in the morning, wearing green khakis, short pants, playing the role of the police. Sometimes they gather some information about one of the neighborhood residents and then forward it to the military rulers and their civil servants.

The neighborhood says farewell to the German soldiers who, it seemed, deserved victory. The cause of their failure is their alliance with the Italian Bashka and the plumed soldiers, those peacocks who prance about the city streets and are beaten up in the wild. They say good-bye to them, "Auf wiedersehen, Kamerad," and greet those who come after them.

They greet those who sent gifts to the innocent, gifts hurled from above the clouds. Those who covered the city with a horizon of fire, blazing flames that were neither well-aimed nor necessary. The shrapnel melted the bodies of women and men and children. Never reaching the Italians, for they had shelters, the flames targeted the Arabs who sat out in the open. They greet them with sarcastic songs, for they were not horsemen, wearing no plumes, a strange mixture of people, a lump:

O Arabs, Kaman has arrived among you.

THE PLACE WILL FIT EVERYTHING

Ashur Etwebi

TRANSLATED FROM THE ARABIC
BY KHALED MATTAWA

Ashur Etwebi was born in Tripoli in 1952. He received a PhD in medicine from the University of Dublin, and now practices medicine and teaches at Zawia University west of Tripoli. Etwebi is the author of four books of poetry, Qasaed Al Shorfa *(*Poems from a Balcony*),* Asdikauka Marru Min Hunna *(*Your Friends Passed This Way*),* Nahr Al Musiqa *(*River of Music*),* Sunduk Aldihakat Alkadima *(*A Box of Old Laughs*), and a novel,* Dardanin (2000).

The sound of the wind stretches its limbs.
The jazz music withholds some of its ruckus.
Hands move something in the dark.
I say: just an old romanticism . . .
No matter, the place will fit everything.

Vision descends upon flaccid pathways
and rides them on cheap metal.

Dried out trees and others take their water
from the drowned sand by force.
I say: only a passing depression.
No matter, the place will fit everything.
During the day the sun approaches the mountain,
places its hand upon it,
its cold hand of lovers,
strikes stone with stone.
Mountain scrub dances behind the stone.
The sun does not see it.
Only the moon shines upon it all the way beyond the bend
and the guardian stones watch from afar.
I say: a passing coincidence.
No matter, the place will fit everything.

Sudan

Sudanese literature reflects the country's distinctive cultural and geographic diversity. Sudan brings together some 600 indigenous groups that comprise some 114 languages and dialects. This very diversity has led to bloody conflict and social fragmentation.

In cultural and geographical terms, Sudan straddles the so-called North African line, and is thus sometimes included among the countries that comprise the Mediterranean basin. At the same time, Sudan is considered Arab—and yet this attribution is not a pure one, for its "Arab" people are mixed with deep-rooted African races. Sudan has thus adopted, at various times in its history, a superficial religious cover in order to rid itself of any pagan "Africanism." In this manner, Sudan occupies a space that is considered African, yet not "pure" African.

Sudanese writers of the recent past commanded distinctive rhythmic styles, influenced by many of the greats from English literature: Samuel Taylor Coleridge, William Wordsworth, Lord Byron, Sir Walter Scott, and (from the later period) Jane Austen. The gems of Russian literature—Tolstoy, Pushkin, Dostoyevsky,

Chekhov, Turgenev, and Maxim Gorky—were also not unknown to them, to say nothing of the influence of Arabic literature, particularly from Egypt, Lebanon, and Syria.

In the period from 1930 until 1975, many weekly and biweekly literary journals appeared, and this resulted in an unprecedented circulation of literature, a high point that may not be reached again. At the beginning of the 1960s, the "forest and desert school" revived a traditional current of literature in an attempt to delve into the subject of Sudanese identity. Its most prominent members were An-Nour Othman Abbakar, Mohammad Al-Makki Ibrahim, and Mohammad Abd Al-Hai.

Western culture did not digest the writings of this intelligent elite at the time, but rather feverishly sought authentic insight into both the oral and written Sudanese heritage. During the "May" era—the period of Jafar An-Nameeri's sixteen-year rule (from 1969 to 1984), which began as leftist and ended as right-wing—Sudan oscillated between the Eastern and Western military camps. In the meantime, Sudanese literature swayed between two contradictory poles—the popular conservative religious milieu and the secular cultural milieu—and gradually gave way to political influences. In 1983, the government declared Islamic Sharia law, suddenly and without any warning. Thus the larger project of uniting all elements of Sudanese society was done away with. The country was once again thrown into civil war, which lasted until the arrival of the National Islamic Front and the military coup of 1989 and its many consequences. And so literature disappeared into the shadows, and the features of the greater Sudan were lost within this narrower country incapable of diversity. Literature, theater, and cinema all regressed, along with the rest of the arts. Many people were driven into exile, and their cultural projects died out or were abandoned.

Sudanese romanticism gave rise to many exemplars of literary excellence, though only a handful of them were known outside of Sudan's borders. The most prominent ones are the poet At-Tajani Yousef Bashir (1910–37), the novelist Tayeb Saleh (b. 1927), and the poet Mohammad Al-Faytouri (b. 1936). They were the first Sudanese writers whose works enjoyed a wide readership outside of their country.

Much of the best Sudanese literature of the past two decades has been published beyond Sudan's borders, most notably in Egypt and some of the other Arab countries, as well as in Europe. In spite of the scattered nature of the cultural elite outside Sudan, literature is still being produced, even if it is not gathered together in one country and even if it is not found in the usual cultural vessels. (The Internet, however, is now helping to gradually provide a cohesive image to this diaspora.) Yet most of Sudan's writers, as children of a "confiscated" country, work for others rather than for themselves. We can find them everywhere: they are the ones serving, not the ones being served. They participate in both Arab and non-Arab projects, yet benefit from neither of them.

At the outset of the new century, as part of the American discourse on "enemies" and "the axis of evil," the adjective "Sudanese" came to be confusedly identified with terrorism, without any differentiation between Sudan's "hostile" politicians and its unfortunate citizens. Sudanese writers today, then, endure two bitter conditions: first, the pain of a mother country that forbids the spread of our ideas of innovation and freedom, a country that does not grant us literary immunity; and second, the pain inflicted by "unfriendly" nations that do not know us, that offer no cooperation, and that will not treat us like human beings, in complete disregard of what these countries call "human rights."

Will the time come when it is possible for the ordinary reader to first read the text and then—afterwards—seek out (for example) the nationality of the writer, as something secondary to the rest of his curiosity, as a means of modifying and improving the overall picture of the text? Or at the very least, will the time come when this reader will possess a great enough faculty for research and knowledge to be able to read objectively and without prejudice? Or will the writer from the countries of "evil" remain perpetually accused, always attempting to rid himself of charges he knows nothing about? Will he always have to rush to follow the advice of his countrymen, to work incessantly for "the improvement of our image in the eyes of the other" until we finally appear like ordinary men, respected and free of guilt?

Tarek Eltayeb
Translated from the German by Wolfgang Astelbauer

COFFEE AND WATER

Tarek Eltayeb

TRANSLATED FROM THE ARABIC
BY KAREEM JAMES ABU-ZEID

Tarek Eltayeb was born to Sudanese émigré parents in Cairo, Egypt, in 1959. He lives in Vienna, and has made numerous contributions to Arabic newspapers and magazines both in Europe and in Arab countries. Since 1992, his books have been published in Arabic, French, and German. His two volumes of poetry, Ein mit Tauben und Gurren gefüllter Koffer (A Suitcase Filled with Doves and Cooing, *1999) and* Aus dem Teppich meiner Schatten (*From the Carpet of My Shadows, 2001), appeared in German and Arabic, and his novel,* Städte ohne Dattelpalmen (Cities Without Dark Palms*), appeared in Arabic in 1992, in French in 1999, and in German in 2000. After receiving various literary scholarships in the 1990s, Eltayeb was granted the Federal Chancellery's project scholarship for 2000–2001, 2001–2002, and 2002–2003. He has held numerous readings in Vienna, Saalfelden, Frankfurt, Aachen, Washington, Cairo, La Rochelle, Poitier, Strega, Dublin, and Lemberg.*

"Coffee and Water" was first published in the aforemen-

tioned Ein mit Tauben und Gurren gefüllter Koffer, *and*
"The Sweetest Tea with the Most Beautiful Woman in the
World" is from an earlier collection of stories, Al-Gamal La
Yaqif Khalfa Ishara Hamra (A Camel Does Not Stop on
Red) *from 1993.*

A hundred times a day, he says,
"I'll have to return. Here, there is no mercy.
There, there is kindness and warmth and . . ."
Then he falls silent.

I ask him, "There?
Where is that?"
He points somewhere.
His face is expressionless,
and he does not say anything anymore.

I take his hand.
We go to a café
and sit down at a quiet corner table.
I order coffee for him
and water for me.

I speak to him in Arabic
and mix water into the coffee.
He is annoyed, "Are you crazy?"

He tries to remove the water
from the coffee.

He tries to.

He tries to get the water back
into the water.

Café Griensteidl, Vienna, June 27, 1997

THE SWEETEST TEA WITH THE MOST BEAUTIFUL WOMAN IN THE WORLD

Tarek Eltayeb

TRANSLATED FROM THE GERMAN
BY REBECCA PORTEOUS

Listening to the radio is prohibited.
Smoking is prohibited.
Drinking tea is prohibited.
Laughter and jokes are prohibited.
Sleep is prohibited.
Sitting down is prohibited.
Even dreams are prohibited.

The list of prohibited things is long and embraces anything new. We know nothing of permissions. Before making any movement or action we must ask which list it comes under. Things that are permitted can shift to the list of prohibitions on a whim, and they don't go back the other way. This is what life has become: rigid, fixed, and as interminable as the list of prohibitions. And the place has become restricting and depressing in this wide, empty tract of land.

I take up my weapon now and take my turn on guard. The final shift. My hasty companion wakes me, snatches my dream, and goes to sleep with it. He leaves me with my eyes open in shock. Every awakening here is to shock, we don't wake up to anything else. I sigh to relieve some of the anxiety that is spreading in my chest and it stops in my throat. I get up, take my weapon, and go to my place of duty where the snoring reverberates in my ears like the mockery of devils.

I am trying to recall my dream. It was a fabulous dream. I don't know exactly what it was. Before the moment of shock I was in another world completely from this roughness and coarseness. There was some woman in my usurped dream. I cannot remember her features. That idiot, if he'd left me a moment longer I'd be able to get hold of her now. She was repeating my name in a soft voice when the loathsome sound of, "Eh you, soldier boy! . . . Private! Get up! . . . Goddamn this place!" merged with her voice. It'll be nine weeks and two days today. I see nothing of the world but this god-forsaken army camp and these scowling faces. The voices are vile, the looks are crazed, the language foul, the food repulsive, the drinks worse, and sleep is disturbed. Nothing but orders. Orders or punishments. And our compliance always expressed in polite, prepared utterances; memorized and hypocritical. Nine weeks, two days, and I, with five others, have been sentenced to an indefinite revocation of my holiday for some unwarranted offense.

The officer is happy with these offenses. He sees his importance in terms of the harsh penalties he metes out. To humiliate others gives him a sense of a certain prominence in the hierarchy of coercion and humiliation issuing from on high. He gives vent to the dejection of his spirit on our bodies and our souls, for there are none lower in the pecking order than we. Sometimes we look for the weak among us to pour what we can of the venom of our humiliation upon them. Together we all eat, and together we laugh. Each one of us curses another at the slightest excuse. We take sides, we break allegiances, we steal things from one another, we plot against each other. And the humiliation remains part of us.

————

Nine weeks, five days, and everything repeats itself with a deathly boredom. It is August and we are in the desert, in a military camp in the desert. The sun and the officers ravage us by day, and the night-shifts and insects complete the matter at night. Nothing of our humanity is left but past memories. We combine what we can recall of these with a little patience and song, and sham laughter—prohibited of course. Here I hear daily of the failures of every soldier and the struggles of every officer. Occasionally I am nailed to the spot by the fantasizers as one of us begins to tell a story with the scent of woman in it—even if he has beautified it with lies and stuffed it with exaggeration. We listen to him closely on our evening gatherings. We wander off with his stories, wandering ever more freely if it is a story about a loved one. On such nights, each one of us is She-herezade, and in the mornings, with our orders, every one of us is sacrificed to the homeland.

In this detention I have almost forgotten the voice and scent of a woman. I live off the false stories that I hear and the recollection of remnants of the dreams that are stolen from me. I transform the stolen dreams into my daydreams, and complete the delusion of the days.

What could be more miserable than this, this separation from women? What are we supposed to do, kept away from them like this? Are we preparing ourselves for war just to be able to win for ourselves as many as possible? It is laughable. Give me myself, alone, with just one; that would be enough. I'll leave this war and weapons and destruction, and killing to the lot of you, just for the winning of the greatest number of women possible. Madness draws nearer, and an admission of numbness rises from tortured humanity. I have nothing left of my humanity but the weakened threads of feeling. I have become like the lamb limping before the wolf. There is no running any more. Just an attempt to satisfy the grovelling bleats and lecherous howls.

"Wake up, soldier!"

The officer raps it out in a voice that makes the whole camp quake. I am next to him, about five paces away. The words pierce me and kill all that is left.

Nine weeks, five days. The day has got stuck and it doesn't want to pass. It is now five P.M. I go into the officer's room to submit three letters that have arrived for the soldiers. He must open them himself and read them before they can reach the boys. Maybe he'll find in them plans for a plot against state security, and thus his promotion. I find a three-day permit, without a name on it, signed on his desk. Without much deliberation I shove it into my tunic pocket and leave.

I leave the camp at a run, having first checked up on the movement of traffic coming in and going out, and the whereabouts of the officer and guards. I run for three miles and then stop a truck coming out of one of the camps. I don't know where it will head, but I jump up into it. I want to disappear and let it go wherever it wants, even if it is going back to the camp.

I'm in the back for about half an hour. The truck driver stops and knocks on the inner window at me, asking if I'm getting down here or whether he should take me with him into the western camp. I hear him mention the word camp and jump down without replying, thanking him in his wing mirror with a wave of my hand.

I see a tree and houses in the distance. I hear the chirping of birds, and dogs' barking, and then the indistinct voices of people. I hasten cautiously in the direction of the voices. I finger the permit so that no antagonist from the military police can hinder my way and I am reassured by its presence. I run faster and then stop, suddenly, next to a school from which rises the clamor of schoolkids. I feel drunk on the voices of the childhood I have lost, and even more drunk when I see her. The most beautiful of all the things I see in this place; no, the most beautiful thing I have ever laid eyes on in this world. There she is, sitting, making tea. And no one is there but an old man, a few meters away from her, who looks into nothing and sips from his cup with great slurps, enjoying the taste, daydreams and fantasies. I ask for a cup of tea.

"Pleasure, my love."

Thus she replies in a voice that makes me tremble; a more beautiful voice than this I have never heard and never shall. For she is the woman for whose sake and with whom we stayed up all those nights. She is the Sheherezade of the stories, the smile of the sad ones. I look at her before me. Nine weeks and five days. I do not move my eyes from her face. She looks at me and smiles. The smile is for me alone. I want to hear her voice once more, so I say,

"I'd like four spoons of sugar."

"Pleasure, my love!"

She repeats what she'd said in an even sweeter tone, as though saying something new. I am addicted to her voice. I search for another question, that I may hear that tone again. I find nothing. I go mute and leave the listening to my eyes. I contemplate the veins of her life, long and prominent, on the back of her hand. She wants to cover her head, and a few wisps of hair fall out from under her bedouin-worked scarf onto her forehead, enhancing her grace. She puts her hand out to me with a glass of hot tea. Intentionally, I touch the hand. I grasp the glass with both hands. At that moment I recall the dream that the loathsome soldier stole from me.

I savor the sweetest tea I have ever drunk in my life, I smile at her with a smile that speaks louder than words, and I awaken to the tones of her voice, honeyed with that tremor of the voices of kind grandmothers, saying, "Here you are son! Is it enough sugar?"

Cuba

The Cuban revolution that took place in 1959 and is, by official accounts, still actively underway, is filled with contradictions. One of the Cuban revolution's first pursuits was the institutionalization of culture, taking the form of diverse publishing houses and cultural institutions, as well as elaborate systems of prizes for the "best" artists in a variety of genres. As is the case in many countries around the world, critics and judges rely on political ideologies to evaluate the "best." The state also sponsors workshops, giving the untrained opportunities to become good artists, so long as they also become good revolutionaries.

The rhetorical positions of both the U.S. and Cuban governments make it very difficult for English-language readers to familiarize themselves with the everyday realities of Cubans' lives. These writings speak of a sense of out-of-placeness and abandonment not only by the Americans but also by the Cubans, the Soviets, and the world; they do so through the representations of intimate experiences that one would be hard-pressed to locate outside of fiction and poetry. These intimacies resist being read in a political context.

Sometimes, as in Anna Lidía Vega Serova's "Project for a Commemorative Mural (Mixed Media)," they speak of the terror of exposing one's poetic verses that are not yet bound in a book. Vega Serova creates a post-Soviet world that is inhabited by what she calls an "extraterrestrial," a poetic subject who is unable to separate, to say good-bye to the Russians, given her status as a *palavina* (a child of a mixed marriage between a Russian and a Cuban).

Francisco García González's "Women of the Federation" is a burlesque rendering of a male protagonist who regards his female lovers with a combination of adoration and disgust. It explores the limits of heroism through a discussion of the female body and, at the same time, challenges the concept of international solidarity on many levels, most notably through an imagined dialogue between the pope and the vendors of a popular sugar-cane drink.

It is in Raúl Rivero's "I Don't Want Anyone Coming Around to Save Me" that the anguish of repression is most unmistakable. The poem challenges the efficacy of rescue and calls for the need to speak out and stand up. What makes the poem especially interesting is the ironic way in which Rivero dissents in a language that is perhaps the closest of the selections to revolutionary rhetoric. Thus Cuban writers today often find themselves engaged with the language and the events of revolution, even to the extent their writing critiques some of its most stringent policies.

Jacqueline Loss

PROJECT FOR A COMMEMORATIVE MURAL (MIXED MEDIA)

Anna Lidía Vega Serova

TRANSLATED FROM THE SPANISH BY

ALEXANDRA BLAIR

Anna Lidía Vega Serova (born in 1968 in what was then Leningrad) spent the bulk of her early childhood in Cuba and, at the age of nine, returned to the Soviet Union, where she studied plastic arts. At twenty-one she returned to Cuba, where she currently resides. She is the author of three books of short stories, Bad Painting *(1997),* Catálogo de mascotas *(Catalog of Mascots, 1998), and* Limpiando ventanas y espejos *(Cleaning Windows and Mirrors, 2001). She is also the author of three novels,* Noche de ronda *(Party Night, 2001),* Legión de sombras miserables *(Legion of Miserable Shadows, 2004), and* Imperio doméstico *(Domestic Empire, 2004), among other works.*

That the luckier of Cuban intellectuals and artists forged ties with book industries and publics outside the nation is one of the more positive outcomes of the crisis that Cubans faced in the 1990s after the disintegration of the Soviet Union. In addition, some critics on the island began to question the uniformity of the Cuban revolutionary subject, turning their attention to literature of the diaspora as well as "marginal literatures," a vast and rather heterogeneous body that includes writing addressing experiences of homosexuals, rockeros, Afro-Cubans, and women. The second half of the decade witnessed a considerable outpouring of women-authored works. In an interview with the translator of this piece, however, Vega Serova said, "If I was asked whether or not I believe women's writing exists, I would say that Literature exists, and what men and women have is a difference of languages."

Vega Serova's "Project for a Commemorative Mural (Mixed Media)," published in 2001 in Limpiando ventanas y espejos, *conveys the complexities of a very particular bicultural existence, the product of an intimate affair of a Cuban man and Russian woman that mirrors the Soviet Union's abandonment of Cuba through the use of "mixed media," a highly poetic prose. As it explores the impossibilities of ever feeling "at home" in a single place, it carves out a space called "home" through language.*

1

The woman wearing headphones, who looks like an extraterrestrial, paints with temperas phosphorescent suns and animals and a few primitive landscapes on strictly rectangular canvases.
She does this mechanically, almost blindly.
The woman wearing headphones, who looks like an extraterrestrial, listens to songs in a foreign language and cries.

2

I'm tired of waiting for letters.
Fernan brought me cassettes from Vizbor and asked,

Haven't you thought of going there?*
Maybe he even asked, Haven't you thought of returning there?
I felt dizzy. A door that the wind plays with.
Very far away. A strange melody. A lullaby?

3

Don't show your poems to anyone. Edel decreed: your poems are
naive. To show these poems is an indecent and shameless act. He
stepped on my throat; grunts escaped from my mouth, he analyzed
them beneath a microscope and decreed: they are naive. Keep your
poems inside empty bottles, seal them with the wax of candles burnt
in the hours of the blackouts and throw them outside. I smiled at
him, drowning: thank you for your judgment. Let them fall softly
from the window and listen how they shatter on the pavement
among banana peels, used condoms and sanitary pads, pieces of broken toys, and all kinds of garbage that your neighbors have thrown
out since the building was inaugurated.

4

Nobody can be sure that the woman wearing headphones, who
looks like an extraterrestrial, is not an extraterrestrial.

5

It's possible that there exists some place called HOME. A door that
the wind plays with. Very far away. Men with dark beards and
women with scarves around their heads. Black bread and tea. Songs
in a foreign language. It's possible that it doesn't exist.

---

* Fernan (Andrés Mir) is a great guy, a poet and a good friend. He comes often to my
house, we have tea together, we talk. But the reason I have included him in this story is
that both of us were born in Russia and he understands.

6

A tall black man. In the city of bridges, the consumptive city of bridges, the gray and swampy city of bridges.

A black man watched her from his height and she fell fascinated into his arms.

It couldn't be more pathetic.

7

So he shot the jet of sperm inside her fascinated vagina. Perhaps he thought he would engender a beautiful, sublime being, something like an extraterrestrial being, between so many ancient bridges. It's a lie, he engendered me.

A tall black man, a fascinated woman, a pathetic embryo in the rotting city of bridges.

8

Never, never show your poems to anyone, not even to your closest friends. You would be better off farting during public meetings, better off if your son shouted, "My mother farts during public meetings!" You'd be better off even if they were not simple farts, rather an avalanche of uncontrollable diarrhea from the parasites that inhabit your intestines and your son announced in a loud voice, "My mother shits during public meetings where the minister and two or three vice ministers are present!" but abstain from the insufferable fault of showing your unpublished poems, your rigorously unpublished poems, the original and two copies, senior members of the jury, here is my soul.*

---

* I live on the second floor and the trash that my neighbors on the upper floors throw out enters through my open window often.

9

And when the pathetic embryo finally made its way through the tunnel of the fascinated vagina toward the light, in the snowy city of bridges.

10

The man's voice in the headphones pronounces simple, musical phrases in a foreign language.
The woman who looks like an extraterrestrial cries when she recognizes words with ambiguous meanings.

11

The tall black man took his fascinated lover with the pathetic product of their fornication far away from the miserable city of bridges, across the seven seas, to an island that could be called deserted if not for its animals, suns, and a few million inhabitants.
This will be your home, he announced.
Maybe there exists a place called HOME, she thought.
Maybe not, she could have thought.

12

It did not snow on the island.

13

The woman who looks like an extraterrestrial cries onto the strictly rectangular canvasses and her tears make the phosphorescent colors opaque, dilute the outlines, imbue the figures with ambiguous meanings.

14

The voracious rats that night after night dine beneath the windows of your building will indifferently devour the remains of your unpublished poems scattered among banana peels, pieces of broken bottles, used condoms, and sanitary pads.

15

The fascinated woman loved the tall black man in the island of primitive landscapes.
The tall black man loved another woman (other women).
The pathetic creature torn from the roots of the cloudy city of bridges loved the island of primitive landscapes: it did not snow on the island.*

16

Then becoming bored with the remains of your unpublished poems, the original and two copies, the indifferent rats with lazy faces will lie down to take a siesta and dream of strange melodies, a door that the wind plays with, nightmares, nightmares.

17

Not even when the tall black man disappointed the fascinated woman did it snow in the island of primitive landscapes.
Nor when she packed her suitcase to leave toward any other place called HOME.
Nor when she tore up from the roots the daughter who was already torn up from the roots to go somewhere else called HOME.

---

* *Is chewing snow like chewing sugar? asked Cristian. My eight-year-old son often puts me in predicaments with his questions.*

Nor when the tall black man knelt before the two of them.
Perhaps the sky clouded over.
At most, it rained.
But it did not snow.

18

Even so, the woman who looks like an extraterrestrial neglects her strictly rectangular canvasses. Outward from her ears grow the headphones and the cables. Inward grow her torn roots.

19

No, I said to Fernan, for now I don't think I'll go there.
Maybe, I even told him: no, no I don't think I'll return there.
I didn't explain anything to him of the fear nor of the letters that never arrive nor of the lullaby. But he heard it. I'm sure that he heard it.

20

And the rats will wake up bathed in cold sweat, they will drink leaning over puddles, they will sigh deeply, and they will defecate on your unpublished poems among all the garbage that your neighbors have thrown from their windows since the building's inauguration.

21

The tall black man loved another woman (other women) in the island of primitive landscapes. From time to time he sent ambiguous letters in the foreign language across the seven seas, until it bored him.
There is nothing more boring than sending letters whose destiny is uncertain.

22

The disappointed woman read the letters from the light of a candle, drank strong liquors, cried.

23

They will feel empty, so empty they will howl at the night.
Have you heard the rats howl beneath the windows of your building?
It's a good pretext for two or three new unpublished poems, ladies and gentlemen, members of the jury.

24

Then she would keep the ambiguous letters inside empty bottles, she sealed them using the wax of burnt candles and threw them into outside.

25

Why would I have to return? I responded to Fernan.
I don't know, he said, your home is there.
I laughed surprised covering the emptiness with a smile.
Does there exist a place called HOME?

26

From the strictly rectangle canvasses emerge diffuse and abstract figures that might recall the faces of men with dark beards and women with scarves around their heads, images of other times and places, dreamt by rats driven mad.*

---

* I have gone to Leningrad, now that I am older. It's a tremendous city, but for some inexplicable reason, each time I have visited it, I've gotten incredibly high fevers: I don't know why . . .

27

The pathetic daughter of the disappointed woman had nothing better to do than rummage behind the building through the snow for the pieces of illegible letters in order to smell them. She was sure she could inhale the perfume of suns, animals, and primitive landscapes of the island across the seven seas.

28

The howls of rats heard beneath the windows of your building might recall songs in a foreign language, words with ambiguous meanings, the sounds of other times and places, possibly extraterrestrial.

29

When the tall black man grew tired of writing letters with uncertain destinies, the pathetic daughter announced to her disappointed mother her decision to return home.

30

It was snowing.

31

Smell deeply each one of your poems before guarding them in the interior of empty bottles. Don't show them to anyone, not even to your most loyal enemy, ladies and gentlemen, members of the jury, nor to anyone.

32

To which HOME? said the mother.

33

Don't reread them either, forget them, forget them quickly after smelling them; not a single poem, nor song nor word deserves to be remembered nor to be dreamt by the voracious rats driven mad nor by anyone.

34

The tall black man that the daughter torn up from the roots encountered anew was not the same tall black man she had met in the island of primitive landscapes.

35

The woman wearing headphones, who looks like an extraterrestrial, listens to the silence born from the strictly rectangular canvasses.

36

The island of primitive landscapes that the pathetic daughter torn up from the roots encountered anew was not the same island of primitive landscapes that could be called a desert if not for its animals and suns and some million inhabitants.

37

But never forget the smell of your unpublished poems, the original and two copies.
Keep in your head a catalogue of smells to classify the excrement of the sad rats outside your building: here is my soul.

38

To whom might it occur that the woman wearing headphones, who looks like an extraterrestrial, might be an extraterrestrial?

39

Neither can I admit that I want to receive letters. It bothers me that so much time passes without a single one arriving. But it would bother me much more if one did arrive. I would be dizzy. A door that the wind plays with. Very far away. A strange melody. A lullaby?

WOMEN OF THE FEDERATION

Francisco García González

TRANSLATED FROM THE SPANISH
BY MARY G. BERG

*Francisco García González was born in Havana in 1965
and has a degree in history from Havana University. He is a
writer, editor, and screenwriter. His short story collections
include* Juegos permitidos *(Games Allowed, 1994),* Color
local *(Local Color, 1999), and* ¿Qué quieren las mujeres?
*(What Do Women Want? 2003), from which "Women of
the Federation" is taken. He has also published a historical
essay,* Presidio Modelo, temas escondidos *(Model Prison,
Hidden Agendas, 2002). His stories have appeared in anthologies in Cuba and in Spain. He won Cuba's Heming-
way Short Story Prize in 1999, and has served as editor of
the cultural journal* Habáname. *His articles have appeared
in periodicals in Cuba, Mexico, Chile, and the United
States.*

*"Women of the Federation" is about the rueful and joyful
thoughts of a young man in current day Havana who is
struggling with his attraction to two very different young
women, while coping with the ups and downs of daily life:
shortages, power outages, crowded buses, the adventures of*

riding a bicycle (left to him by a friend who emigrated)
through traffic, as he fantasizes a vivid life of the imagina-
tion.

She's stretched out on her back on the bed and I know she's having a lousy day. She has the complexion of a fresh apple. Sometimes I keep this to myself and other times I get a kick out of telling
her so, depending on how things are going. Pretty corny. I'm always
thinking it, but I only say it out loud once in a while. I look at the
magazine that hides her face. I run my eyes over the sweet fingers of
her sweet hands and the sweet freckles where her shoulders begin
and the sweet breasts drifting toward her armpits. I look at the magazine and I wonder what she can be reading since she only knows
about five words of English. "Good-bye." "Boy." "Girl." Maybe
"Nike" if not "night," because women are so smart—about brand
names. I'm sure she's gazing at the barefoot models or reading the
names of the face creams and vitamins for the skin, or just casting
her eyes over the pictures of overflowing platters of luscious-looking
food. She loves lotions and constantly frets about the sun because
her complexion is so fair. She's an active member of the Federation
of Cuban Women, a food service worker, wears a uniform and black
stockings, and, contrary to what you might think or she might hope,
she is always ravenously hungry. I love her complexion and her ap-
petite, her sweaty sheathed legs. I call her my yummy Pudge, my
scrumptious pink Piggy, and watch how her nostrils dilate. Because
Pudge or my little Piggy are invocations, triggers that unleash whirl-
winds of desire. Followed by stiffening nipples, pupils rolled back,
uncontrollable gasping until the spasm of release, feet kicking the air
beneath or on top of me. I give her a whistle, ask how she's doing
just to say something. I see her legs poking out from under the sheet

and her underpants bulging around the double sanitary pads, so I know it's the third day, when her flow always seems even heavier than last month's. She doesn't answer. I go into the bathroom. Poor baby; I know she's having a bad day. I open the window. The book of word games is on the toilet tank. She's good at word puzzles. She left the last Find the Word page half done. Topic: soccer. Words to spot: goal, contract, penalty, score, winger, corner, line . . . I reach into the hamper and touch her soiled clothes. I pull out her work stockings and some white panties, yellowed by pee stains. I suck in my breath until my lungs are filled. Man, this is my girl's smell. I look around for the toothpaste and my toothbrush among the empty face cream jars and shampoo bottles, then I go back to smelling those yellow pee stains on her panties and I think how intimate and tender my girl's world is. Sometimes I'm part of her world, but other times I feel like an intruder. I give my dick a shake and the last drops spill onto the floor and onto the edges of the toilet. Pudge threatens that someday she'll stick a hose onto me every time I take a leak. Men's pee stinks worse than women's, she claims, and she says I manage to drip all over the place so it reeks like a bus station latrine. That's what she says and I get a kick out of thinking how wise women are and how they can do everything better. I finish brushing my teeth and count the napkins in the open packet: Pudge should have enough for this month. She's still got one more un-opened packet. So she'll get by until next time. It doesn't help to tell her to think positively. She's cheerful, even joyful and optimistic, until two days before the cataclysm strikes. And then, all of a sud-den, she wakes up one day and her breath smells different and she's got that look on her face that neither one of us likes. And sure enough, the next day the bleeding starts. Spotting at first and then a heavy flow, with clots in it. I've seen them on the tiles in the shower and in the toilet bowl when the water's off. The image of a clot on a tile floor is the very embodiment of abandonment and desolation.

But a clot floating in water is something else, it remains diaphanous and intact even while those little protuberances like the pseudopodia of a handsome amoeba are swaying around. With time it begins to dissolve and tints the water until it becomes an intense purple as the clot disappears. It's beautiful. She finds it disgusting. I like it, but I don't tell her so, any more than I tell her I smell her panties, pee-stained and unwashed. I leave the towel on the rod and count the napkins in the packet again, and the used ones in the wastebasket. The total, figuring in the two she has on, confirms my guess: she'll have enough for this month. So that's good. I stand on the scale. From the bathroom I can see the magazine and her fingers. She's lying on her back on the bed and I know she's having a lousy day. I give her a whistle, but she doesn't answer. She goes on gazing at the barefoot models and the delicious platters of food, even though I can't imagine that she's feeling very hungry right now. On days like this I exempt her from everything. Pudge, I'll make my own breakfast, and I'll leave a nice lunch all ready for you, and you can just stay there in bed until I get back, my lady love, my madonna, my nymph, and that way you can listen to the soap operas and watch the noon preview programs and finish your word game and listen to all the tapes you want. Anything, Pudge, just don't look out the window to see if the smokestack off in the distance is belching smoke up into the sky or if it remains silent and lifeless, shut down yet again. Because, Pudge, today is a gray day which is doubly bad for you, so tell the world to go to hell and just stay here resting until your *papi* comes back. I never knew what that distant chimney was until she moved in with me. It was during our first menstrual period together. On the third day I found her on her knees, gazing out the window. She gestured for me to come over and asked me if I knew what that chimney was, the one we could see in the distance between the gray stone buildings. And here I'd been thinking that she was engrossed in the trees in the park, or watching the kids running around benches in the little plaza. "That's the smokestack of the sanitary pad factory." I looked and saw how lifeless it was, without a single plume of smoke against the sky. She didn't have to explain anything to me. I rinse out the glass and go back into the bathroom. A new pad count, more drops on the floor and on the edge of the toilet bowl, again the fragrance of Pudge's pee. She gives me a hug and says not to be late, I tell her I'll call her at noon. I feel her fetid, familiar breath on me and I think if a guy can feel desire for someone who smells this bad, he should be called a hero. I avoid the second kiss with a loving bite on her right ear and I tell her that I can't wait to get past the next few days so I can nibble on her little ear again and see her panting with her eyes rolled up. She believes me and hugs me and I believe me too and I hug her back and I don't avoid the third kiss because I am a hero and tomorrow or this afternoon I'll desire Pudge even though she doesn't like it this way in the midst of so much blood. And in the midst of the kiss and hug it occurs to me that if, as we've been taught, heroism is based on the amount of blood spilled for a worthwhile cause, among other things, then women are the true heroines. The fact that they menstruate just because they are what they are, well, we men should not only tip our hats, but take them off altogether. They are the true heroines, women are, and I shouldn't say I'm a hero just for breathing in her infernal stinking breath. What does it matter that women, at least some women, turn on the tears easily. At first, every time we'd find ourselves at the climactic moment of the primordial act, Pudge would burst into tears. Her sobs drained my enthusiasm and I lost my momentum. I never figured out whether she meant it or not. If it was a farce, I was sorry I was taking it seriously, and if it wasn't, it was just too pathetic. The only interesting part was the taste of her tears: salty sweetness of a landlocked sea. But all that spilled blood, and having to put up with it! Pudge, I forgive you the ocean and for drowning me in your eyes. The topic gets me hot again, and Pudge complains that I could break her ribs. I blow her a kiss from the doorway and she tells me to watch out for cars. I blow her another kiss. She's the one having a lousy day, not her bicyclist.

Pudge isn't pudgy at all, and she has apple skin and she's a heroine because of all that spilled blood.

But the street is something else, man. Another part of the same thing. The air is just right today because the cold wind has blown away the last of the fog. This is something only a cyclist would notice. He's on a bike. She's on a bike. They're on bikes. So are we, so are you. The asshole pal I inherited the bike from when he decided to leave is still up there in the States, far away, and since he's a sentimental guy he writes to me once in a while. In his last letter, he told me about how he'd had a dream where I was riding my, *his*, bike thinking about fucking every woman who crossed my path. Just then, like those things that happen in dreams, the person who crossed my path was the Pope, who was here on a visit. A truck goes by almost sideswiping my bike and leaves me wrapped in a dense cloud of black fumes. The guys riding in the back yell at me— either they want to encourage me or else they're just making sure I notice that they're moving a lot faster than the guy they're leaving in the dust. It's a show of strength. *"Tarrú,"* I manage to make out, "Asshole!" In the dream of the pal who left me the bike, nothing else happened. I think about what it would be like to meet the Pope somewhere along this highway. His Holiness the Pontiff comes along in his special popemobile, going the opposite direction, and something—he never tells me what—makes him notice me. His motorcade comes to a halt. The sun gleams on the keys of Saint Peter's emblem on his limousine. His aides lead me over to the Vicar and I try to act as natural as possible. He still hasn't opened his mouth and I ask him how's he doing and what's he doing on this highway. He tells me he's going to the hospital, because today is the day of his encounter with the world of pain. Then he asks about my bicycle and I tell him that it was left to me by an asshole pal who feels bad every time he remembers that he had no choice but to go off and leave me this pile of shit, this junk heap. Junkip? His Holiness asks what "junkip" means. I explain to him and his mouth twitches in what looks like a laugh. Then he asks where the owner of the "junkip" (like that, all one word) is and says something about the grievous separation of the family. He too had had to pedal hard in Krakow. I laugh thinking about the Pope having to ride a bicycle back then, and in Krakow because it's the only city in Poland, besides Warsaw, that I've heard people talking about. If the Pope and I met, there'd be lots of photos. Before he goes on, he asks me first if I've been baptized by the Holy Mother Church and I tell him yes, I have, and he says that will do. And then, if I fear God. Yes, sir, sometimes I'm scared of God. That, too, is sufficient. Since the motorcade is going in the opposite direction, to its encounter with the world of pain, no one offers to give me a tow. The Pontiff makes one more joke about my "junkip" (like that, all one word). I should skip over the fact that one of the aides gives me a T-shirt with Saint Peter's keys on it, and a cloth patch with the image of Mary on it. Once again, the same fumes on the road and the same or other shirtless black guys are yelling at me. This time I do understand. There, from the truck, proletarian-truck, the black guys yell that I'm an asshole and that I should get out of the way and they're also going in the opposite direction from the Pontiff. Although they (the black guys) and I are going along another road (which is the same one, not the only one) toward the world of pain. And what if I'd told the Pontiff that my girl's home in bed and if I'd told him about the sanitary pads and about the worst days when my heroine just stays in bed? For sure he'd scratch one ear and would recommend me to his pupil, Mother Teresa, who might well be here and not so far away, unreachable Mother of Calcutta. Today the north wind has blown off the fog and the wind shoves me along, and I catch up with other cyclists. An old man. Another old man. A guy with a bored expression, even though the north wind pushes him the same as yesterday and tomorrow. By now Pudge has probably tired of her magazine and gone back to the Find a Word game. Penalty. Contract. Run. Goal. Pudge is really good at finding the words. The cyclists are left behind and the bright, soft sun, cooled by the north wind, gleams not on the emblem of Saint Peter's keys, but on the roadside stand where they sell cane juice, *guarapo,* to people coming and going along the highway. I might invite the Pontiff to have a *guarapo* with me. I'll bet no Pope has ever had a *guarapo.* The Pontiff's in luck: they have ice. I order two *guarapos.* The kiosk owners refuse to charge the visitor. His Holiness admires the machinery that crushes the cane and spits the stalks out in bits. The owners recommend we add lemon. We do so. Tasty. Delicious. The aides try the drink, too. The owners tell the Pontiff that they work in a cooperative named "Cuba-Laos Friendship." Cuba-Laos Friendship? Wow, he says to me, that must be very important. It is. I ask the owners if they know where Laos is, and they answer that they do not, that when they got there, that was the name of the place. "I understand," says the Pontiff. This machine is a "junkip" (like that, all one word). We all laugh. I almost laugh and I finish drinking the *guarapo.* No ice today, the guy in the cap tells a taxi driver. Did any Pope ever really drink *guarapo?* What will the friend who left me the bike think if I tell him how I've improved upon his dream? The taxi driver doesn't much like warm *guarapo,* either, so he orders just one. While he drinks, he notices that the business belongs to the "Cuba-Laos Friendship" cooperative. He asks about it. No clue, pal, when we got here the place was already named that. The taxi driver and I pay. Tomorrow there will be ice, then we'll each have two and eventually someone will tell the owners where Laos is. Tomorrow or never.

The other item in my friend's dream isn't quite true. While I pedal along, I'm not thinking that I want to go to bed with every woman who comes into view. I'd have gone to bed with Pudge if today were a good day for her. And there are no women hitch-hiking, standing in the shade of the trees along the side of the road. No. It's Lisanka I'm thinking of. I should admit it, the dream is partly about her. I've given Lisanka the best thrusts of all in my mind and on this bicycle. Once I told her about it and she told me I had a sick mind and that's what she liked about me. Lisanka is different from Pudge. At least that gives our relationship some meaning. Otherwise, why bother? I met Lisanka not long ago on a bus. I met Pudge at some friends' house. When I saw Lisanka hang-ing onto the bar trying to read a book, I stood right behind her, leaving just enough space so it could be accidental or on purpose on my part. It was a book of poetry. "If everyone riding a bus read a book, we'd be closer to the sun." She laughed. You couldn't begin on a higher note. The day I met Pudge, I had to use the bathroom. That underwear couldn't belong to anyone else. The olfactory memory, the girl they had introduced me to had to be menstruat-ing. That may not have been her day, and that's why she hardly paid any attention to me, there are meetings and then there are meetings. Lisanka tells me not to exaggerate, the fact is we were pretty close to the sun in that bus, otherwise why would we have been sweating so much. And since sometimes I manage some men-tal agility, I scolded her and said she shouldn't confuse hell with the sun. In hell, it could be cold, too. Cold and hot. I asked her to read me a poem. Just then we were pressed tight against each other. Lisanka closed the book. *If some day the waters / drown my memory / from the first scolding / to the final holocaust* . . . the poem was hers. Lisanka belonged to the "Rabindranath Tagore" literary workshop. Lisanka was a writer. Pudge was studying gastronomic science when we met. The day after we met, she had a practical exam and had to present a main dish. She was complaining that she wanted to make stuffed peppers and she couldn't find the two peppers anywhere. Everyone in the room was complaining. Pudge never suspected that her smell and her skin interested me. I offered to look for the peppers. They tried gently to dissuade me: it was a pretty risky business. Pudge was having a really bad day. Lisanka said that Rabindranath Tagore was a Turkish poet with a very long beard. I could get into that. *Like the pocked sea / the waves boiled / in such gray display / close by other rocks.* You just can't let a poet with such an elevated idea of Turkish poets get away. I pressed her on the nationality of the poet. Right. Turkey, over there by India. If I hadn't seen her eyes I'd have thought Lisanka might be leading me on. But Lisanka is incapable of lying, I picked up on that right away. Rabindranath Tagore was Turkish, from over there by India. Women do things that just kill you. I didn't wait for my bus stop. Want to go sit in the park? Lisanka's skin was white with delicate black fuzz on it. It was a risky enterprise, something that added to her attractions. I spent the afternoon walking the city, and Pudge ended up with not two but five handsome peppers. Under the trees, Lisanka read the poem again . . . *And perhaps you will arrive invading / before and after, you / alone at the helm, your back to time.* Things wouldn't—a question of chance—have progressed past the enchantment of listening to each other, if Lisanka hadn't revealed the mystery of her name. Lisanka was the name of the mare that belonged to a character in a Soviet novel, a book we'd all read in the crowded military barracks in the '60s. *Whipping his gallop / quick to retreat / like the pocked sea.* A shame not to be the Ivan or Boris who could go for a gallop on this Lisanka. The woman laughed and I thought how long her face was, and what big, strong teeth she had, and what a black and gleaming mane. And the image of desire was a woman-mare who wrote poems and trotted in the solitude of my bicycle journeys. But I knew that no matter how much the poet aroused me with her neighing, it was my displaced apple I really wanted to bed, although sometimes with desire stimulated elsewhere. A week after the exam, Pudge came to my house and repeated every detail of the exam in my kitchen, barefoot and aproned. Pudge laughed her way around the house, inspecting and tidying up. I followed her around because I was so taken with her legs and her barefootedness, until she stopped in front of the window and pointed at the dreary smokeless chimney. She didn't explain then what it was about. I'd rather gallop and savor an apple, says a banal—that is, astute—pop tune.

I swerve around an ambulance and turn my attention back to my pal's dream. I had never thought so much about a Pontiff before. We ordered two *guarapo*s and stood back from the counter. Behind the *guarapo* stand, the slaughterhouse butchers of the "Cuba-Laos Friendship" cooperative have done their usual stuff. Right by our feet runs a stream of water red with the blood of just-butchered hogs. I'm afraid my guest will ruin his white cassock on his day to visit the world of pain. We stand there looking at the blood, and I'm sure his thoughts flow toward the earth where the blood will turn to dust tomorrow or the next day. And maybe because I see him so deep in thought, I ask him if by any chance he remembers a Soviet novel where a character had a mare named Lisanka. He sighs, stands there gazing at his glass, and then confesses that he has never been able to get through a Soviet novel. I trade confessions with him: I haven't either. What do you think we've missed, Your Holiness? What do you think we've been spared, son? Eating apples? A good gallop?

The street is one thing and work is quite another, man. I don't know who the hell this "man" is. It's not Pope John Paul or my bicycle buddy. The secretary has left me a note. She's had to go to the hospital with an asthma attack and won't be back until afternoon. Clients won't come either, which makes me pretty happy. You can expect all the extremes of behavior, good and bad, from these guys, never the normal thing. I shuffle through my papers and a picture of my pal with the bicycle falls out onto the floor. He rode that bike to work for two years. He had a job in a cemetery. When he walked into his office to deal with death, he'd say hello to the woman in charge of death certificates. At noon, she'd come in and they'd screw on his desk. She complained about this a little. Afterward, they'd pee in a potted plant. The plant seemed to thrive on this. It's complicated, but we've kept in touch. He's never met Pudge. I'd like to tell him about Lisanka and her poems, about how, contrary to all expectation, we've never gone beyond some affectionate making out, even though my ideal desire fantasy is the woman-mare strumming a harp and neighing in my ears. Ah, Lisanka's mouth. On the back of the picture, my pal wrote that someday we'll have to compare notes. He's put on so much weight that he looks like a different person. He and Pudge could cook up some good dishes in the kitchen. What would it be like to have a three-way conversation between him, the Pope, and the heir to the bicycle? We'd talk and we'd drink *guarapo*, watching the blood—the hogs' blood—run along the side of the road until it soaked into the earth and the dust. For sure we'd tell two or three good jokes that we'd have to explain to the priest. I put the picture and the papers away. I take a look at the newspaper. Italian Robbers Drugged Their Victims. Police detained four Albanians who had been breaking into victims' houses and knocking them out with drugs so they could get away with all kinds of bad stuff. Rape, robbery. New members appointed to the Socialist International. Alleged fraud in Special Oympics disputed in Mexico City. "Troyano" disguised as Y2K error. Called FIX2001, the virus infiltrates computers, disguised as an innocent electronic message. Before I folded the paper back up, a letter to the editor caught my attention. A lady's companion has gone from one province to another on account of a death in her family. The wake has made her realize that coffin manufacturing is a disaster in her town, while at the same time she praises the good taste and efficiency of the operations of the funeral home that tended to her relative. The list of manufacturers' shortcomings in her native Guantánamo falls like hammer blows on stone. Green wood. Skimping on nails. Poor quality lining cloth. Delays in delivery to the family. A shoddy product. Her complaint is going to the sanitary authorities of her town. She ends by congratulating her colleagues in Bijarú. Bijarú: now there's a place where they know how to treat you right on your final journey. Bitter words from a *compañera* now sitting in her armchair, sipping coffee after coffee. The moment comes for us all, and one coffin is not the same as any other. We want to do it right when we die. A letter like this merits serious action. This heroine, apart from the blood she has spilled during her life, is the defender of a cause that is surely transcendent. I cut the letter out carefully. I'll send it to my bicycle buddy, so he can see. Better to send him the entire paper. I put water on to boil. Just as I put the kettle on, the electricity goes off. I look over the clients' requests one more time. It would be better if they didn't come, at least not today. At first sight, the operation doesn't seem complicated. I go through the document and by the end I can hardly believe how tortuous and eccentric a procedure it is. New winds of consumer awareness are blowing. Someday everyone everywhere will have coffins like the ones in Bijarú. At noon I call my heroine. Nothing new, the word search for soccer terms is giving her a headache. I cheer her up by suggesting that she look for a topic she likes better. Before hanging up she reminds me to bring her the magazine with the article about Lady Di's death, she wants to read it again and loan it to some friends. The day they issued Cuban stamps with Diana on them, Pudge wanted me to get her some. Neither one of us has ever collected a stamp. The Diana stamps are under the glass top of the dresser with some postcards of the movie *Titanic*. I promise her I won't be late and I'll bring her the magazine. A little while later the phone rings. Neighing on the other end, that seductive voice reels me in. Lisanka is alone and wants me to have lunch with her. I feel like I'm throwing myself off the top of a roller coaster. I feel bad about Pudge, but the poet mare is my vivid, single image of desire right this instant. Despite her pleas, I detect a sad tone in her voice. I'm a pushover. There's a silence after we hang up. Behind the indecipherable noise I know there lurk surprise and the mystery of poems I'll never understand. I feel bad again. Without victims or perpetrators, how could heroines exist?

The street is one thing, and work something else, and this chasing after another woman, can't even talk about that one, man. I hadn't seen or talked to Lisanka for three days. Down the roller coaster I slide, and my hard-on is the bicycle's horse. Nothing matters, not her sad tone of voice, not the war in my diaphragm, not Pudge or the Pope or the dust soaking up the blood spilled by the slaughterhouse butchers and by my heroines. This chasing after another woman, man. This hiding my desperation when I get to her door. The exquisite detail of Lisanka's white fingers on the brass doorknob. "Hi there." The silky mane brushes against my cheeks and the scent, that distinctive scent of this Lisanka, who stands there with her hand on the knob, tells me her body fluids are awash in an elemental mix of woman and beast. Down the roller coaster, man. Excuses, but there's no action brewing here, nothing to excuse. And before Lisanka even says a word, I know, feel sure of it, that today's not her day. Lunch was just a pretext, even though the french fries, canned meat, rice and beans, and the two beers are right there. I dish some up for her and help myself. Great potatoes and meat, and Lisanka watches me chew as though seeing me eat were a banquet for her. Today is not her day. Yeah, I know, I tell her. She smells different. The Soviet hero's mare runs her fingertip through the sweat on the glass. The mare isn't hungry. Her parents

get home tomorrow. She asks me if I think she's fat and if I want
her lunch, she doesn't feel well. It's all a terribly domestic, and even
heroic, scene. I feel the tension in my diaphragm subsiding. Will
Lisanka's clots, on the bathroom tiles, be the very image of desolation or will they waft like beautiful amoebas in the water in the toilet bowl? I tell her it's fine with me and I'm glad she felt she could
call me when she feels this way. I get her to stand up and I pull her
onto my lap. Lisanka relaxes against my body, I stroke her mane
and she lifts my hand to her lips. She kisses my fingers. She bites
them with her square, equine teeth. If she has called me today, it's
because she takes me seriously, she assures me and that, for now,
seems okay to me. She has several things to tell me. Things she
can't tell anyone else. On days like this, she thinks nothing she does
matters. The last poem she read at the "Rabindranath Tagore"
workshop, named for the Turkish poet, was a great success. But she
doesn't believe it. *This December day, / the forest is so heavy / it hides
mockingly / amidst sips of solitude.* How can she have any doubt
about such moving images. The weight of a forest hiding mockingly. Lisanka shouldn't even question the beauty of something like
that, I assure her, hugging her. And it's not that I'm being an asshole, leading her on, but right this moment, a heavy forest hiding
mockingly amidst sips of solitudes are words that embody a beauty
that is total, possible . . . *often piling up debris / beside old ants /
hanging from my eyes.* I think Lisanka has talent, and I hug her close
again with my arms that have been the victims of simultaneous
natural cycles. Lisanka's weight on my knees begins to bother me.
Sustained by the gaze / of sterile rains. We kiss, a key move, man,
when you're trying to keep from inhaling bad breath. *Perhaps
wisely / I could bear no more.* Man, I like this poem, what does it
matter whether R. T. is Turkish or Malay or Australian. I move out
from under Lisanka's weight. In vain, I look in the bathroom for
trophy by-products, the package with whatever napkins are left,

clots, old pee-stained underpants. Then we sit on the bed. Will the day ever come when we won't doubt what we do? Doubt has no sex (SHE) (THEY), Lisanka. I've written a story, too. A story, Lisanka? It's called "Blame the River." Hardly letting me ask about it, the mare cleared the next hurdle without a hitch. Marisol meets Miguel at a meeting, Marisol goes to live at the guy's house. One day, without any explanation, Miguel commits suicide. Marisol, who is pregnant, is rejected by Miguel's parents. She goes to see the dead man's aunt and uncle. Miguel was HIV-positive. Shock. Then I . . . ? Positive. Marisol-Ophelia-Alfonsina Storni (the river connection), instead of heading home to her parents, leaps into the river believing that she sees Miguel's face in a small, luminous window in the middle of the rapids. Miguel is calling her: "Come on, darling, come on." Marisol-Alfonsina-Ophelia doesn't know how to swim. The end. She hasn't read the story yet in the R. T. Workshop. I scratch my head. Lisanka is waiting for my reaction. I don't know, right on the spot. I'd have to reread it. You should let me have it, and tomorrow I'll tell you. Lisanka moves her ears and her mane. From this angle she looks more attractive. We fall into each other's arms again. I liked your story, but I don't know. The heroine opens her legs and makes space for me down there. We can't do this, I don't feel well. You don't have to tell me, Lisanka, today's a bad day for everyone. About that guy with AIDS, that's strong stuff, man. Strong stuff. The heroine pushes me away slowly: now my weight bothers her. I go back to variations on my buddy's dream. The Pontiff swirls his *guarapo* around. The hogs' blood runs right by our feet. All rivers flow into the sea. Even the one Marisol leapt into, without first checking with the Center for Hygiene and Epidemiology just in case. I tell the priest I'd like to confide in him. I'm attracted to two women, sir. My guest finished his drink and shrugged his shoulders. There's sin along all of life's roads, son. He tells me this, he, a priest, a man, an old man. Then he says good-bye to me through the window of the popemobile. At my side, my pal drinks his *guarapo*. It's been years since I've had such good *guarapo*. We both gaze at the mix of blood and water running into the ditch. Cuba and Laos can do a lot together. No one laughs. I tell my pal I'd like to confide in him. I'm attracted to two women, bro. My pal finishes his drink and shrugs his shoulders. Don't leave the main road for a detour, my friend. He's saying this as a man who's monogamous and who's seen the sun set over the mouth of the Hudson River. I get off of Lisanka. We'll have our trot another day. That's strong stuff about AIDS, man. Nothing more demoralizing, man, than AIDS and pornography. The one castrates you, and the other is too perfect, and excludes you. Now Lisanka can breathe better and asks me what kind of music I'd like. The mare walks past me and her strong odor hits me in the stomach. Anyone who is capable of desiring someone who stinks like this is either a hero or out of his mind. This is the second time I've thought this. And while Lisanka fusses over the music, I inflate a condom and paint little eyes on it, and a smile, and an "I Love Lisanka" and below that, the head of a mare with very long eyelashes. When Lisanka comes back, I toss the zeppelin into the air. The poet neighs with pleasure and I'm glad she's pleased. We play a little volleyball. A condom, man. A condom for Lisanka. I hear the sound of Silvio Rodríguez on the record player. I tell Lisanka I didn't think anyone paid attention to Silvio Rodríguez any longer. I think he's great. I bet you do - I can't stand him, I think he's really trite. How could I have guessed that such a casual remark would upset her so. I got tangled in a stupid explanation and I finally said she was right. Silvio Rodríguez is a great guy. If my friend the midget heard you, he'd throw a brick at your head. The midget, Lisanka? But no one else counts here but us, and certainly not a midget, right, my mare? *How could it be / how could it be / a steed without a rider* . . . A great guy, Lisanka, just like that midget who heaves bricks. Anything you want. Silvio Rodríguez is the best Turkish crooner I know, no matter what the midget says. Anything you want, go on and bleed today, and tomorrow then, we'll get on with it with spurs and riding boots and the bridle that's . . .

The breeze wafts the condom from one side of the room to the other. Lisanka goes back to bed, her ovaries are still aching. She's glad I'm keeping her company. With her legs half open and lying on her back, obviously every month she wishes the earth would swallow her up. Again she apologizes for taking advantage of my patience and my time. I tell her that if it were up to me, I'd spend all afternoon with her, but I'd better get back to work. Just a minute, and the mare heaves up on her haunches and goes over to the cupboard. Help me, would you, before you go. Lisanka spreads a sheet on the bed. If she cuts it into strips, she'll have enough for the rest of this period and next month, too. Okay. We set to work. If the Pontiff and the pal with the bicycle saw us, they'd for sure insist on the road of life, sin and the detour. Two heroines are too much. So far Pudge-Apple hasn't had to resort to this extreme. We finally count up sixty strips. At this rate, I'll sleep on the bare mattress, she tells me, and it sounds frivolous and absurd to me. As absurd as asking the Pope in the middle of the highway how things are going. Once again in each other's arms. Pats on the haunch. The heroine will end up with no sheets. If I offered her Pudge's contacts for buying contraband napkins or cotton, it would be a double betrayal. One is enough. And before I leave, I go over to the window and I ask her if she sees that tall tower there in the distance. Well, that's a sanitary products factory, they make napkins. *White on the outside close up / not from far away . . .*

I leave and Lisanka remains standing in the window. I look from the street and to my surprise the smokestack begins to emit swirls of smoke. Then on my bicycle without a Pontiff and without a pal, without *guarapo* or seeing the blood run along the earth, I think about what I'm like, and it seems to me that I, too, am the very image of abandonment. A clot on the tiles, an inflated condom, pulled here, pushed there, pushed and pulled. It's all one thing, man, and this is something else.

November 1999

I DON'T WANT ANYONE COMING
AROUND TO SAVE ME

Raúl Rivero

TRANSLATED FROM THE SPANISH
BY DIANA ALVAREZ-AMELL

Raúl Rivero is one of Cuba's best-known dissident journalists and a figurehead of the country's beleaguered independent press. Rivero was born in 1945 in Morón, Camagüey, in central Cuba. He was among the first generation of journalists trained at Havana University's School of Journalism after the 1959 revolution, and he co-founded the cultural magazine of the Cuban youth Caimán Barbudo *in 1966. He worked as Moscow correspondent for the government news agency,* Prensa Latina, *from 1973 to 1976 before returning to Cuba to head the agency's science and culture service. Rivero resigned from the National Union of Cuban Writers and Artists in 1989. In 1991, he signed, along with nine other writers and intellectuals, an open letter petitioning for reform in Cuba. In 1995 Rivero founded* CubaPress, *one of a handful of independent, and illegal, news agencies set up by dissident journalists in order to provide an alternative to Cuba's state-owned media. He was arrested in 2003 and sentenced to twenty years' imprisonment, but was released in November 2004 and moved to Spain. Rivero is viewed as a political dissident and*

*cannot publish or broadcast in Cuba. Instead, he sends his
work abroad for circulation on the Internet and in U.S. and
European publications, although publishing abroad can result
in a jail sentence for spreading "enemy propaganda." Rivero
was awarded the World Press Freedom Prize in 2004. He has
published several books of poetry, journalism, and interviews.*

*"I Don't Want Anyone Coming Around to Save Me" was
originally published in 2002 in a Mexican edition of Rivero's
poems,* Puente de Guitarra *(*Bridge of the Guitar*).*

I don't want anyone coming around to save me

So, whoever is sending me those nice thoughts,
those smug little messages,
—take it elsewhere.

Cut off the oxygen now.
I don't want to suffer the agony of the mask.

And that black paint
from the stone path
is not going to hide
my fatigue nor my headstrong,
parsimonious way of putting up with it.

The gauze, the tight gauze,
saves just the burns
on the surface of my skin
So there is nothing to do
about the burning branded in my memory,

about the open wound that's not a spot in my body,
but a country where harmony is banned.

Take away the light
—since this anguish began
I've turned into a soothsayer.

Keep off the cotton swabs.
To me they seem only clouds of quicksilver
and preordained snow
and now
—as it was when I was small and loved—
I'm afraid of the rain
and cold things can hurt me.

Don't get near me.
I may end up becoming majestic
and that in itself can be another danger.

Now that death is all dressed up,
(they are fixing her hair just about now)
pressing her field uniform,
coloring her cheeks and burnishing her medals.
I don't want anyone coming around to save me.
I want to try and see
if I am able to stand up
all by myself.

About the Translators and Advisers

Kareem James Abu-Zeid, half-Egyptian and half-American by blood, has lived in Kuwait, the United Arab Emirates, France, Germany, Egypt, and the United States. He received his BA in French from Princeton University in 2003 and has held a Fulbright fellowship in Germany and a CASA fellowship at the American University in Cairo. He has taught English at the University of Mannheim, Germany, and in Poitiers, France. He is currently a PhD student in comparative literature at the University of California, Berkeley, where his research focuses on the links between phenomenology and modern poetry.

Hanadi Al-Samman, advisory editor for the Syria section of this anthology, was born in Aleppo, Syria, in 1966. Al-Samman is an assistant professor of English at Appalachian State University. She earned her PhD in comparative literature from Indiana University in 2000 under the auspices of a joint Fulbright and Syrian scholarship. Her research focuses on Middle Eastern and Arab Women's Studies as well as on literature of the diaspora.

Diana Alvarez-Amell teaches Spanish at Seton Hall University. She writes for cultural publications and scholarly journals in the United States and abroad.

Wolfgang Astelbauer is a translator who lives in Vienna, Austria.

Mary G. Berg's recent translations from Spanish include the edited volume *Open Your Eyes and Soar: Cuban Women Writing Now* (2003) and the novels *I've Forgotten Your Name* (2004) by the Dominican Martha Rivera; *River of Sorrows* (2000) by the Argentinean Libertad Demitrópulos; and *Ximena at the Crossroads* (1998) by the Peruvian Laura Riesco; as well as stories, women's travel accounts, literary criticism, and collections of poetry, most recently *Quincunx* and *The Book of Giulio Camillo* by the Cuban Carlota Caulfield. She and Dennis Maloney have translated twentieth-century Spanish poetry, including Antonio Machado's *There Is No Road* (2003) and *The Landscape of Castile* (bilingual, 2005). She teaches at Harvard Extension and is a resident scholar at the Women's Studies Research Center at Brandeis University, where she writes about Latin American writers, including Clorinda Matto de Turner, Juana Manuela Gorriti, Soledad Acosta de Samper, and contemporary Cubans.

Alexandra Blair graduated from Brown University, where she translated the stories of three Cuban women writers for her honors thesis, "A Translation and Discussion of Contemporary Cuban Women Writers." She received the Arnold Fellowship to travel to Cuba to collect the stories and thoughts of Cubans defining their relationship to their natural resources and to their environment via documentary photography, audio documentary, and writing. She recently returned from working with Tibetan refugee communities in India, and is working on several documentary projects and urban garden programs in California.

Constance Bobroff is currently a graduate student in Persian language and literature at the University of Texas at Austin. She is active in all issues concerning the implementation of Persian language on the Internet. In addition to "The Vice Principal," she has published a short story by Mohammad-Ali Jamalzadeh, "A Day in Rostamabad of Shemiran," on the Internet (http://lib.washington.edu/neareast/yekruz), complete with notes and exercises as well as the Persian and English text.

Marilyn Booth is visiting associate professor at the University of Illinois, Urbana-Champaign, in the Program in Comparative and World Literature. Author most recently of *May Her Likes Be Multiplied: Biography and Gender Politics in Egypt*, she has also translated fiction and autobiography from Egypt and Lebanon by Hoda Barakat, Somaya Ramadan, Ibtihal Salem, Nawal al-Sa'dawi, Sahar Tawfiq, and Latifa al-Zayyat. She received her BA from Harvard-Radcliffe and her D.Phil. from Oxford University, and has also taught at Brown University and the American University in Cairo.

C. Dickson is the translator of Shams Nadir's *The Astrolabe of the Sea*, Mohamed Dib's *Savage Night*, J. M. G. Le Clézio's *Round and Other Cold Hard Facts* and *Wandering Star*, and Gisèle Pineau's *Macadam Dreams*. Her forthcoming translations include Ann Riquier's *Voices of Tibetan Women*, Laure Adler's *Life in the Bordellos (1830–1930)*, and Gisèle Pineau's *Chair Piment*. Her prizes and awards include the ALTA Fellowship and scholarships to the Collège International des Traducterus Littéraires. She lived for five years in West Africa and now lives in France.

Tarek Eltayeb, advisory editor for the Sudan section of this anthology, was born to Sudanese émigré parents in Cairo, Egypt, in 1959. He lives in Vienna, and has made numerous contributions to Arabic newspapers and magazines both in Europe and in Arab countries. Since 1992, his books have been published in Arabic, French, and German. His two volumes of poetry, *Ein mit Tauben und Gurren gefüllter Koffer* (*A Suitcase Filled with Doves and Cooing*) and *Aus dem Teppich meiner Schatten* (*From the Carpet of My Shadows*), appeared in German and Arabic, and his novel, *Städte ohne Dattelpalmen* (*Cities Without Dark Palms*), appeared in Arabic in 1992, in French in 1999, and in German in 2000. After receiving various literary scholarships in the 1990s, Eltayeb was granted the Federal Chancellery's project scholarship for 2000–2001, 2001–2002, and 2002–2003. He has held numerous readings in Vienna, Saalfelden, Frankfurt, Aachen, Washington, Cairo, La Rochelle, Poitier, Struga, Dublin, and Lemberg.

Lilian Friedberg is a performing artist, translator, and visiting assistant professor at the University of Illinois at Chicago (PhD, Germanic studies). Her translations have appeared in the *Denver Quarterly*, the *Chicago Review*, *Transition*, *Trivia*, and elsewhere. She is the co-editor, with Sander L. Gilman, of *A Jew in the New Germany: Selected Writings of Henryk Broder* and recently completed translations of the original source documents for the forthcoming *Sourcebook of Nazi Culture*, edited by Gilman and Anson Rabinbach. Her translations of Ingeborg Bachmann (*Last Living Words: The Ingeborg Bachmann Reader*, 2005) received the Kayden National Translation Award. She has been commissioned to translate several works by Nobel Prize–winner Elfriede Jelinek.

M. R. Ghanoonparvar is a professor of Persian and comparative literature and Persian language at the University of Texas at Austin.

He served as the president of the American Association of Teachers of Persian and is an active member of many academic and scholarly societies and organizations. He has published widely on Persian literature and culture in both English and Persian and is the author of *Prophets of Doom: Literature as a Socio-Political Phenomenon in Modern Iran* (1984), *In a Persian Mirror: Images of the West and Westerners in Iranian Fiction* (1993), *Translating the Garden* (2001), and *Reading Chubak* (2005). His translations include Jalal Al-e Ahmad's *By the Pen*, Sadeq Chubak's *The Patient Stone*, Simin Daneshvar's *Savushun*, and Sadeq Hedayat's *The Myth of Creation*, and his edited volumes include *Iranian Drama: An Anthology*, *In Transition: Essays on Culture and Identity in Middle Eastern Societies*, Gholamhoseyn Sa'edi's *Othello in Wonderland* and *Mirror-Polishing Storytellers*, and Moniru Ravanipur's *Satan Stones* and *Kanizu*.

Yasmeen S. Hanoosh was born in Basra, Iraq, in 1978, and lived in Baghdad until 1995. She holds a BA in philosophy and religion and an MA in Arabic language and literature, both from the University of Michigan, and will soon complete a PhD in contemporary Arabic literature there. She teaches Arabic at the University of Virginia.

Andrea Heyde is the former head of the German Book Office in New York (1998–2002). In 1998 she was the German recipient of the Frankfurt Book Fair Fellowship, which assembles editors from sixteen countries to build international relationships in publishing. She holds a PhD in German literature of the twentieth century, and she now lives in Zürich.

Zara Houshmand, advisory editor for the Iran section of this anthology, is an Iranian American writer and theater artist. She has studied Balinese shadow puppetry and Tibetan performing arts, and her plays have been produced in Los Angeles, San Francisco, New

York, and at the Spoleto Festival. She was awarded the first commissioning grant from the National Theatre Translation Fund for her work on Bijan Mofid's plays. Her poetry, essays, and translations from Rumi are featured in the Internet magazine Iranian.com (www.Iranian.com/ZaraHoushmand). She is also a pioneer in the development of virtual reality as an art form; her installation *Beyond Manzanar* has been exhibited internationally and is now in the permanent collection of the San Jose Museum of Art. As editor for the Mind and Life Institute, she has been responsible for several books representing a long-term dialogue between Buddhism and Western science.

William Maynard Hutchins was born in Berea, Kentucky, in 1944. He was the recipient of a 2005–2006 NEA award for literary translation for *The Seven Veils of Seth* by the Libyan Tuareg author Ibrahim al-Koni, whose novel *Anubis* he has also translated. Hutchins was the principal translator of *The Cairo Trilogy* by the Egyptian Nobel Laureate Naguib Mahfouz.

Ha-yun Jung, advisory editor for the North Korean section of this anthology, is a writer and translator whose work has appeared in journals and anthologies including *Prairie Schooner*, the *Threepenny Review*, the *New York Times*, and *Best New American Voices 2001*. She is the recipient of awards and grants including the Korean Literature Translation Award and the Carol Houck Smith Fiction Fellowship from the University of Wisconsin–Madison. In 2002, she was a fellow at the Radcliffe Institute for Advanced Study. She currently lives in Seoul, Korea, where she is at work on a novel.

Won-Chung Kim is a professor of English literature at Sungkyunkwan University in Seoul, Korea, where he teaches contemporary American poetry, ecological literature, and translation. He earned his PhD in English at the University of Iowa in 1993. He has translated Kim Chiha's *Heart's Agony* and Choi Seungho's *Flowers in the Toilet Bowl*. He will soon publish translations of Chong Hyonjong's *Trees of the World* and an anthology of Korean ecological poets. He has also translated E. T. Seton's *The Gospel of the Redman* and Bernd Heinrich's *In a Patch of Fireweed* into Korean.

Jacqueline Loss, advisory editor for the Cuban section of this anthology, earned her PhD in comparative literature from the University of Texas at Austin in 2000. She teaches Latin American and Comparative Literary and Cultural Studies at the University of Connecticut in Storrs. Her book *Cosmopolitanisms and Latin America: Against the Destiny of Place* was published by Palgrave in 2005. She is the co-editor of an anthology of Cuban short stories to be published by Northwestern University Press in 2006 and has translated texts by Cuban writers Víctor Fowler Calzada, Ernesto René Rodríguez, and Jorge Miralles into English. Her critical essays have appeared in *Nepantla: Views from South, Miradas, Chasqui, Latino and Latina Writers, Mandorla,* and *New Centennial Review,* among other publications. She is currently preparing a manuscript with the working title *Cultural Memory: Cuba and the Soviet Bloc.*

Khaled Mattawa, advisory editor for the Libya section of this anthology, was born in Benghazi, Libya, in 1964 and came to the United States in his teens. He is the author of two books of poems, *Ismailia Eclipse* and *Zodiac of Echoes*. He has translated five books of contemporary Arabic poetry and co-edited two anthologies of Arab American literature. He has been awarded a Guggenheim fellowship, the Alfred Hodder Fellowship at Princeton University, an NEA translation grant, and two Pushcart Prizes. He teaches in the MFA creative writing program at the University of Michigan, Ann Arbor.

Christopher Merrill has published four collections of poetry, including *Watch Fire*, for which he received the Peter I. B. Lavan Younger Poets Award from the Academy of American Poets; several edited volumes, including *The Forgotten Language: Contemporary Poets and Nature*; and four books of nonfiction, *The Grass of Another Country: A Journey Through the World of Soccer*, *The Old Bridge: The Third Balkan War and the Age of the Refugee*, *Only the Nails Remain: Scenes from the Balkan Wars*, and *Things of the Hidden God: Journey to the Holy Mountain*. He directs the international writing program at the University of Iowa.

Rebecca Porteous is a translator who divides her time between London and Cairo.

Brother Anthony of Taizé is a professor in the English department at Sogang University, Seoul. He is also a leading translator of Korean literature. Born in England, he is now a Korean national with the name An Sonjae.

Najem Wali, introducer for the Iraq section of this anthology, was born in Al-Amarah, Iraq, in 1956, and earned a degree in German literature from Baghdad University in 1978. Shortly after the outbreak of the Iraq-Iran war, he emigrated to Hamburg, Germany, where he was awarded an MA in German literature and Islam in 1987. From 1987 to 1990 he lived in Madrid, where he studied Spanish and Latin American literature; he also lived in Oxford for six months in 1993 and in Florence for six months in 1995. Wali now lives in Hamburg, where he works as a freelance journalist and cultural correspondent for the largest Arab newspaper, *Al-Hayat*. Wali is the author of the novels *War in the Destruction of Pleasure*, *The Least Night to Marry*, *Place Names Kumait* (also published in French and Swedish translations), and *Tel Al Leham* (*The Trip to Tel*

Al Leham), and the short story collections *There in the Strange City* and *Waltzing Matilda*.

Yu Young-nan is a freelance translator living in Seoul. Her most recent literary translation is Yom Sang-seop's *Three Generations*, published in 2005 by Archipelago Books.

About Words Without Borders

Words Without Borders is an online magazine for literature in translation that undertakes to promote international communication through publication of the world's best writing—selected and translated by a distinguished group of writers, translators, and publishing professionals. We also serve as an advocacy organization for literature in translation, producing events that feature the work of foreign writers and working with print and broadcast media to foster a cultural engagement and exchange that allows voices in many languages to prosper. As part of a large educational initiative, we are developing curricular units, reading lists, and lesson plans for high school and college use. (If interested in our educational outreach projects, please contact us at wwbinfo@bard.edu.)

Our monthly publications of fiction, nonfiction, poetry, and contextual essays are continually available online and searchable by author, title, country, language, region, and environment. Visit our Web site to participate in discussions with an international group of literary bloggers and forums on great works of international literature and translation and publishing issues. Please sign up for our free monthly newsletter at www.wordswithoutborders.org.